Gendering Mental Health

Gendering Mental Health
Knowledges, Identities, and Institutions

edited by

Bhargavi V. Davar

and

T.K. Sundari Ravindran

OXFORD
UNIVERSITY PRESS

OXFORD
UNIVERSITY PRESS

Oxford University Press is a department of the University of Oxford.
It furthers the University's objective of excellence in research, scholarship,
and education by publishing worldwide. Oxford is a registered trademark of
Oxford University Press in the UK and in certain other countries

Published in India by
Oxford University Press
YMCA Library Building, 1 Jai Singh Road, New Delhi 110 001, India

ISBN-13: 978-0-19-945353-5
ISBN-10: 0-19-945353-5

Typeset in Adobe Garamond Pro 11/13
by Tranistics Data Technologies, New Delhi 110 019
Printed in India at Rakmo Press, New Delhi 110 020

Contents

Preface

The idea for this book emerged at the 'National Review Workshop on Gender and Mental Health', held in Goa, in July 2007. At this workshop, a small group of feminist researchers met to set a frame for research on new thinking and practice in the field of gender and mental health. Among those resource persons, a few writers emerged who worked on updating the knowledge and information on some thematic areas.

New areas of thinking have come into the field of gender and mental health, such as on sexuality, sexual identities, and orientation, posing a challenge to conventional feminist thinking on women's identities and experiences. The emerging areas of stress, trauma, physical/immunological health, and psychosomatic problems need to be understood better with an integrated health framework. The study of women's traditional knowledge and indigenous psychological resources used to maintain positive mental health and prevent mental ill health is also a new development. Women's spirituality and access to spiritual spaces have been theorized more as a harmonizing principle rather than a divisive principle. The knowledge pool on various subjects relating to women and mental health, which are in the mainstream now—domestic violence and mental health; child sexual abuse and mental health; reproductive health of both men and women and mental health; social determinants of well-being and mental health; gender, social power, vulnerability, and mental health; and gender, poverty, and mental health—also needed upgradation in the light of recent research. With this broad programmatic thinking, we started soliciting papers, peer reviewed them, and finalized a manuscript. When we finished the review project, we had around 20 review reports in hand.

From 2005 onwards, the United Nations (UN) was engaged in stakeholder consultations to develop a 'Convention' on the rights of people with disabilities. A new framework for those rights emerged in 2007, with the Convention on the Rights of Persons with Disabilities (CRPD), signed and ratified by India. New concepts have come into the mental health sector, from a social perspective, such as 'psychosocial disability', 'inclusion', and 'quality of life', as well as new medico-legal terms such as 'reasonable accommodation', 'non-discrimination', 'full legal capacity', and 'integrity'.

By the time we finalized our report in 2009, the CRPD was entrenched in policy discussions within the mental health sector, and the readied manuscript already looked dated! So, as editors, we made a selection of articles from the voluminous first version, and kept those that would present primary research and also respond to the present policy debates around CRPD. That is the origin of this volume.

Bhargavi V. Davar
T. K. Sundari Ravindran

Acknowledgements

We are very grateful to the Royal Netherlands Embassy, particularly Mr Rushi Bakshi, for his continuous support during the project period. We thank all the experts who attended the National Review Workshop, the many contributors to this volume, as well as the peer reviewer, Professor T.S. Saraswathi, from Bangalore. We are also grateful for the patience and persistence exhibited by the editors of Oxford University Press during this whole process.

Abbreviations

AIDS	acquired immunodeficiency syndrome
BIC	best interests of the child
CALERI	Campaign for Lesbian Rights
CAM	complementary and alternative medicine
CEDAW	Committee on the Elimination of Discrimination against Women
CREA	Creating Resources for Empowerment and Action
CrPC	Code of Criminal Procedure
CRPD	Convention on the Rights of Persons with Disabilities
DPO	disabled people's organization
DSM	*Diagnostic and Statistical Manual*
ECT	electroconvulsive therapy
FDA	Food and Drug Administration
FIR	First Information Report
GWA	Guardians and Wards Act
HIV	human immunodeficiency virus
HMSO	Her Majesty's Stationery Office
ICF	International Classification of Functioning Disability and Health
ICIDH	International Classification of Impairments, Disabilities and Handicaps
ICTR	International Criminal Tribunal for Rwanda
IDEAS	Indian Disability Evaluation Assessment Scale
IIM	Indian Institute of Management
IIT	Indian Institute of Technology
IPC	Indian Penal Code
IQ	intelligence quotient
LABIA	Lesbians and Bisexuals in Action
LG	lesbian and gay
LGBT	lesbian, gay, bisexual, and transgender
LGBTQ	lesbian, gay, bisexual, transgender, and queer
MHA	Mental Health Act

MSM	men who have sex with men
NGO	non-governmental organization
NHRC	National Human Rights Commission
NIVH	National Institute for the Visually Handicapped
PIL	public interest litigation
PTSD	post-traumatic stress disorder
PUCL-K	People's Union for Civil Liberties (Karnataka)
RN	registered nurse
RUWSEC	Rural Women's Social Education Centre
SAFE	Sexual Assault Forensic Examination
SANE	sexual assault nurse examiner
SC	Supreme Court
SSRI	selective serotonin reuptake inhibitor
STI	sexually transmitted infection
SVRI	Sexual Violence Research Initiative
TISS	Tata Institute of Social Sciences
UNCRPD	United Nations Convention on the Rights of Persons with Disabilities
UPIAS	Union of the Physically Impaired against Segregation
WHO	World Health Organization

1

Delivering Justice, Withdrawing Care

The Norms and Etiquettes of
'Having' a Mental Illness

Bhargavi V. Davar

The women's movement has, over many decades, engaged patriarchal institutions with foundational critiques, describing the consequences of these institutions on women's lives, occupations, and health. Here, 'institutions' mean family, science, community, religion, state institutions, and other such organized collectives representing and reinforcing patriarchy through the production of privileged knowledge systems. Such foundational critiques examining institutions, the relationships among them, and how they stand in contrast to women's identities, knowledge(s), and lived experiences need to be described with respect to the mental health sector in India.

Various questions, dilemmas, and paradoxes need to be addressed, particularly in the context of the United Nations' (UN) Convention on the Rights of Persons with Disabilities (CRPD), which India ratified in the year 2008. Among these dilemmas are the following. What is the genealogy of mental illness? Is it a social construct, a medical construct, a legal construct, a historical construct, or a personal construct, or some mix of each of the above? Is 'schizophrenia', 'attention deficit and hyperactivity disorder', or any other diagnosed mental illness purely a product of capitalism, the neo-liberal Indian economy, encapsulated in the freely marketed cosmetic drugs to enliven the humdrum of daily life? Is mental illness a disability? Do families cause mental illness, as Ronald Laing and others suggested five decades earlier; or are they a supportive institution; or, for that matter, is this question itself posing a false dichotomy? Do people living with a mental illness have a memory and/or the 'insight' to tell their own stories? When told, are such stories 'true'? If someone were to pursue religious prayer, as a part of their everyday practice of staying mentally well, is this a choice or is this the press of conventional religion? Why do we still have mental institutions, which operate on penal principles, in a free society? Is mental health a public health issue at all, as it rarely figures in the public health literature or public health policies?

Within the scope of this volume, institutional responses to such complex questions in contemporary India are being considered. Institutions include the state, families, courts, and media, other than the mental hospitals, which, in the 200 years of its existence, never ascended to the status of 'public health hospital', but have remained 'asylums' (National Human Rights Commission 1999). A sustained argument that runs through each of the chapters relates to the palpable need for a substantial overhaul of the mental health and other organized systems in India. Women's narratives of their experiences within these institutions are meagre, with exceptions such as Addlakha (2008). Earlier writings in the field of gender and mental health did not sufficiently appreciate the fact that institutions, especially law, overdetermined the mental health sector, its norms, and ground-level care practices (Davar 2012). The many lived experiences of women, documented by writers in different institutional contexts in this volume, provide abundant evidence of an urgent need to critique the penal approach that treats mental illness as a crime, and those afflicted by it as criminals, to one where the highest priority is placed on the provision of humane care that protects and respects the humanity of the women experiencing distress and disability.

The prototype of 'institution', as we know them in contemporary India, is the mental asylum, a product of complex exchanges between colonialism and modernity (described by Ernst 1991; Mills 2000, 2004). Most mental asylums were built in the late colonial period, along with other penal institutions (prisons, pauper homes, and lepers' homes). 'Treatment' for 'mental disorder' began in these institutions in our country in the last 150 years of colonial rule. These historical processes gave some peculiarities to the mental health sector, and to medical ethics regarding mental health patients, not found in health, disability, social welfare, or other sectors. They left an enduring colonial and custodial legacy within the public imagination, the Indian society at large, legislations, and within the care delivery sector. An asylum model continues to be the service delivery prototype till today, even though community-based practices have existed for two decades, mainly through non-governmental organization (NGO) work (for recent critiques of the mental health system in India, see Goel *et al.* 2005; Cremin 2007; Basu 2008; Sebastia 2009; Davar 2012).

The mental asylums are regulated by the Mental Health Act (MHA) of 1987. The MHA follows from its colonial precursors: the Indian Lunatic Asylums Act, 1858; and the Indian Lunacy Act, 1912. As in the earlier Acts, the MHA provides an expansive medico-legal context for the incarceration of people living with a mental illness, through a set of procedures colloquially known as 'involuntary commitment'. Comparable to the 'arrest' procedure of the Code of Criminal Procedure (CrPC), the involuntary commitment process is dehumanizing and may involve multiple state authorities, such as the local police, prison officials, the security personnel of asylums, and other statutory authorities. The National Human Rights Commission report (1999) recorded a high percentage of involuntary commitment practices in the state asylums. Cremin (2007) recorded the 'catch' and commit methods adopted by various private agencies in involuntary commitment.

Recent writers (Andrew and Digby 2004) in the field of gender and psychiatry have noted that asylum practice is indicative of societal practices of labelling and marginalization, leading up to a demand for spaces where people can be put away in confinement. The labelling and stigmatization of a woman as 'crazy' begins within familial and societal spaces and, over a period of time, leads to her removal from society into seclusion. The endurance of a custodial architecture and legal norms has ensured the seepage of a custodial outlook into all public discourses. Stereotypes about 'mentally ill' women (as incapable people who need to be forced into treatments) abound in many non-custodial institutions as well, as evidenced by several chapters in this volume. 'Institution', then, is not just a physical structure but also an attitude or an approach towards people that can be found in all kinds of spaces.

In the extant literature, narrations of women's lived experiences of institutions, for critical theorizing, cannot be found. This volume addresses the impact of institutions and institutional relationships on women's well-being, as they have experienced it. It presents critical outlooks on the institutional norms, their social derivatives, public cultures, and institutional etiquettes relating to those determined to be 'mentally ill'. 'Etiquette', in this context, is defined as a set of entrenched habits and behaviours determining the norm for relating to people who live with, are diagnosed of, or otherwise accused of 'mental illness'. These institutionalized habits are contrasted against women's stories of the experience of psychosocial disability; or attribution of 'mental illness'. Being determined to be 'mentally ill' is taken as more of an indication of social and legal customs, rather than disease status; and we try to recall this position throughout the volume in various institutional settings.

The contrast in the chapters between the privileged voices of health professionals and the voices of those with the most intimate, lived experience of mental health, namely, the women themselves, is a significant development that sets this volume apart from other edited Indian collections that may have appeared in the last decade. An interesting finding, as the volume developed, was how institutional pressure (within the psychiatric clinic, the mental asylum, the families, the courts, and other public discourses) itself causes mental agony and trauma. While the health system also causes such mental traumas, it is paradoxical that the mental health care institutions exacerbate, rather than abate, mental trauma.

Vindhya (2007: 340) writes, '[D]espite the proliferation of studies on women and the benefit from the increasing visibility being accorded to issues related to women, the original objective of the women's studies perspective to provide a critical cutting-edge in all disciplines has remained rather sidelined in mainstream psychological research'. As an editor, the excitement has been about being a part of a growing collective of young and senior gender researchers on mental health, and to be able to present recent, primary data and social theory on the subject, in this volume. Each of these chapters in the volume is questioning of mainstream institutions, while expanding the frontiers of critical theory and practice on gender and mental health.

Intersectionality has recently begun to engage the attention of both gender and disability researchers. Women and men are not homogeneous categories, and each constituency is stratified by race, ethnicity, gender orientation, sexuality, age, caste, or class. Gender is a social stratifier, and is an ascribed characteristic of individuals; and gender interacts with other social stratifiers, and also with the structural determinants of health and disability, to constitute structural determinants which are dynamic. Structural factors also include 'macro' factors such as globalization, demographic transition, urbanization, dominant ideologies governing relationships between and within countries, the increasing role of human rights and women's movements, and so on. The consequences are inequalities in health outcomes in terms of mortality, morbidity, and long-term disability. A social, political, and environmental influence over health and disability is more clearly understood these days. The CRPD also reinforces this view that disability is not what is found simply as impairments in the individual, but includes the structural barriers created by society. In case of some groups of people with disabilities, especially those with intellectual or psychosocial disabilities, the disability caused by social and normative barriers to inclusion and to enjoyment of equality and equal opportunity may outweigh the disability caused by impairment.

In gendering the mental health discourse, other layers of individuation with respect to social stratification, discrimination, and access to resources need to be added, that make disability experiences visible and also variable, as a set of interacting political, social, economic, and individual factors. The distribution of class and capital in urban spaces adds a further layer for nuanced analysis. For example, voice-hearing young, middle-class women run the risk of being 'early intervened' with expensive and often unnecessary antipsychotics; while the homeless women with unusual or bizarre experiences are rounded up for institutionalization within asylums or beggars' homes through the courts. Lesbian/bisexual/androgynous or transgendered people with disabilities face multiple social risks, as women, homosexual, and disabled; and all have more than an equal chance in society to be picked out as 'mentally ill'. Young 'anorexic' women or women with eating disorders, receiving psychiatric/psychotherapeutic care in private clinics, are at one end of the spectrum; malnourished poor women lie at the other end, as if there were no issues to be addressed in the case of the latter except the right to food. The poor Dalit and tribal women approach the *dargahs* (healing shrines based on the Sufi way of life) for cures from psychosocial afflictions, while affluent women seek out the psychoanalyst or the many new-age therapies now widely available at a high price in urban areas and the metropolises. Battered women who were diagnosed and treated; married non-conforming and assertive women who were certified insane through psychiatry and the family courts system in India; women with physical disabilities as well as diagnosed mental illness; elderly and disabled women; lesbian disabled women; and women with other age or development-linked disadvantages had a diversity of contexts defying generalization. Also, notice the disparities in care between Hindu women and Muslim women, particularly in contexts of communal violence or regional conflicts. Nursing or caregiving women from the lower class may face an emotional burnout in their role in caring for a disabled or elderly woman from higher classes. There are also women untouched by any kind of psychosocial support, such as homeless women, women providing sexual services, and those living within institutions.

The conflict-torn regions of the country and the regional political scenario bring their own inequalities and serious mental health concerns. Consider, also, the large number of women arriving from the developed West seeking 'Eastern' healing in India, and establishing Western enclaves around ashrams and temples, while the 'modern' Indian families seek psychiatry, against the background of stigma reduction campaigns by psycho-pharmacy. A universal theory of mental illness or disability is not useful herein and we need more studies to reflect such intersectionalities and complex locally operating structural ramifications within the gender, mental health, and disability discourse. The question of who is choosing what, at which social strata, where, and at what costs, for getting 'cured' of what, is a complex one.

Building appropriate mental health care for a woman is not simply reforming psychiatry from a gender perspective; nor is it persuading distressed or disturbed women to join the movement ranks for getting 'empowered'. The assumptions within the medical disciplines need to be stood on their head, and the path paved for a more socially and politically informed, mind–body integrated, psychosocial and spiritual knowledge on health, well-being, and disability. At the same time, the women's movement and other political spaces need to become a space not only for strong, rational, and angry women but also for those with vulnerabilities, fragilities, and disabilities—who are no less able to be thinking, feeling persons with 'fight' in them.

The play in the volume can be imagined as spiralling around the themes of knowledges, identities, institutions, and public spheres by establishing a critique and attempting, where possible, a reconstruction and a future proposal for engaged knowledge(s) and praxes. The volume traverses the three discursive elements. The next three chapters by Ranjita Biswas, Vasudha Nagaraj, and Jayasree Kalathil derive critiques of the normality/pathology dichotomy as it applies to women within the sciences, courts, and the media. Shazneen Limjerwala, Renu Addlakha, Ketki Ranade and Yogita Hastak fill data gaps and develop new theories and methods from bottom-up, that is, from women's self-storying and addressal of identity questions as a researcher, disabled woman, and a lesbian. Finally, Anubha Sood and Bhargavi Davar address the question of choice vis-à-vis policy perspectives for the care of women living with psychosocial disabilities.

Gender Norming and Mental Illness

Writers have been concerned about the control of behavioural, attitudinal manifestations, expressions of individuality, grooming and personhood, defiance and resistance, through new categories of psychopathology. Ian Hacking (1995) presents a hilarious account of the rise and fall of 'multiple personality disorders'. He writes:

> In 1972, multiple personalities were almost invisible. Ten years later, they were noticeable enough for there to be talk of an epidemic. In

1992, they are a thoroughly visible minority. This is the fourth and greatest coming. It provides an extraordinary opportunity to observe a kind of illness, a kind of behaviour, a kind of treatment, a kind of doctor, and a kind of person in the making. (Hacking 1995: 3)

In the making of the *Diagnostic and Statistical Manual* (*DSM*), Ian Hacking (1998) has referred to the invention of the individual self in categorical and pathological terms, as having 'looping effects', that is, 'providing actionable *DSM* self identifications for the people taking up such self descriptions' (Strong 2012). We become that which is projected on us textually, through the *DSM*. Absent, any kind of purely physiological markers of mental illness, the historicity and gendering of psychiatric diagnosis in different sites of medical, psychiatric, social, legal, and cultural application become interesting subjects of study.

Society judges and marginalizes women on the basis of judgements and values about what constitutes 'normalcy'. This is a truism in the case of health and disease also. Judgements of abnormal mental health could be about behaviours, whimsical expressions, intensities of feelings, creative surges, surges of pleasure and desire, unusual thoughts, medically unexplained bodily pains, worries about reproductive experiences, existential worries, unusual, bizarre, or intense spiritual experiences, deviance from sexual stereotypes, being too 'racy' or 'wayward', an enduring feeling of malaise, disease, or disturbance, being unemployed, and so on.

Chapter 2 by Ranjita Biswas examines the genealogies of scientific notions of the 'normal' and the 'pathological'. She challenges the very assumption of conceptualizing 'mental illness' as a legitimate object of knowledge. The 'history' of psychiatry and psychology, it has been said, has no object of study and therefore is a pseudo-discipline within history. Rose (1996: 380) also cautions thus:

It would indeed be ironic if, in our renewed attention to the history of psychiatry, we were to forget the processes that brought its object into existence and inscribed it in our modern imagination as pathology, negativity, incompetence and deficiency, the processes that still today, in different ways, continue to thrust all that we call madness, and all those we call mad, into oblivion.

Similarly, Smith (2008) writes forthrightly, as a counter to Michel Foucault, that a history of psychology is not possible, and whatever the scientific construct of 'psyche', it can be dissolved into earlier philosophical, social, or other everyday matters relating to how people engage each other.

When, why, and how, as a part of the evolution of animal species, did human beings start classifying each other as 'normal'/'pathological'? When did our everyday caregiving functions as a human society become 'specialized', leading to university curricula and special groups of licensed caregivers? How and when did the everyday construction of our humanness, for example, 'sexuality', reconstitute itself as a medical psychiatric problem? Savoia (2010) argues that sexuality is a discursive equation: on one side is the subject and on the other side, the object of knowledge. Sexuality gets constructed on the grounds of the articulation between conceptual spaces, power relations, the evolving technologies of the self, and 'scientific' clinical practices. She looks at how a psychiatric and a psychological pathway developed in different ways because these relationships were different for the scientists of the nineteenth century. Braslow (1997), an American psychiatrist, makes a similar claim in another context, that the 'mental illness' gets constructed in the interaction between the doctor and the patient, the evolving medical gaze, and its technologies. Braslow shows convincingly, piecing together patient records at a North American asylum, that the doctor's diagnosis of insanity changed with each kind of treatment: each new and promising treatment (for example, lobotomy) led the doctor and his peers to 'see' the psychopathology (*delirium tremens*) that necessitated that treatment. In these historical forays into diagnostic categories, we see a human penchant, unlike the rest of the animal kingdom, for classifying and dividing ourselves, for establishing sameness and exploding difference, and when encountering difference, finding ways of controlling it. Biswas's chapter sets the critical tone for analysis in the two following chapters, by Vasudha Nagaraj (Chapter 3) and Jayasree Kalathil (Chapter 4), on the application of normality/psychopathology in two other sites of public discourse and the shaping of public consciousness: media and the courts.

Discussing the two instances of hysteria and homosexuality and arriving at 'anorexia nervosa' and 'gender identity disorder', Biswas' chapter takes up gender and sexuality as the two sites to examine how 'difference' is reconstituted into 'lack', both before the beginning of the psychiatric diagnostic manuals as well as in contemporary codifications. Even when a certain clinical category has been removed from the diagnostic systems used in psychiatric practice, for being less objective or more biased, the apparent disappearance of a definition has opened up the space for a more incisive continuation of its 'function'. The chapter establishes that normative construction of gender and sexual roles continues to operate not only in social spaces: they are also naturalized through scientific categories—categories that are considered to be objective truths and thereby more resistant to critical questioning.

Mixing Justice with Care

Societal attribution of 'crazy' and 'insane', and variations thereof, being widespread, determination of psychopathology becomes a social and justice issue. Within the public health system, people do not 'charge' or 'accuse' each other of being 'diabetic' or 'cancerous'. The court of justice issue comes much later in the health system, when maltreatment happens. In mental health, the very 'finding' of 'mental illness' sets up a close medico-legal environment for that person, where justice and care get mixed up. A diagnosis of mental illness determines citizenship status and access to constitutional rights. The Constitution of India explicitly denies franchise rights to persons of 'unsound mind'. Various family and community laws (relating to marriage, maintenance, custody, civil contracting, holding public office, standing for elections, voting, and so on) disempower all dimensions of women's lives (reviewed in Davar 2012). There is a personal, legal, and social cost to receiving a diagnosis of mental illness, not comparable to any other medical or disability diagnosis that women may receive.

What leads to a homemaker, or for that matter a homeless woman, being seen as 'mentally ill'? The claim that is being made here, that 'mental illness' is first a 'charge' or an 'accusation' made by the immediate social circuit—be it family, friend, or neighbour—has excellent consequences for any further social theory building or analysis, as this volume testifies. From this claim, we can map the many paths that women traverse in social, public, and healing spaces, trying to challenge the finding of mental illness and to reclaim their self-attested 'sanity'. Particularly within marital spaces, it is not uncommon to find mutual accusations of the others' 'abnormality', leading to everyday contests of establishing control over the immediate household resources and authority: children, household budgets and gadgets, property, and day-to-day decisions. Issues become really complex when the family unit goes before a professional, who will then 'certify' insanity, and the whole issue goes before a court.

One marriage was annulled by a lower court on the basis of a finding of 'moderate depressive episode with somatic syndrome'.[1] The history of this case shows that the husband filed nullity of marriage petition on the grounds of insanity and fraud due to non-disclosure, in the Pune family court. He alleged that his wife had had 'as many as six previous sexual relationships' and had kept him in the dark about it. Not revealing these past relationships was construed by the lower court as 'deception', the ground of 'insanity' admitted, and the marriage was rendered null and void. The judgement was squashed by the High Court, which however engaged in serious violation of the right to bodily and mental integrity and the right to privacy. The woman was repeatedly sent for different gynaecological tests and psychiatric tests. The husband had alleged that her 'vaginal opening was enlarged and vaginal muscles laxed'. After two independent gynaecologists found that the vaginal muscles were indeed 'laxed', the gynaecologists directed that both of them should see a psychiatrist. The woman in question had reported child sexual abuse by a male cousin who had raped her in childhood, which the court noted in its judgement. Other than this, the woman also was evidently distressed and had mentioned sleep disturbance, crying spells, and other symptoms before the court. Not empathetic at all to the history of childhood sexual abuse and nor to its mental health consequences in the woman's adult life,[2] the court ordered several medical tests. After several subsequent referrals, she was diagnosed with 'severe subjective distress' and 'moderate depression with somatic complaints'. A study of case law from the family court provides many such examples.

Unlike other health patients, once a person is identified as 'mentally ill', there is a huge 'downward mobility' process, from the first step of social identification of deviance to social censure, exclusion within community spaces, to a medical certification of mental disorder, and then on to institutional life or a severely restricted community life. The first entry into the institution may well result in a 'life cycle' of this process: release, deviance, conflict, censure, treatment, exclusion, and institutionalization.

In the health system, nuanced debates on proof of disease and effectiveness of treatment are possible and do happen, and cases of human rights violations reach the courts usually with petitions against the doctor. In mental health, the judicial contest begins with the very assertion of a finding of 'mental illness' and it is the patients who go before the court, not the doctor, to be adjudged for their mental status! Where 'mental illness' is a social claim to be established before a court of law, women risk higher disempowerments of their health status as well as rights, as in the above-mentioned case and as Nagaraj's chapter in this volume testifies. A social attribution of 'mental illness' leads to disbelief, dissociation, shame, anger, negativity, self-doubt, 'self-talk', psychosomatic problems, and a range of coping or adaptive responses, which then get stamped through psychiatric clinics as 'mental illness'. Women so disempowered also face other emotional and psychological scars of just entering and exiting 'the system': the doctors, institutions, family members, media (sometimes), and courts. These aspects of disbelief and personal trauma of entering and exiting both the psychiatric system as well as the court process are presented in killing detail by Vasudha Nagaraj.

As her chapter testifies, when a family member or a community member brings the subject before a court on a 'charge' of insanity, the courts do not have any way of figuring out whether 'mental illness' is 'real', 'imputed', or 'feigned'. The legal system is prejudiced about women's supposed propensity to mental illness and, especially at the lower court level, is quick to label them as mentally ill in case of any departure from the cultural norms of a 'wife' or 'mother'. The chapter challenges the rationality of the legal process by which it arrives at a decision related to a woman's claim and, at the same time, portrays the dilemmas inherent in petitioning the law—known to be gender biased in the domain of the family—to seek justice for wrongs suffered.

Vasudha Nagaraj's chapter shows the path traversed by many women in India, though perhaps not always as successfully as her client. Her chapter shows that, in the mental health sector, unlike general health care, there is a curious mix-up of justice and care, a mix-up which has survived over 200 years of colonial legal history into this millennium.

The Business of Psychopathology

Vasudha Nagaraj's chapter describes the pathway of a woman labelled mentally ill within the familial context and how that process of 'insanitization' is amplified through a court system; Jayasree Kalathil's chapter describes how women are constructed as mentally ill through popular media, specifically drug advertisements found in various psychiatric journals in the last few decades.

In 1988, late Dr Channabasavanna, a psychiatrist, wrote in the editorial of the *Indian Journal of Psychiatry* about the irrational drug prescribing practices found in India. He lamented that doctors prescribe 10–12 drugs per patient. Further, he cautioned against the routine prescribing of antipsychotic drugs with anti-Parkinsonian medication, a quick-fix method doctors often use to deal with the incorrigible motor side effects of the antipsychotics. Other than warning against mass prescribing of tranquillizers, anti-anxiety and antidepressant drugs, he noted the malpractice of narco analysis and the extensive use of 'electronic gadgets' (euphemism for shock treatment) and 'uncommon treatment methods' (Channabasavanna 1988). Nunley (1996) had also remarked on the overprescription of psychoactive substances almost two decades ago. Nunley wrote that psychiatrists' motives and attitudes are shaped by the culture in which they live, and that cultural factors may contribute to the heavy reliance on multiple drug prescriptions and on electroconvulsive therapy (ECT) in north India. Later, a study from Goa (Patel *et al.* 2005) found widespread irrational drug prescribing in a pharmacy they studied, corroborating studies from elsewhere in the country. In 80 per cent of the prescriptions they studied, polypharmacy was the norm, with a significant number of prescriptions having five or more medicines in a single prescription. More recently, Jain and Jadhav (2009) provided an ethnographic account of how the (psychiatric) 'pill' serves as the key metaphor transacted in rural outreach clinics of the District Mental Health Programme in Kanpur. The paper provides glaring and rare insights about the National Community Mental Health Policy, which, as the title suggests, is swallowed by the 'pill' (also, see Trivedi *et al.* 2010, on a finding of polypharmacy).

There isn't a voluminous history of Indian writings on gender and advertisements, though post-colonial theory and literary studies have a strong intellectual tradition. The study of gender in advertisements has pointed to the ways in which images of men and women in advertisements influence and propagate existing ideologies, and create new ideals to meet the needs of a changing world economy, thus institutionalizing these ideologies in new formats. Classic works in this area (Goffman 1979; Wex 1979) have inspired much of the literary, social, and political analyses around advertisements. Marianne Wex studied visual images through history and analysed gendered poses/posturing. Goffman reviewed six gendered dimensions of advertisements: the comparative size of men and women; on gendered aspects of touching—'feminine touch'; role and function; family; on posturing subordination; and finally, license to withdraw. Writers have looked at advertisements for house products, perfumes, car advertisements, stressing the patriarchal and stereotyped depiction of women. In India, Meenakshi Thapan (2004) analysed *Femina*, a popular women's glamour journal, and noted the recolonization of women's bodies in the transition period of the last decade. She found that *Femina* projects a view of the female body as desirable and as a product that can be commercialized for international consumption.

Jayasree Kalathil's chapter in this volume is on gendered psychotropic advertisements. Kalathil develops a further challenge to the objective reality and proof of mental illness by showing that public discourse, as much as the normative ones, is shaped by gendered notions of normality and psychopathology. Her chapter examines how psychoactive drug advertisements of the 1990s and until mid-2000s represented women. Kalathil's chapter is witness to the construction, consolidation, and propagation of patriarchal ideologies about transitioning women as found in psychopharmacological advertisements. Ads of the 1990s tended to portray men as psychotic and women as neurotic, and to portray drug effectiveness in terms of helping women effectively play their roles as housewives. While women's depression remained unexplained, men's depression was portrayed as being associated with organic diseases. Advertisements in 2006 were very different: the emphasis had shifted to portraying mental illness as just another illness that can be cured by drugs, thereby reifying mental illness and offering medication as essential.

A study of psychiatric drug ads, which are usually aimed at doctors, helps understand what gendered notions of illness, treatment, and doctor–patient relationships are employed. Such a study also provides insights into the implications of these ads for how drugs are prescribed and where the doctors obtain their research information from. In the late 1990s and through the last decade, several 'whistleblowers' such as Peter Breggin, David Healy, and others have spoken out against ghostwriting: a psychiatrist hired by pharmaceuticals for writing papers validating their drug (Kallivayalil 2008). The United Kingdom (UK) House of Commons publicly denounced these practices in 2005.

Together, Chapters 2, 3, and 4 attest to the historical and epistemological indeterminacy of 'mental illness', and leave us pondering over the question of whether mental illness 'really' exists. Women experiencing emotional swings, hearing voices, or contemplating suicide will talk about profound mental pain and confusing experiences, which is perhaps what is signified by 'mental illness'. However, diagnostic concepts are far removed from experientially shared knowledge, compounded by the politics of the mental health institutions and the drug industries. It is this distance that Ranjita Biswas, Jayasree Kalathil, and Vasudha Nagaraj describe in their foundational challenge to psychiatry.

Knowledge(s), Marginalities, and Identities

The disability paradigm gives an alternative discursive space for women experiencing psychosocial disability to reconstruct their experiences of marginality. Empowerment, inclusion, interdependence, autonomy, difference with dignity, acceptance of vulnerability, the inherent meaningfulness of lived experiences, and the expertise of people living with a disability are some key features of the contemporary disability paradigm, as found in the CRPD. The CRPD moves our understanding of mental illness from a medical, institutional conceptualization to a social, community understanding, suggesting that lack of access and marginality exacerbates the disability experience, particularly intellectual and mental disabilities.

But is mental illness a disability? Women who have had transient experiences with psychological distress may not see themselves as either mentally ill or as disabled. Women living with a mental illness may or may not see themselves as living with a disability. Women who have survived mental illness in the past, and who are presently living the lives of the well-coping abled, may not even consider that they were disabled in the past. Women diagnosed with schizophrenia often view their problem as medical or as an illness, and may or may not acknowledge the disability. Many others may be struggling with the disability, without necessarily having a name for their situation. Medical professionals, too, have had difficulties in casting psychosocial problems in terms of disability, and in making an instrumental or clinical shift from the medical to the social. Psychotherapists, who are taught 'abnormal psychology' as part of their training, see themselves as sub-serving the medical profession, not the disability sector, unless they are working with children. Few sensitive instruments on the 'measurement' of psychosocial disability exist and the Indian Disability Evaluation Assessment Scale (IDEAS), while being used, is much criticized for being a purely medical instrument, not at all reflecting the disability ethic or experience.

Disabled people's organizations (DPOs) are well organized with respect to the blind, the deaf, and people with mobility impairments. People with other disabilities, including mental and psychosocial disabilities, suffer a very high degree of stigma and discrimination, creating barriers to their accessing any kind of resources or opportunities. Legal barriers also exist, disallowing formation of organizations. Disabling features of mental illness are not due only to the primary condition, but also due to the social layering of barriers. The CRPD recognizes this fact, and disability caused by social barriers is considered as a significant contribution to estimates of disability. In the mental health sector, studies linking disability with mental illness from this social perspective are very meagre.

The disability discourse has been based on physical disabilities conceptually. A theoretical leap is required to include people with mental and psychosocial disability. The disabled people's movement in India has worked towards inclusion of people with psychosocial disabilities in their cadres and in leadership roles. The groups working on other disabilities may sometimes express disdain for people living with a mental illness, or further stigma ('Our wards have cerebral palsy, they are not mad'...). Various central and state-level committees on disability, and local committees at the panchayat level, have little to offer people with mental health problems. Looming large in the disability sector is the metaphor of ability and disability as having physical qualities: access to roads, buildings; work and livelihood; education; among others. Psychosocial dimensions such as selfhood, spirituality, intimacy, privacy, and creativity have not yet been fully conceived in terms of rights within the larger movement. For example, for a woman who hears voices, not being crowded by people and requiring private space is an important accessibility need. Her confusion increases if there are people around trying to help her in ways that are actually not helping, but only increasing her sense of fear and panic. However, the physical parameters of the disability discourse have not been stretched to include these internal psychological dimensions of access as well.

Chapter 5 by Renu Addlakha builds on the conceptualization of mental illness as psychosocial disability. Specifically, the chapter juxtaposes the narrative of a woman with a physical disability with that of a woman diagnosed with a mental illness. Disability is framed as the interface between personhood, biology, culture, and society, and this definition bridges the gap between physical disabilities and the emerging category of psychosocial disability. It is significant that 'disability refers to the specific social restrictions imposed on persons with impairments through the discriminatory practices and attitudes of society'. With this definition, disability moves from a medical to a social model. Among all the social variables that frame disability causation and experience, gender plays perhaps the most critical role. Patriarchy imposes additional multiple burdens on the woman with a disability. Cast as the 'other', when compared to a 'normal' woman, she experiences asexual objectification and pervasive rolelessness, as being unfit to care and nurture and to be a homemaker. She is at a disadvantage in comparison to non-disabled women and disabled men, throwing her into a socially residual category that is yet to be clearly articulated. Her chapter describes the lives and worlds of two women—one with a visual impairment and another suffering from schizophrenia—and highlights the similarities underlying the two. Gender, socio-economic status, marital status, and a certain north Indian cultural ethos combine to create very similar experiences of selfhood, relationship with the material and social worlds, and perspectives on family life, marriage, and the future in general. The purpose of this chapter is to present personal stories of disability within a holistic perspective, with equal emphasis on its biological and social dimensions. Renu Addlakha's chapter in this volume makes a beginning in moving the concept of mental illness into theories of disability, within the context of reference set up by the CRPD.

Just as women's mental health has been treated as a footnote in mainstream mental health literature in India, lesbian women's mental health has been a footnote or maybe even invisible in writings on women and mental health in India. Lesbian women, like women with disabilities, occupy the space of marginalization within society. Lesbian and gay youth face a greater number of stressful events and have access to less social support than their heterosexual peers. As they are invisible and lack social support systems, their everyday grief and losses, friendships, relationships, their personal attributes of presentation, grooming, mobility, personal development needs, need for intimacy, sexuality, the special needs of ageing, among other factors, do not have any public space for even mundane conversations. The needs of disabled, or ageing, or psychosocially disabled lesbian or bisexual women add multiple layers of discrimination and are only recently becoming articulated. While dating and meeting in intimate spaces is difficult even for young heterosexual people, it becomes near impossible for the gay community. Gay meeting places are targets for the moral vigilante, including the police. Lesbian women are usually forbidden to meet friends, kept under house arrest, quickly married off, and so on, often against their will and under duress. Some of them may go before psychiatrists and be treated for their deviance with psychiatric medication, hormonal therapies, or even unmindful surgeries. Gay men are at high risk for inhuman and degrading treatments within the mental health system even now, three decades after the *DSM* of the American Psychiatric Association removed homosexuality as a mental illness. Gay men are subjected to treatments such as aversion therapy, shock treatment, and other unnecessary treatments. Section 377 was repealed at the time of writing this chapter, but whether this repeal will change ground-level mental health practice is a moot question.

Chapter 6 by Ketki Ranade and Yogita Hastak fills this gap in knowledge of the mental health of lesbian and bisexual women. The chapter approaches women's mental health from a growth and development perspective. It is based on the premise that being attracted to individuals of the same sex can elicit familial and societal responses that can impact all aspects of living, across the lifespan, having detrimental effects on the women's sexual identity and fulfilment as sexual beings. The authors present the experiences of adult women with same-sex desires as they narrate what it was like to be different during their growing up years and socialization. Some of the themes covered in the chapter include questions about sexual desire and identity, sense of isolation, gender atypicality as seen in play, choice of clothes, correction of this from self, family, and peers, stressors due to sexual preference, and so on. The chapter attests to the various processes, barriers, challenges, tasks, and stressors that lesbian women go through in the process of growing up, in a predominantly heterocentric world. In the case of women with disabilities as well as lesbian, bisexual women, integrating mental health hopefully will result in community-based psychosocial services.

Following these chapters is a researcher's diary, with Shazneen Limjerwala writing on her own experience of fears and terrors brought on by her encounter with rape (Chapter 7). Women who are raped are yet another class of women living on the margins of society, often carrying the scars of the violation well into adulthood and old age, reliving the trauma, or surviving it through silence, coping, resilience, and resistance. However, the initial touchstone on the subject of rape seems to be fear, a fear born of years of zealous socialization into patriarchy, a fear that reveals layers of nuanced emotions and cognitions, and sometimes, a fear that paralyses all thought and emotion, leaving the researcher bereft of words. Shazneen Limjerwala's experiential account describes, in detail, the embodied, spatial, emotional, and cognitive dimensions of pursuing the subject of rape as an object of study. Here, as in most other experiences of marginality, we cannot take the subject out of the object, and in the end, are left with lingering doubts about the pursuit of 'pure' knowledge without empathy or emotion.

Identities, Voices, and Choices

This volume is also set against the background of various legal, policy, and other regulatory developments in the mental health sector in the last decade and the present, which have presented insurmountable barriers to community mental health care and to community choice in seeking local resources for healing (see Goel *et al.* 2005; Sebastia 2009, for debates on community mental health). Community choice and access to mental health care is more for faith healing, as found in dargahs, churches, mandirs, and other religious institutions. Community mental health and human rights have been a subject of debate since the Erwadi tragedy of 2001, which set off Supreme Court (SC) and other regulatory actions (Basu 2008; Davar and Lohokare 2008; also, see Chapter 8 by Sood, in this volume, for detailed discussions). A fire broke out at one of the private shelters in the precincts of the Erwadi dargah, Ramanathapuram district, in Tamil Nadu. On 6 August 2001, the hutments in which the inmates were housed, chained to their beds, caught fire. Eleven women and 14 men died when the fire broke out early in the morning. In all, 43 persons were kept there; three persons died later in the hospital.

After this incident, the SC initiated *suo moto* action against the state government of Tamil Nadu and all other states of India (vide Writ Petition Civil No. 334 of 2001), which invited Saarthak, an NGO from New Delhi, to file a petition. Saarthak's petition challenged the use of solitary confinement, direct ECT, and research without consent. The Saarthak petition had several ramifications, but one main outcome was the SC's directive for the construction of more mental hospitals in states where none existed. The MHA provided for such a facility, and the SC did not examine the constitutionality of the MHA in upholding Article 21, 'Right to Liberty'. While the rest of the world was moving towards community mental health, recovery, and complementary and alternative medicine (CAM) alternatives, why did the SC order the construction of penal institutions for the mentally ill? The SC paid little heed to the various public interest litigations (PILs), inquiries, and other legal interventions that emanated out of its own jurisprudence, or from other High Courts in the country. The SC also overrode the choice that people were making in seeking out places of faith healing.

The SC directed communities from faith healing centres to nearby mental hospitals.

The question is not so much about the reform of these institutions, but whether their architectural design and framework of service delivery needs to be totally condemned as obsolete. Just like the MHA, the asylums are a legacy from the colonial times and must be superseded by more humane institutional designs. Davar and Lohokare (2008) observed that mental asylums, while establishing a stiff legal regime, were legally non-compliant themselves. They argued for resourcing local designs of healing institutions, which are appropriate for community-based healing (Lohokare and Davar 2010). Anubha Sood, in Chapter 8, directly addresses the paradoxes that the state is caught in: offering 'modern' care through the mental hospitals, with their obsolete designs, while phasing out the indigenous healing systems. Anubha Sood's chapter builds on the claim that women do seem to choose indigenous healing systems, and also the open, voluntary community spaces. The chapter presents a comparison of the two systems of care from the point of view of women, and links it up with debates within feminism. Anubha Sood shows the role of the state in its unquestioning support to psychiatry, presenting it as the only legitimate choice in addressing mental health needs of the population. The chapter focuses on the implications of a transitioning mental health policy scenario post-Erwadi for the mental health needs of Indian women. It concludes by reiterating the urgent need to foreground women's mental health-seeking strategies and their choices as a crucial factor in formulating future mental health policy in the country. In order to do so, a shift in perspective is required to see how women's help-seeking choices may signify a deliberate response to the positive role indigenous mental health systems play in women's lives and well-being rather than simply an effect of women's lack of choices vis-à-vis psychiatric care or of their ignorance. To see women as ignorant masses who need to be educated into modern psychiatry is the limitation of modernity: Anubha Sood's chapter highlights the possibility of choice in seeking traditional healing sites for emotional well-being.

The CRPD opens up the question of identities of women with disabilities and their choices, unlike ever before. The rallying cry of 'Nothing about us without us' of people with disabilities brought the topic of identities as disabled people, and the question of autonomy and legal capacity, to the forefront. It opened up the possibility of sharing personal stories, building a collective rationale for activism, coming together in supportive spaces, and creating a living memory of the histories and struggles of women living with (psychosocial) disabilities in contemporary Indian society. The final chapter in this volume (Chapter 9) by me, amplifies the voices of women living with psychosocial disability, what the experience was like, and how it impacted their lives and decision-making.

As far as the epistemological structure of diseases go, mental health is different from health, as there is no 'thermometer' or 'evidence' for well-being, and subjective/interpersonal experiences and mental or psychosomatic events of everyday life serve as a good measure of mental health. When environmental factors are not facilitative, we suffer everyday afflictions and a sense of malaise: not sleeping too well, losing appetite, having a headache or stomach problems, burning sensations in the chest, fatigue, cramps and pains, irritability, being querulous, and so on. We take this to be an everyday affair and tolerate it well; and when it gets beyond our levels of tolerance, we may characterize our experiences as 'stress'. We may or may not take measures to deal with it, but nowhere would it consume our 'selves' or our experiences of who we are, or what we do, in the everyday world.

If such stresses have endured over many years, and the intensity of the environmental factors is more intense or complex, these would determine who we are and what we do. Analogy from general health could come from people who suffer chronic anaemia, cancer, human immunodeficiency virus (HIV), multiple sclerosis, or other grave illnesses. Some of us, a small percentage perhaps, do construct our identities around our experiences of disability and well-being. However, we may not always seek medical or psychological 'expertise' to deal with these issues because they fall within our everyday repertoire of living our lives, describable in our everyday-shared language. Friendships, support systems, relief spaces available in the locality, leisure, play and other entertainments, local healing spaces, lifestyle changes, spiritual or philosophical pursuits, joining political groups, sports and other physical regimens, and creative pursuits...often, one or more of these serve our purpose of acceptance, adaptation, and recovery from personal traumas and instability. 'Healthing' is a process and an everyday practice, and we struggle with establishing a routine about it, which we can repeat every day. More than these, what brings sustaining states of wellness and freedom from a sense of malaise is insight and self-reflection, and for some who have been through psychosocial stresses, this is a life career, of living in mindfulness, building insight, and experiencing the self as so many thresholds of transition and transformation. We then search for knowledge(s) which reflect our lived realities of disability and wellness, and which respond to our identity questions. My chapter in this volume talks about the everydayness of emotional suffering and the measures we take to cope with it, accept it, or overcome it. These are different choices that women with psychosocial disabilities make, and all are equally legitimate.

***

There are areas in the field of gender and mental health where gaps have been experienced in knowledge as well as in teaching and programme development. In the last decade, new areas of thinking have come into the field, such as marginality, disability, spirituality, sexuality, and sexual identities and orientation, posing a challenge to conventional thinking on women's identities and experiences. A discourse of women as evergreen victims of patriarchy has been challenged by this new paradigm, which celebrates women's being, lived experience, resilience, and their agency. The emerging areas of stress, trauma, physical/immunological health, and mind/body medicine need to be understood better if mental health interventions must be community friendly. The linkages between women's health, nutritional and reproductive health, and mental health are barely understood. There is a need to create a knowledge/skill pool in these intersectional areas, which cut across specializations. Women's traditional knowledge and indigenous psychological resources used to experience states of well-being, to maintain positive mental health, and to prevent mental ill health also are new developments. While this volume does not address the many new emerging areas, we hope to have brought into public discourse, the voices of women on the subject of psychosocial health and disability, as the women experience them and also as constructed by various institutions which impact their lives. In doing so, the volume may seem to indulge in a kind of doublespeak: is mental illness a myth, or is it lived reality? The spectrum of views presented in the volume may shift from one side to the other without resolving all dilemmas encountered along the way. However, from the narratives, it can only be concluded that the responses to this question are complex, providing opportunities for women to make choices. As a truism, it is acknowledged that there is a need to deconstruct traditionally given medical knowledge on mental illness, while attempting to reconstruct fresh knowledge from the experience of women with disabilities.

Notes

1. Mr. Vinand Vilas Arabale *vs* Ms Shilpa Vinand Arabale, Petition A.NO.487/2011, for annulment of marriage under Section 12(1)(c) in the court of Principal Judge, Family Court of Pune, at Pune. Judgement was delivered on 29 July 2012.
2. The Child Welfare Information Gateway, in Washington, DC, has useful resources on the subject of childhood sexual abuse. Available at: https://www.childwelfare.gov/pubs/issue_briefs/cm_prevention.pdf.

References

Addlakha, R. 2008. *Deconstructing Mental Illness: An Ethnography of Psychiatry, Women and the Family*. New Delhi: Zubaan Books.

Andrews, J. and A. Digby (eds). 2004. *Sex and Seclusion, Class and Custody: Perspectives on Gender and Class in the History of British and Irish Psychiatry*. Amsterdam: Editions Rodopi B.V.

Basu, H. 2008. 'Contested Practices of Control', *Journal of Medical Anthropology*. 32 (1 and 2): 28–39.

Braslow, J. 1997. *Mental Ills and Bodily Cures: Psychiatric Treatment in the First Half of the Twentieth Century (Medicine and Society)*. California: University of California Press.

Channabasavanna, S.M. 1988. 'Editorial: Drug Prescriptions in Psychiatry', *Indian Journal of Psychiatry*, 30(3): 209–10.

Cremin, K.M. 2007. *General Hospital Psychiatric Units and Rehabilitation Centers in India: Do Law and Public Policy Present Barriers to Community*

Based Mental Health Services. Pune: Bapu Trust for Research on Mind & Discourse.

Davar, B. 2012. 'Legal Frameworks for and against People with Psychosocial Disabilities', *Economic and Political Weekly*, XLVI(52): 123–31.

Davar, B and M. Lohokare. 2008. 'Recovering from Psychosocial Traumas: The Place of Dargahs in Maharashtra', *Economic and Political Weekly*, XLIV(16): 60–8.

Ernst, W. 1991. *Mad Tales from the Raj: The European Insane in British India 1800–1858*. London: Routledge.

Goel, D.S., S. P. Agarwal, R. L. Ichhpujani, and S. Srivastav. 2005. 'Mental Health 2003: The Indian Scene', in S. P. Agarwal, R. L. Ichhpujani, and S. Srivastav. (ed.) *Mental health: An Indian Perspective*. New Delhi: Ministry of Health and Family Welfare.

Goffman, Erving. 1979. *Gender Advertisements*. Cambridge, MA: Harvard University Press.

Hacking, I. 1992. 'Multiple personality disorder and its hosts', *History of the Human Sciences* 5: 3–31.

———. 1995. *Rewriting the Soul: Multiple Personality and the Sciences of Memory*. Princeton: Princeton University Press.

———. 1998. *Mad Travelers: Reflections on the Reality of Transient Mental Illness*. Cambridge, MA: Harvard University Press.

Jain, S. and S. Jadhav. 2009. 'Pills that Swallow Policy: Clinical Ethnography of a Community Mental Health Program in Northern India', *Transcultural Psychiatry*, 46(1): 60–85.

Kallivayalil, R.A. 2008. 'Guest Editorial: Are We Over-dependent on Pharmacotherapy?', *Indian Journal of Psychiatry*, 50(10), 7–9.

Lohokare, Madhura and Bhargavi Davar. 2010. 'Community role of indigenous healers', in Kabir Sheikh and Asha George (eds). *Health Providers in India: On the Frontiers of Change*. pp.161–181. New Delhi: Routledge.

Mills, J. 2000. *Madness, Cannabis and Colonialism: The 'Native-only' Lunatic Asylums of British India, 1857–1900*. London: Macmillan.

———. 2004. 'Body as Target, Violence as Treatment: Psychiatric Regimes in Colonial and Post Colonial India', in J. Mills and S. Sen (eds), *Confronting the Body: The Politics of Physicality in Colonial and Post-colonial India*, pp. 80–101. London: Anthem South Asian Studies.

National Human Rights Commission. 1999. *Quality Assurance in Mental Health*. New Delhi: National Human Rights Commission.

Nunley, M. 1996. 'Why Psychiatrists in India Prescribe So Many Drugs', *Culture, Medicine and Psychiatry*, 20(2): 165–97.

Patel V., R. Vaidya, D. Naik, and P. Borker 'Irrational drug use in India: A prescription survey from Goa', J Postgrad Med [serial online]. 2005 [cited 2015 Mar 6]; 51: 9–12. Available at: http://www.jpgmonline. com/text.asp?2005/51/1/9/14015.

Rose, Nikolas. 1996. *Inventing Our Selves*. London: Cambridge University Press.

Savoia, P. 2010. 'Sexual Science and Self Narrative: Epistemology and Narrative Technologies of the Self between Krafft-Ebing and Freud', *History of the Human Sciences*, 23(5): 17–41.

Sebastia, B. 2009. *Restoring Mental Health in India: Pluralistic Therapies and Concepts*. New Delhi: Oxford University Press.

Shidhaye, R. and V. Patel. 2010. 'Association of socio-economic, gender and health factors with common mental disorders in women: a population-based study of 5703 married rural women in India'. *International Journal of Epidemiology*, 39: 1510–21.

Smith, R. 2008. 'Does history of psychology have a subject?', *History of the Human Sciences*, 1(2): 147–77.

Strong, T. 2012. 'Talking about the DSM-V', based on a paper presented to the Therapeutic Conversations X Conference, 12 May, Vancouver, Canada. Available at http://www.taosinstitute.net/Websites/taos/images/ ResourcesManuscripts/Strong_Talking_about_the_DSM-V.pdf

Strong, T., J. Gaete Silva, I. Sametband, J. French, and J. Eeson. 2012. 'Counsellors respond to the DSM-IV-TR.'. *Canadian Journal of Counseling and Psychotherapy*, 46(2): 85–106.

Thapan, M. 2004. 'Embodiment and Identity in Contemporary Society: *Femina* and the 'New' Indian Woman', *Contributions to Indian Sociology*, 38(3): 411–44.

Thornborrow, J. 1998. 'Playing hard to get: Metaphor and representation in the discourse of car advertisements', *Language & Literature, 7(3)*, 254–72.

Trivedi, J.K., M. Dhyani, V.S. Yadav, and S.B. Rai. 2010. 'Anti-psychotic Drug Prescription Pattern for Schizophrenia: Observation from a General Hospital Psychiatry Unit', *Indian Journal of Psychiatry*, 52(3): 279.

Vindhya, U. 2007. 'Psychological Research on Gender Quality of Women's Lives in India: Some Findings from Two Decades of psychological Research on Gender', *Feminism and Psychology*, 17: 337–56.

Wex, M. 1979. *Let's Take Back Our Space: "Female" and "Male" Body Language as a Result of Patriarchal Structures*. Germany: Frauenliteratur Verlag.

2

(Un)making Madness

Delving into the Depths of Knowledge

Ranjita Biswas

This chapter takes a critical look at a few clinical diagnostic categories used in psychiatry that describe and help diagnose certain pathological conditions said to be found frequently among a given population. Through this revision of clinical categories, the chapter examines the notion of the 'normal' and the 'pathological' and asks: how does the spectre of normality loom large over our beings? Do the purportedly 'normal' and the 'pathological' have a life of their own; or do these categories have a certain history to their definitions? Moreover, how do these notions function to subsume difference? In the clinical setting, one constantly comes face-to-face with the question of 'difference'—all our clients are different, however much we may try to homogenize them under diagnostic categories. The difference within the respective sexes is undeniable and the difference in 'sexuation'[1] is particularly acute. How then does the question of difference, or for that matter, of 'sexual difference', figure in the mental health clinic? In this chapter, I specifically take up gender and sexuality as the two sites to examine how 'difference' is reconstituted into 'lack', both before the psychiatric diagnostic manuals were in use as well as in contemporary codifications. I argue that even when a certain clinical category has been removed from the diagnostic systems used in psychiatric practice for being less objective or more biased, the creation of newer categories subsequently has however retained the 'function' of the previous category in defining the normal/normative figure of the woman and the heterosexual. In fact, the apparent disappearance of a diagnostic category opens up the space for a more incisive continuation of its defining function. Discussing the two instances of hysteria and homosexuality, and arriving at anorexia nervosa and gender identity disorder, this chapter attempts to draw attention to how normative construction of behaviour continues to operate not just in social spaces, but within the domain of science as well. In other words, the chapter argues that gender and sexual roles and identities are not just perpetuated by social cultural institutions, but also naturalized through scientific categories. These categories are then considered to be objective truths and thereby more resistant to critical questioning.

Women in Psychiatry

Representations of women as 'mad' have conjured up images like the crazy wife languishing in the attic[2] or the young mother who, unable to cope with the pressures of her new responsibility of child rearing, starts crawling up the wall, literally.[3] The intimate tie between a woman and unreason is believed to be justified in her many 'performances'—sometimes an enigma, sometimes a seductress, and sometimes a witch. In all such descriptions, woman and femininity are seen as synonymous with madness, symbolizing the potential mysteries and dangers said to be lurking behind her countenance— believed to have the power to launch a thousand ships. In a world of binaries—human/non-human, mind/body, reason/affect–unreason, man/woman—woman is always already deemed the underside, the abject, the 'dark continent' symbolizing unreason and madness—signifying the potential mysteries and dangers said to make up all that a woman is.

Explanations of women's 'madness' have undergone numerous transitions over the ages. From the wanderings of a dissatisfied womb to vapours emanating from a suffocated uterus in antiquity, from the witches' unholy designs in the Middle Ages to a case of weakened nerves in the age of empiricism, from repressed sexual fantasies in Freud's time to a disturbed hormonal balance in the discipline of gynaecology, a woman's mental health has been understood in terms of her biological and psychological vulnerability. Aetiological explanations of her mental distress have vacillated between the 'female body' and the 'feminine psyche'. While discussions on her physical health have centred on reproduction-related issues—her capacity to 'procreate'—analysis of her mental health has focused on her hormones and their tendency to disrupt her capacity to 'create'. Whether it is her sex, her hormones, or her psyche, a woman is believed to bear an intimate relation with insanity.

In the last century, mental health sciences, but more particularly psychiatry, have crossed new frontiers in research, evident through ever-increasing insights about the brain and its functioning. Several new psychotropic drugs have populated the market and the clinician's vocabulary. These have reconfigured, in a large way, mental health, mental ill health, and cure. Terms like 'lunacy' and 'madness' have come to be reconstituted as 'mental illness' or, more fashionably, as 'mental disorder'. When it comes to women's mental health, two trends can be identified in this scientific fervour apparent within the psychiatric fraternity. On the one hand, women have featured significantly in epidemiological statistics, giving a fair description of the disorders found more commonly among the women population, as well as in accounting the different sociocultural risk factors that predispose them to ailments such as depression, post-traumatic stress disorder, and conversion disorder (previously known as hysteria). Thus, psychiatry talks of women's distress in terms of incidence and prevalence rates among the general population that gets divided along biological lines. On the other hand, women's distress gets located in the three-dimensional space of the body—in the hormones, tissue spaces, and the sex chromosomes—thereby erasing the sociocultural and economic–political factors. Such scientific studies apparently analyse a woman's mental illness in terms of her constitutional proneness to unreason/disorder. This emerging awareness about women's mental health issues, and the preoccupation with the same, has been lauded in certain quarters as a step in the right direction. But also inherent in such preoccupation is the attempt to institutionalize female disease/distress/experience through a process of biologizing and psychologizing in the disciplines of psychiatry and psychology. Both the biological and psychological schools of thought share the positivist/realist standpoint with an emphasis on a homogenous use of hypothetico-deductive methodologies. Efforts at both biomedical cures and psychological interventions focus on the individual woman positioned as passive. The social space gets reduced to the body space, which is seen to be determining the manifestation of mental illness in a linear fashion. This has resulted in the marginalization of historical and cultural factors that come to define women's lived experiences in significant ways.

Using the lens of gender as a tool of analysis, feminists have drawn attention to the structural and institutional misogyny that not only trivializes women's experiences of health/illness but also structures their distress only in terms of disease. The difficulties of women surrounding their experiences of pregnancy, childbirth, menopause, social marginalization, and the subsequent indifference of the health care system towards these issues, have often left them with a sense of helplessness. The advent of feminist theory in the 1970s in the West ushered in a sustained inquiry into the ways in which conventional disciplines have been shaped through the historic exclusions and mis-representations of the lives and experiences of women. The conceptual schemes that inform the production of scientific knowledge—the notions of detachment, objectivity, rationality, and neutrality—were shown to be biased in that they celebrated, in actuality, masculine systems of thought and premised themselves on the necessary exclusion of women's perspectives and life experiences (Harding 1986). Gender thus became a critical category for asking unasked questions about the content and practice of the sciences, for showing how the sciences were surreptitiously privileging a male perspective. The mainstream philosophical notion of rationality was shown to have been conceived as a transcendence of what is feminine, which, in other words, meant a disavowal of all that is characteristic of women's lives. Women have been traditionally seen as having a lesser presence of reason; they are seen as tied to affect and body. Affect or emotion that finds an easy comparison with non-reason, even unreason/madness, is seen as disruptive and is treated as an obfuscating layer between social reality and reasoned understanding. This gender bias, found to operate at a deeper conceptual level, is said to shape our apparently objective and value-neural scientific truths, more so in our dealings with women and issues related to their everyday lives and thought worlds. Discussed in the following section is one instance where a woman's distress is understood and theorized in terms of her constitutional imbalance, said to be emanating from her sexual–reproductive character.

Dora to Diana

Nineteenth-century medical and psychoanalytic discourse called hysteria[4] a somatic illness without organic cause—a neurotic symptom par excellence. Hysteria as a category has been variously described as a medical disorder, a spiritual malady, a social symptom, and as a psychosexual riddle. Through the successive explanatory models and contemplative theories, however, hysteria never lost its hint of a gendered essence—a certain specific association with feminine sexuality.

In ancient times, hysteria was linked to female generative organs and women were warned against subjecting their bodies to the vagaries of an uncontrolled sexual desire. Hysteria was believed to occur due to either a suffocated womb or a restless womb wandering inside the body and giving rise to the symptoms (Bronfen 1998: 105). Women were urged to follow the strict regime of maintaining their state of virginity till the time when the womb is ready to conceive. They were advised to avoid both the dangers of a premature defloration as also a lengthy postponement of reproduction, since both conditions could result in the state of hysteria. The Middle Ages saw hysteria shifting from a case of 'dissatisfied sexuality' to 'demonic possession' (Bronfen 1998: 106). Commonly seen as 'beings' that could travel between two worlds—the world of innocent femininity and the world of satanic mischief—without remorse or reticence, women were branded as 'witches' and hunted down. Thus, the stage was set whereby hysteria came to be associated with deceit, the ability to mimic and mislead. The age of empiricism saw hysteria undergoing a major change in its vocabulary. Hysteria was no longer thought to result from an actually displaced uterus. Rather, it was believed to originate from the uterus and affect all the organs by a diffusion of vapours and animal spirits.[5] The brain was thought to act as a 'relay station' in sympathetic involvement with the uterus (Bronfen 1998: 108). Hysteric affliction was now thought to be dependent on the integrity of body (and soul). The more penetrable the spaces to external 'spirits', the more frequent the possibility of hysteria. Women, by virtue of their weaker nerves and frail and rarefied corporeal spaces and souls, were seen to be more prone to hysteria.

With modernity, the emergence of the 'new woman' and her newly acquired attribute—education—provoked the anxiety of clinicians. Wanton emotion and intellectual exercise, alike, were seen as fatal for the female. Women's reproductive physiology, the space of the 'womb', captured the attention and imagination of the sciences,[6] but what remained most enigmatic was menstruation, which was believed to be 'the moral and physical barometer of the female constitution' (Jacobus et al. 1990: 47). It was believed that menstruation and its disorders, including the local diseases of the female reproductive organ, played a major role in the development of mental illness. Menstruation could be disrupted by emotional instability and this could, in turn, be followed by hysteria. What occupied the minds of the medical establishments then was not so much the flow of menstrual blood, but rather the state of its obstruction and retention. The notion of women's health consisted in continuously needing to sluice her internal drains so that she does not retain inside her the internal secretions—the disruptive and chaotic forces of sexual energy.[7] Only a regular draining of the superabundant circulating fluid could restore emotional tranquillity. This is because '[W]hen the growth of the form is nearly completed, the circulating fluid necessary for the future support of the body is in superabundance, and unless corrected in the delicate system of the female, must... necessarily acquire a power of rendering unduly intense the feelings of the mind' (Samuel Hibbert 1825, quoted in Jacobus et al. 1990: 57). Thus, women's bodies, their emotions and feelings, became a subject of constant monitoring, surveillance, and control through medical prescription.

The category of hysteria came to permeate intellectual discussion in India too. Mention of hysteria is found in a couple of early writings on psychology in Bengal. As Pradip Bose writes in his introduction to the section on 'Psychology' in Samoyikee, articles on psychology in Bengali periodicals were few and far between in the nineteenth century. The first, an incomplete article, was published in 1896, and the second in 1901, in *Swashthya*. They are mostly articles on philosophy and human nature, and it is only by some retroactive extrapolation today that we make a case for these articles and brand them as 'early' writings (Bose 1998: 357). As Bose (1998: 366; translation mine) quotes from one of the articles:

> Hysteria has become a very common disease; especially among the educated community of the city. The male youth suffer from short sight—the female from hysteria. There is not a single affluent household in the city, where one will not find one or two patients of hysteria. What is the reason for this? There were not so many hysterics previously.

The article from which the given excerpt is taken was written in 1901 and it brings out the author's anxiety for an increase in the incidence of 'hysteria'. Here, the author makes a number of observations, at times contradictory, on a possible aetiology of 'hysteria'. He discards the notion of hysteria being a disease of the womb. He mentions that current scientific research indicates that hysteria need not have a relationship with the uterus and in the absence of such proof, it can be clearly concluded that hysteria is primarily and 'generally a disease of the nervous system'. The author, thus, questions the age-old association of hysteria with the uterus and asserts that hysteria is not a disease of a specific organ or a 'specific space' of the body. Rather, the disease primarily develops due to 'weakness' of the nervous system (Bose 1998).

The author also states that hysteria is also not restricted to unmarried young women: 'Even a number of hysterics can be found among married and happy couples.' To further his point about the lack of association of hysteria with the uterus, the author cites cases of women who are born without the uterus and yet show signs of the disease and the fact that 'Hysteria is observed among the male as well' (Bose 1998: 367). The reasons given by the author behind hysteria, however, reflect those of the West:

> A deficiency of the flow of blood or impurities in blood within the nervous system
> Abnormal physical growth of organs among women

Menstrual irregularities
Excitement of the uterus
Pregnancy
Gynaecological disorders
Happenings against or contrary to one's wish
General ill health
Depression, fear or too much anxiety over some issue
Loss of husband or son or friend
Failure in love
Education of women
Reading of drama and novels that generate excitement
Social, cultural and moral upheaval and crisis among women's lives
due to English education
Wearing of tight dress
Lack of sleep (Bose 1998: 367)

The 'womb' had already been given up in Europe as the seat of hysteria. Both education of women and menstrual disorders were seen as causes of hysteria in Europe in those days. We see in this article of *Swashthya*, the uncritical reproduction of those same gendered notions that were in circulation in Europe in the eighteenth and nineteenth centuries. The European notion of education being the 'shame of (the) times' is reiterated in Indian conditions by relating it to the education of Bengali women—especially English education—of a few 'Bidhumukhi, Chandramukhi' (names of women) who get their BA degree and a few 'Sarala, Chapala' who get their MA degree. The author laments in true European style that this system of education only leads to their being affected by hysteria (Bose 1998: 368).

With the birth of psychoanalysis, a new chapter came to be inaugurated in the celebrated history of hysteria. The male anxiety about women's 'radical instability' and 'chaotic sexuality' in the nineteenth century came to be epitomized with Freud's invention of the talking cure, whereby one's distressed psyche comes to be liberated through confession in free association. Psychoanalysis was born out of the need to find 'the truth' behind hysteria, which was believed to be the conversion symptom of repressed childhood sexual experience (Freud 1956). Freud (1991[1905]: 144) writes on the differentiation between men and women in the following terms: 'The fact that women change their leading erotogenic zone...together with the wave of repression at puberty which as it were puts aside their childish masculinity, are the chief determinants of the greater proneness of women to neurosis and especially to hysteria.'[8] The male anxiety regarding feminine sexual excess of the nineteenth century gave way to the discovery of a feminine 'lack' in the twentieth century. Psychoanalysis defined woman as a figure of castration and hysteria as a 'feminine neurosis'. It maintained that only women were in danger of losing the love object (first, the mother's separation and then, the fear of losing the phallus).

The works of Girindrasekhar Bose, the first non-Western psychoanalyst, have served as an example of 'critical engagement with received theory' of the mind in colonial India. Besides his discussion of the Freudian dream theory in *Swapna* with the example of one of Josef Breuer's most discussed patients, Anna O., Bose also describes three patients with hysteria (in sections 125 and 142). All his three patients were women. Although his overall analysis is Freudian, in the classical sense of the term, he does not really discuss any specific (sexual) aetiology for these three patients of hysteria. He is rather more interested in positing 'hysteria' as a scientific category against popular belief in possession and in the supernatural. Bose, in a way, establishes that in all these three cases, the women were not possessed but were, in fact, suffering from 'hysteria'. The unconscious of the hysteric serves less as the repository of a possible sexual aetiology and more as the 'scientific' trope. It is the convenient conceptual tool for explaining occurrences that defy comprehension of the conscious; that negates the ready belief of the colonized in 'possession by spirits'.

In his articles in English in *Samiksha: Journal of the Indian Psychoanalytic Society*, Girindrasekhar Bose, however, does discuss a possible aetiology of hysteria. He writes, 'This difference in the development of the sexual life between a boy and a girl has got an important bearing on the genesis of mental disorders. The greater liability of girls to hysteria is to be explained on the basis of this factor' (Bose 1950a: 71). Recognizing an element of intense identification with the mother and a passive attitude towards the father, in the girl, he goes on to say:

The girl more than the boy loves to play with dolls and to act like the mother towards the father...The strong fixation of the libido on the father and the active homosexuality are invariably unearthed in the analysis of hysterics...In some cases the action of homosexual trend might completely inhibit the development of the *normal passive feminine cravings* and sexual anaesthesia might result. (Bose 1950a: 71; emphasis added)

In another article in the same volume (about a 35-year-old male sufferer of 'a very severe type of anxiety hysteria'), he writes, 'This case is of interest to us because it showed very clearly the existence *in a male* of a *female wish* to bear a child and at the same time the relationship of this wish to anal eroticism, homosexuality, castration complex and the small penis complex' (Bose 1950b: 84; emphasis added). The patient's improvement was said to happen after he came to appreciate 'the similarity of his symptoms to those of pregnancy and delivery' (Bose 1950b: 85). The analysis comes to an end by pinning down the patient's symptoms of apparent impotency and small penis complex to 'the tussle between his male and female tendencies', and ends by stating, 'the complete analysis of the case clearly proved the existence of the *female wish* in the patient as a result of identification with the mother' (Bose 1950b: 85; emphasis added).

In another issue of *Samiksha*, one comes across an article on hysteria by Nagendranath De (1947). De writes:

...[T]he mind of the hysteric...retains many of the characters of childhood...Hysterics are selfish at heart...due to domination in the mind of the selfish unconscious...What becomes deeply buried in the unconscious in a normal individual remains more or less superficial in the hysteric...[T]he inhibitory influence of the conscious...is very limited in the hysteric and so emotions are easily aroused...The preponderance of hysteria among prostitutes is not because they are more liable to it but because many of the hysterics as a result of their emotional instability in sex sphere fall into trouble...They do not develop a moral code of life...Chastity is not valued above pleasures of life. Discrimination between truth and falsehood is imperfect...Many of the stories told by adult hysterics about sexual assaults in early childhood are proved on investigation to be false. (De 1947: 299–301)

Hysteria thus serves, on the one hand, as a convenient tool of modern scientific criticism of the belief system of the colonized and, on the other, as the ready trope for redefining the woman of the colony—her psyche, her madness—in terms and language set by a Western psychoanalyst.

The clinical category of hysteria came to be used widely in psychiatric practice to define and treat women's mental health problems. However, with the appearance of better diagnostic tools and more detailed knowledge of the functioning of the brain and nervous system, the category seemed inadequate to capture the wide range of women's psychiatric manifestations. In 1952, in the first edition of the diagnostic manual formulated by the American Psychiatric Association that is followed the world over, *Diagnostic and Statistical Manual (DSM I)*,[9] hysteria became subdivided into two categories: hysterical neurosis, conversion type; and hysterical neurosis, dissociative type. This was again brought together in *DSM II* (1968). The *DSM III* (1980) decided to abandon the use of the word hysteria and included two new categories, somatization disorder and conversion disorder, under the heading 'Somatoform Disorders'. This broad category, still in use today, contains information about disorders (which have no organic pathology) and their physical symptoms, manifested solely as a result of repressed psychological conflicts. Dissociative disorders appear as a separate category.

Today, hysteria is not a recognized pathological condition in the mental health sciences. The apparent 'demise' of hysteria as a category has been accompanied by the birth of certain other more exhaustive and specifically codified categories such as somatization disorder, conversion disorder, dissociative disorders, and multiple personality disorders in *DSM IV*. These new descriptions of mental illnesses appear ostensibly gender-neutral and more objective, having replaced the older condition of hysteria, and with it, the notion of a disordered femininity. But even though the said association of hysteria and feminine sexuality has been apparently given up in scientific discourse (dominant biomedical psychiatry, to be precise), there is a subversive, surreptitious trickling of the 'same' cultural ideals into scientific space as evident in other late twentieth-century diagnostic categories like anorexia nervosa. Hysteria has ceased to function as *the* category typifying mental illness. But the 'function' of the category as defining of woman and her sexuality has been as operative as before. In fact, it has found a plurality of expressions in both scientific and sociocultural spaces. Hysteria has supposedly outlived its association with the female sex and with feminine sexuality. Or has it? Has hysteria freed itself of its cultural–sexist moorings or can similar cultural–sexist ideals be still located as 'displaced' into new scientific categories?

Any study of hysteria, the nineteenth-century female malady, cannot but arrive at anorexia, its twentieth-century counterpart. Or in other words, a study on anorexia cannot but trace its journey from hysteria. A curious counter-pull of representations brings both notions precariously close: both try to define a certain woman's malady, albeit in different spatio-temporal contexts; both, in other words, define 'woman'.

A new variety of disorders came to be recognized in the mental health sciences in the 1960s. Clubbed under one umbrella term—the 'Eating Disorders'—anorexia nervosa, bulimia, and binge eating signified those disorders where one constantly fought with hunger, the desire to eat, to carve out or keep intact a sharp, chiselled, contained body margin. Medical science discusses anorexia nervosa as an emergency condition experienced by women mostly, driven as they are by an inner delusional idea regarding their body shape.

> Anorexia nervosa is characterized by a *profound disturbance* of body image and the relentless pursuit of thinness, often to the point of starvation...[M]uch more prevalent in females...has its onset in adolescence...[W]ith greatest frequency among *young women* in professions that *require* thinness, such as modelling and ballet...[A]ppears to be a reaction to the demands on adolescents for more independence and increased social and sexual functioning...[L]*ack a sense of autonomy and selfhood*. Self-starvation may be an effort to gain validation as a unique and special person...through acts of extraordinary *self-discipline*....[U]nable to separate psychologically from their mothers. (Kaplan *et al.* 1994: 689–90; emphasis added)

Assumed in the above-mentioned definition of anorexia nervosa are the following notions:

- It is natural for women to indulge in occupations that spawn body ideals such as slenderness and anorexia emerges out of a conventional feminine practice.

- Women by virtue of some (un)explainable core truth cannot quite manage it all, and a little push or overdoing could well land them in the throes of pathology. Normal femininity and pathology are regarded to be part of the same continuum.
- Independence and increased social, sexual functioning are seen as 'demands on femininity', the underlying assumption being that women are not wont to exercise such options.
- A struggle for selfhood, autonomy, and validation for a special and unique personhood, the hallmarks of the male, is nevertheless a struggle (as embodied in and by the anorexic) fraught with failures and fatalities.

While amenorrhoea, considered one of the four diagnostic criteria required to make a diagnosis of anorexia nervosa, further grounds the sexed nature of the ailment, other more pertinent complications like metabolic, gastrointestinal, cardiac, and haematological disturbances do not find any mention among the main features in the diagnostic category. It is widely believed that a woman's intense desire to play the role of eternal seductress instils in her psyche, a sense of insecurity and causes her to become pathologically obsessed with her body. The result could be a fatal condition of losing weight beyond control.

Concepts about a woman's health bear an intricate–intimate relation to notions of femininity—a fall from femininity is a fall from health; and a fall from femininity is a fall into disease–pathology–madness. 'Hunger' and its control, that is, fasting, have often served as metaphors for sexuality and celibacy respectively. Dominant discourse has sought to portray women as unstable beings, vulnerable to intrusions and disruptions, and thus, hovering precipitously on the thin line between the 'normal' and the 'pathological'. The female body is understood and described as *the* bearer of a restless, dissatisfied sexuality. This sexual excess is believed to disrupt other bodily functions. The management of this devouring appetite is achieved, as if metaphorically, through the control of her 'hunger', her diet, her calorie intake, that is, intake of stuff that produces body heat through metabolism. She is constantly advised to bring and exercise control over a perpetually wandering mind and body, because her self-worth is believed to be very intimately related to her perception of her body. The bulges that must be 'attacked', the fat that should be 'burnt', and the stomach that must be 'busted' come to signify internal processes that must be brought under control.

Women are encouraged to fight relentlessly their consuming passions, their internal(ized) excesses, and their hunger to keep their body in shape. In the process, they starve themselves to insanity. The ordering of their bodies leads to dis-order. Through repeated invocations of terms like 'uncontained desire', 'unrestrained hunger', and 'uncontrolled impulses', women are made to view their bodies as repositories of chaos and disruption: as the harbinger of an 'enemy' that needs to be constantly 'eliminated' to keep the 'borders' of the body in perfect shape—safe, secure, and impenetrable. And yet, women end up prisoners of their passions. They fall back to 'binge' eating, 'binges' of self-indulgence. Then they repent. They try to make amends. They purge themselves of their excess(es). Said to lack the principle of masculinity, which is 'management with mathematical precision', women repeatedly fail to manage themselves. The logic of 'excess' and 'lack' haunts women—a circular logic. One flows into the other. It haunts her sciences.[10] It pervades her culture.

Viewed from a psychoanalytic perspective, women are said to lack the managing authority—the name of the father as an anchoring signifier—and are thus not wholly integrated within the phallic function. This 'lack' drives them to madness. They try to transcend their 'primal lack', but their excess(es) haunts them. They suffer from an unmanageable excess (of sexuality) that keeps cropping up, raising its dirty head from the mud and mire of the Freudian unconscious. Women end up being pathological(mad)—being the hysteric in the nineteenth century and the binge-eating anorexic in the twentieth and twenty-first centuries.

The Magnetic Lure of Opposites

Every day, we hear stories about how different men and women are. They are said to have different brain organizations, different body chemistries, different hormones, and different psyches. They are said to have different ways of knowing, working, and even loving. These differences are, however, recognized and celebrated universally as oppositional *and* hierarchical—as characteristic of 'opposite sexes'; there are two and only two sexes of the human species with exclusive, well-defined, nature-ordained characteristics, such that they can never meet except in heterosexual love (the union of a sperm and an ovum produced by the male and the female respectively) to give rise to a zygote and thereafter, to another male- or female-sexed human being. Heterosexual love (union) with reproduction as its ultimate aim is said to be the law of nature such that any other form of love is proclaimed 'unnatural'.[11]

Common-sense understanding and specialized knowledge operates on the almost naturalized, largely unquestioned assumption of heteropolarity that dictates that there are two sexes (natural: male and female)[12] that express themselves through two genders (cultural: masculine and feminine). The male sex is understood as naturally endowed (with the XY chromosome, the testosterone hormone, and the sex-differentiated brain hemispheres) to be physically strong, intellectually ambitious, and sexually charged—the hallmarks of a masculine gender role. The female, quite complementarily (and complimentarily as well), develops to be physically beautiful, intellectually intuitive, and sexually desirable—the social markers of femininity. Both the assumed linearity of bodies (sex), beings (gender), and desires (sexuality) and the heteropolarity of the two groups of people are considered inevitable, culminating in a mutual attraction between them in accordance to the laws of nature and essential for the propagation of the human species. This compulsory heterosexualization of desire instates a dynamics of self where the internal coherence of either gender identity (male or female) feeds itself on a stable and oppositional heterosexual attraction (men and women are bound to be attracted to each other) that is projected as biologically essential, natural, and universal. Reproduction is considered the ultimate privilege of heterosexual union and by the logic of exclusion, homosexuality is the 'other' of heterosexuality. Further, heterosexuality's naturalization requires that certain kinds of 'identities and desires' can exist only on the margins, that is, those in which gender does not flow from sex and in those in which the practice of desire does not 'follow' the heteropolar curve. While charting this neat taxonomy of bodies, beings, and sexualities, a few 'others' are left by the side—those who are said to 'not fit'. In this list of the 'abnormal', we have the hermaphrodite, the transsexual, the homosexual, the bisexual, the infertile, the impotent, and the queer.[13] These 'queer' moments of sexual desire occupy the domain of the socially abject, as unlivable and unviable.

A certain style of psychiatric reasoning, starting from the mid-nineteenth century (Davidson 2001), codified and categorized certain sexual practices falling outside the norm of reproductive heterosexuality, to produce a whole new set of 'perversions'. This emerging 'science of sexuality' thereafter characterized every instance of deviance from the sexual norm as diagnostic of a specific personality—that of the 'perverted individual'. Same-sex behaviour came to be classified as homosexuality and the homosexual came to be seen as a mentally ill person needing treatment. It fell upon the scientific community to find answers—to (re)search the aetiological basis of such deviant behaviour and accordingly fix the methods of restoring them back to health.

Today, homosexuality is no longer described as a pathological condition. The American Psychiatric Association, in 1973, withdrew homosexuality from the *DSM*, and the World Health Organization (WHO) in 1990 also did the same. This, in a way, marked the culmination of a widespread movement (starting from the late 1960s) by the gay–lesbian population for a depathologization and decriminalization of same-sex behaviour. This was also the result of scientific research that went on to prove that homosexuality was not a mental illness, as also that mental illness did not occur more among the homosexual population. The debate over whether homosexuality could be included as a mental disorder in the *DSM* of the American Psychiatric Association was reflective of a crucial shift in the psychiatric deliberations at that time: 'consequence' and not 'cause' came to be treated as central to the definition of mental disorder. So, following the logic of consequence, homosexuality could no longer be considered inherently pathological and therefore, a mental disorder. The creation of a new category, 'Sexual Orientation Disturbance', in 1973 for those 'disturbed by, in conflict with, or wish to change their sexual orientation' marked the disappearance of the disorder, homosexuality. It was renamed ego-dystonic homosexuality in the *DSM III* in 1980. Ego-dystonic homosexuality was removed entirely from the *DSM III-R* (1987) following the criticism that linking homosexuality with pathology was not desirable as almost all homosexually oriented people go through an ego-dystonic phase, and this could be reflective of the social prejudice that they are bound to encounter.

Today, any standard textbook of psychiatry discusses homosexuality as a subsection of the chapter on normal sexuality, being described as 'an alternative lifestyle' and as 'a variant of human sexuality' (Kaplan *et al.* 1994: 658). However, though considered to be a normal form of sexuality, the quest for a cause continues. The gay gene animates much of the scientific discussion around homosexuality, notwithstanding the fact that no such research for the heterosexual gene is heard of. Scientific theories have, time and again, tried to explain homosexual behaviour in terms of a masculinized uterus, feminized testes, female hormone (to explain male homosexuality) and male hormone (to explain female homosexuality) excesses, and chromosomal weaknesses. Similarly, psychoanalytic accounts of excessive same-sex parent attachment and opposite-sex parent rejection suggesting faulty gender role development have been in circulation for long. Perhaps it is important to note that against a backdrop of institutional primacy and legitimization of the middle-class monogamous reproductive heterosexual economy, all forms of sexual behaviour outside the heterosexual framework, in particular homosexuality, would emerge as deviant and marginal, at best an unviable variant. The hegemony of the heterosexual order functions through a securing of its boundaries. And to do so, it has to create its other. Without a certain precipitation of the 'deviant', heterosexuality cannot prove itself to be normal; without this image of a copy-gone-bad, heterosexuality cannot be called original; without the cultural artefact of a 'queer', heterosexuality cannot perhaps assert its naturalness.

Even though the scientific community, today, posits a certain democratic stand towards this 'other' sexuality, the psychiatrization that persists even after the depathologization of homosexuality gets manifested in other forms of normativization. Those same textbooks that carry homosexuality in a chapter on normal sexuality describe a pathological condition called 'gender identity disorder'. Gender identity disorder was first introduced in the *DSM III*. Textbooks of psychiatry define gender identity disorder as 'a strong and persistent cross-gender identification (not explained merely by a desire for any perceived cultural advantages of being the other sex) with persistent discomfort with his or her sex or sense of inappropriateness in the gender role of that sex and the disturbance not being concurrent with the physical intersex condition' (Kaplan *et al.* 1994: 684). The chapter begins with an introductory note that defines gender identity as: 'a psychological state that reflects the inner sense of oneself as being male or female. Gender identity is based on culturally determined sets of attitudes, behaviour patterns, and other attributes usually associated with masculinity or femininity' (Kaplan *et al.* 1994: 682). The same paragraph defines gender role as 'the external behaviour pattern that reflects the person's inner sense of gender identity. It is a public declaration of gender.' Nowhere in this definition does it become apparent that gender is determined by sex or emerges from it. In fact, the state 'that reflects one's inner sense of oneself' could well be interpreted as a subjective process of development not necessarily tied to one's sex, instead emerging out of social–cultural norms and attitudes as mentioned in the note. Interestingly however, as is always the case, the gender of upbringing is made to match the sex that is assigned at birth. Following this rule, if in any case, the gender of upbringing happens to be contrary to the sex assigned at birth, and later on the person concerned undergoes gender dysphoria,[14] would this person then be liable to a diagnosis of gender identity disorder? In all probability, the person would be encouraged to change over to the 'proper' gender identity without attracting the label of a disorder.

Having got an idea of how sex is believed to be tied to gender both in scientific and non-scientific discourses, one can ask at this point: what is the relation between sex/gender and sexuality?[15] In the chapter on human sexuality in this same textbook on psychiatry, there is, at the very beginning, a section on sexual identity which notes: 'A person's sexuality depends on four interrelated factors: sexual identity, gender identity, sexual orientation, and sexual behaviour' (Kaplan *et al.* 1994: 653). Thus, a relation is drawn between gender identity and sexuality, and consequently, a relation between gender and sex as seen in the following statement: 'Even though family, cultural, and biological influences may complicate the establishment of a sense of masculinity or femininity, the standard and healthy outcome is a relatively secure sense of identification with one's biological sex—a stable gender identity' (Kaplan *et al.* 1994: 654). Thus, any discussion of gender and sexuality is subsumed under a heterosexual heteropolar 'opposite sex' framework, and this framework not only feeds the clinical category of gender identity disorder, it pervades as well, our daily lives and living practices.

Gender identity disorder can be shown to be very closely related to homosexual behaviour and shares many common elements with sexual orientation in terms of mental pathology, social stigma, apprehended disabilities, distress, and disadvantages. The inability to make sense of one's sexual desires that do not conform to the conventional gender stereotypes (heterosexuality as directly flowing from heteropolarity, that is, men falling in love and desiring women) prompt some to try and reconfigure themselves as members of the other sex. For example, if a woman happens to desire a woman, then she might start thinking of herself as a man and thus model herself accordingly since the only available frame of desire is heterosexuality. Thus, an indication of same-sex desire in a woman may cause her to panic at the thought that she may be losing her femininity, that she is no longer a proper woman, nor quite a man, at least physically if not mentally. However, often the inability to adapt completely to this changed gender role might create a sense of gender dysphoria in such people, often ending up wanting to change their sexual preference and return to a more (re)productive sexual economy. Similarly, the presence of gender traits other than what are deemed 'normal' for a certain-sexed individual may cause one to fear the loss of a his/her inherent sexuality. For instance, a man showing feminine traits is not only construed a 'failed' man, he is also immediately condemned as a 'homosexual' and ostracized as a figure of monstrosity.

Sexism–Heterosexism to Androcentrism–Phallocentrism

The gender 'blindness' of the mental health sciences has been a matter of great concern to feminists who have sought to foreground the issue of sexism within the practice of mental health sciences as also in the larger discipline of the philosophy of science. The apparent objectivity of scientific research, the purportedly neutral stance, which, in effect, overlooks important issues such as that of inadequate resources, lack of women's access to mental health services, as also the attitude of the health institutions and its professionals towards women's distress, has come in for criticism (Davar 1999, 2001). But the health of women suffers not just because of the sexism of a few mal-informed professionals; it suffers also due to the sexism of the knowledge system that comes forth with certain preformed theories about women. This pervasive presence of a deeper and inherent gender 'bias' at the level of concepts, that is not overtly palpable, has been described as androcentrism[16] by feminists (Moitra 2002). The gender bias that operates not merely at the level of attitude but also at the level of knowledge, and is inbuilt into the conceptual frameworks of health and illness, is something that has not occupied enough attention in discussions within mainstream psychiatry or in feminist critiques of the mental health sciences. Perhaps, along with an attention to exclusion, suppression, and invisibilization, better understood as sexism–heterosexism, it is also important to attend to the androcentrism–phallocentrism[17] inherent in the apparent value-neutral and objective scientific truths that rule the process of diagnosis and treatment. To do this, a starting point could be to substitute the traditional model of the detached, disinterested individual knower with the dynamic model of the engaged knower, and recognize the epistemic value of affect, emotion, and body/morphology in the very processes of constituting knowledge.

Notes

1. *Sexué* (in French) means 'having a sex, a sexual organ, or being *differentiated* into male and female, i.e. sexually differentiated' (Lacan 1998: 5, emphasis: author). Lacan's way of defining 'man' and 'woman' has nothing to do with biology. For Lacan, 'man' and 'woman' are conceptual categories; the categories are defined separately with respect to language, with respect to the symbolic order. Each person's relation to the signifier and mode of *jouissance* will have to be understood so as to arrive at 'man' and 'woman', at who is 'man' and who is 'woman'; one cannot jump to conclusions on the basis of biological sex. Each person is alienated in and by language in radically different ways, as witnessed by their disparate relations to the Other; as subjects they are split differently, and this difference in splitting accounts for 'sexual difference'; the 'two' of 'sexual difference', of the construction–production of 'man' and 'woman' with respect to their divergent relations to the signifier, is somewhat different from the biological given of sexual difference, from biological man and woman (Dhar 2002).

2. *Jane Eyre*, a nineteenth-century English novel by Charlotte Bronte where Rochester's mad wife, Bertha, stays locked in the attic.
3. *The Yellow Wall Paper*, a short story written by American writer Charlotte Perkins Gilman in 1892 narrates the plight of a mother confined to her bedroom in the name of therapy and who then starts imagining herself crawling up the yellow wallpaper of the room.
4. The word 'hysteria' derives from two root words in the Greek language: *hysterus*, meaning womb; and *usteron*, meaning afterbirth or what comes later. In the popular imagination, 'hysteria' denotes excess, irrationality and crassness, sexual promiscuity, and attention-seeking behaviour.
5. Here, animal is used in the sense of *anima*—soul.
6. This period saw the emergence of a new medical specialty—gynaecology and obstetrics—that brought under its gaze the 'interior space' of the female body. The per-vaginal examination, the touch of the palpating finger, was supplemented by the visions of the 'investigating speculum'. Science was made 'ocular'. There was a slow 'illumination' of obscurity—a reading of the essential. The sovereignty of the gaze gradually established itself—'the eye that knows and decides is the eye that governs'.
7. A direct analogy was drawn between the circulation of blood in the human body and money in the body politic. Just as a blockage in the socio-economic sphere could bring about an overwhelming of profit by waste and threaten to destabilize the entire system, so too, a retention of menstrual blood could lead to a disruption of the uterine economy and further lead to hysteria and insanity.
8. A successful resolution of the girl child's Oedipus complex—the acceptance of her castration—produces the feminine as 'complementary' to the masculine; the feminine in apparent complementary harmony with the masculine. This is 'normal femininity'. One who can normally include herself in 'vaginal heterosexuality' and 'accommodate' masculine sexuality. But this is not the only form. One may refuse her castration. She may think, assert that she is not inferior. She may consider herself phallic. Freud termed this the 'masculinity complex' (discussed in Freud 1991[1905]).
9. The *DSM*, published by the American Psychiatric Association, carries specific diagnostic criteria used for clinical diagnosis. There have been four editions so far. The last one, *DSM IV*, came out in 1994. A 'text revision' of the *DSM IV* was published in 2000.
10. For thousands of years, it was believed that women had the same genitals as men, except that theirs are inside the body and not outside it. In the second century A.D. Galen demonstrated that women were essentially

men in whom a lack of vital heat—of perfection—produced the reten-tion, inside, of structures that in the male are visible without (Lacquer 1990). Women were but men turned outside in. Thus, women were considered as being the inversion/aberration of men—where men were taken as the standard. Present-day knowledge, however, looks at the two sexes as 'opposite'. Starting from the eighteenth and nineteenth centuries, the 'science of sex' sought to situate sexual difference firmly in the various branches of science, such as anatomy, physiology, and biochemistry, with their evidence of organs, hormones, chromosomes, and genetic material that prove, beyond doubt, the scientific basis of ideological exclusiveness.

11. Section 377 of the Indian Penal Code states that whosoever 'volun-tarily' has carnal intercourse against the 'order of nature', with any man, woman, or animal, shall be punished with imprisonment for life or 10 years. Male and female adult homosexual behaviour, however private and consensual, is thus deemed unnatural and, therefore, illegal under this section. On 2 July 2009, a Delhi High Court ruling declared that Section 377 violates Articles 14, 15, and 21 of the Indian Constitution in so much as it criminalizes consensual sexual acts of adults in pri-vate. This ruling marks a turning point in the lesbian, gay, bisexual, and transgender (LGBT) movement and will hopefully help in curbing the unprovoked arrests, harassment, and prosecution of homosexuals. However, while the ruling serves to remove the charge of 'illegality', as read in Section 377, of consensual homosexuality, it does nothing to address the charge of 'unnaturalness' (against the order of nature) as denoted in the same section.

12. The assumption further builds itself on the premise that there are only two socially viable sexes. Though medically a third sex is acknowledged, it is however considered a socially non-viable entity requiring surgical and psychological correction in order to lead a normal life.

13. Perhaps the list is not so easily exhausted and new 'pathological' catego-ries keep appearing by the day.

14. The term 'gender dysphoria' has been used to characterize a person's sense of discomfort or unease about his or her status as male or female.

15. Today, we can further ask the question: what is the relation between sex/gender and reproduction or what is the relation between sexuality and reproduction? Advances in surgical technology have made sex, and thereby gender, malleable and dubious. People can, with the help of surgery and hormones, change at will parts of their body, while leaving other parts intact, in a way loosening the tight bind so far perceived between gender ideology and materiality of bodies, as also the biological

link between the materiality of bodies and the reproduction ideology. On the other hand, advances in reproductive technology have played havoc with the argument that homosexuality is not evolution friendly. Today, there are numerous gay and lesbian couples who have been able to form a biological family with the help of these technologies.

16. Sexism denotes any form of 'overt' male oppression. Androcentrism, on the other hand, denotes the conceptual domain of male domination. 'Andro-centrism is not…an overt case of gender injustice. What makes it interesting to feminist theory is its opacity and covertness… By producing a homogenous model of humanness on the basis of male virtues (androcentrism relegates) women…to a marginal position. Subsequently women internalize this constructed marginalized identity as an ideal one…Internalization is thus a pernicious phenomenon, which complicates women's oppression even further' (Moitra 2002: 30–2).

17. Phallocentrism is the organization and evaluation of thoughts and concepts around the centrality of the male attribute of generative powers. The word 'phallus' is a Greek word meaning penis. Phallocentrism denotes the hierarchization of the conceptual space in a manner that all other ways of thought or ways of life that do not conform to male-gendered virtues are treated as inferior and subordinate. 'Phallocentrism endorses a structural form that can victimize both men and women depending on where they are positioned on the entire phallocentric scale. In a gendered division of conceptual space there is a masculinized position and a feminized position regardless of the anatomical sex of the person in that position' (Moitra 2002: 13).

References

Bose, G. 1950a. 'The Genesis of Homosexuality', *Samiksha: Journal of the Indian Psychoanalytic Society*, 4(2): 66–75.

———. 1950b. 'Notes from the Case History of a Patient "B"', *Samiksha: Journal of the Indian Psychoanalytic Society*, 4(2): 83–101.

———. 1980. Swapna, 4th edition. Calcutta: Bangyia Sahitya Parishad.

Bose, P.K. (ed.). 1998. *Samoyikee: Purono Samoyikpatrer Prabandha Sankalan, Prothom Khanda: Bijnan O Samaj (1850–1901)*. Calcutta: Ananda Publishers Pvt. Ltd.

Bronfen, E. 1998. *The Knotted Subject: Hysteria and its Discontents*. Princeton: Princeton University Press.

Davar, B.V. 1999. *Mental Health of Indian Women: A Feminist Agenda*. New Delhi: Sage.

————. (ed.). 2001. *Mental Health from a Gender Perspective*. New Delhi: Sage.

Davidson, A. 2001. *The Emergence of Sexuality: Historical Epistemology and the Formation of Concepts*. Cambridge, MA: Harvard University Press.

De, N. 1947. 'Some Aspects of the Unconscious in Hysteria', *Samiksha: Journal of the Indian Psychoanalytic Society*, 1(4): 299–301

Dhar, A. 2002. 'Beyond or within the Lacanian Turn: Sexuation... Sexual Difference...Melancholy Gender...', *From the Margins: Bodies, Beings and Gender*, II(1): 143–64.

Freud, S. (trans. by James Strachey). 1991[1905]. *On Sexuality: Three Essays on the Theory of Sexuality and Other Works, Vol. 7*. London: Penguin.

————. (trans. and ed. by James Strachey and Alix Strachey). 1956. *Studies on Hysteria*. London: Hogarth Press.

Harding, S. 1986. *The Science Question in Feminism*. Ithaca: Cornell University Press.

Jacobus, M., E.F. Keller, and S. Shuttleworth. 1990. *Body/Politics: Women and the Discourses of Science*. New York & London: Routledge.

Kaplan, H.I., B.J. Sadock, and J.A. Grebb. 1994. 'Eating Disorders', in *Synopsis of Psychiatry*, 7th edition. New Delhi: Waverly International.

Lacan, J. (trans. with notes by Bruce Fink). 1998. *The Seminar XX, Encore: On Feminine Sexuality, the Limits of Love and Knowledge, 1973*. New York: W.W. Norton & Company.

Lacquer, T. 1990. *Making Sex: Body and Gender from Greeks to Freud*. Cambridge, MA: Harvard University Press.

Moitra, S. 2002. *Feminist Thought: Androcentrism, Communication and Objectivity*. Kolkata: Munshiram Manoharlal Publishers Pvt. Ltd, in association with the Centre of Advanced Study in Philosophy, Jadavpur University.

3

Adjudicating Illness and Capacity

Notes from a Custody Trial

Vasudha Nagaraj

This chapter is a documentation of how women become subjects of the legal system when the process and outcome of a trial is inflected by the category of 'mental illness'. It is about how these women, labelled as 'mentally ill', represent and negotiate their selfhood within the language of law. Further, the chapter also attempts to identify the limits of what the legal recourse actually offers these women, in terms of what they are seeking. Considering that the law enjoys the status of being the primary legitimating discourse of rights and citizenship, how does it conduct itself in such a context?

It is known that legal cognizance of mental illness can nullify contracts, marriages, capacity to hold and manage property, custody of children, etc. In the criminal law, it can even result in non-culpability of the crime and subsequent committal to a mental hospital (Dhanda 2000). In the precincts of the law, any 'evidence' of diagnosis of mental illness can virtually disempower the individual, both legally as well as morally. The significant continuities between sanity and insanity, capacity and incapacity, often go under the radar of the law.

In the corridors of criminal courts, one often overhears intense prejudices concerning women's propensity to suffer mental illness. When women commit suicide due to harassment in their family, criminal law readily accepts defence arguments that the woman was depressed, hysterical, and prone to suicide. Not always are these submissions supported by medical diagnoses. Based on the woman's diaries and letters written to friends and family, or even a single prescription, the law has proffered diagnoses of depression (Dhanda 2001: 352). In such cases, where the husband is on trial for abetting the wife's suicide, the law has accepted several explanations about how women become depressed during menstruation, pregnancy, miscarriage, childlessness, and so on. It is also routinely argued that 'depressed' women cannot withstand the regular wear and tear (read violence) of their marriages. Time and again, the ambiguous link in the circumstantial evidence of such a suicide is the woman's state of mind. 'Proof beyond reasonable doubt', the thumb rule for criminal law, thus develops its chinks: how can a sentence of conviction be sustained against a husband whose wife was 'not all there in her head'?

In another register of law, that of securing divorces, Amita Dhanda notes that there has been a disproportionate and inappropriate use of the insanity provision against women. Dhanda analysed 60 appellate court judgements delivered during 1950–97, and found that 55 were against women. In these judgements, mental illness of the women was variously described as her inability to cook, her refusal to allow consummation of marriage, crying at the wedding, poor household management, disobedience of elders, and so on. Dhanda even found some judgements where divorce was granted merely on the basis of the affidavit of the husband alleging a mental illness of his wife. One of Dhanda's main conclusions about the legal discourse is that any departure from the cultural norms of a 'wife' or 'mother' can be read as mental illness (Dhanda 2001: 356).

Considering the trends in judgements, it may seem a foregone conclusion that the law is inimical to the interests of people accused of or diagnosed as being mentally ill. However, as a legal practitioner in the domain of family, I think it is crucial to investigate the details of the process in which the law decides one way or another with respect to mental illness in family matters. The structure and the limits of the law are discernible more sharply in the process, than either in the statute or in the judgement. Any trial is a wealth of detail, contradictions, and serendipities. Judgements are accounts recorded by the judge: a narration of facts as arranged and prioritized by him. He orders the evidence, borrows (selectively) from precedent judgements in support of his array of facts, weighs the probabilities of evidence, and arrives at a decision. The judge's account, in general, is adopted as data of the legal discourse. However, judgements rarely tell us the many foci of the case: the circumstances under which the law was petitioned; the presentation of 'facts' in the petition; the difficulties of procuring the right kind of evidence; and the possible out-of-court settlements. Attention to these aspects is essential for an enquiry of not only how the law works but also how the law is made in the courtroom.

Close reading of a trial enables us to underscore issues that get generally elided in legal analysis. What are the critical resources that the law demands from its subjects to decide their claims? What are the courtroom cultures that women have to contend with? In what modes do experiences of the procedures of the law rewrite women? What is the politics of legibility demanded by law?

Keeping these questions in mind, I recount here, a particular woman's struggle to retain the custody of her child. Accused of mental illness by her marital family, she appealed to the law to provide protection from her aggressively sane husband. I defended Gauri in this case and as part of this task, I wrote innumerable petitions, pored through volumes of case law, and had a series of discussions with other lawyers. I worked hard to make Gauri's case legible to the law.[1] However, in writing the present account, my objective is not that of telling 'the truth' of the case, because there can be no such truth.[2] I attempt, in this chapter, to:

- reflect on the process of the 'production of legibility' for the trial;
- foreground the disconnect and coldness which characterizes the court's hearing of claims of women in distress;
- document the complex ways in which alleged or real mental illness of a woman constitutes her familial life and legal claims;[3] and
- problematize the inner rationality of the legal process by which it arrives at a decision.

Relevant Laws and the Family Court

Most family trials are anxiety ridden, tedious, and time consuming. They take three to five years for completion. The appellate hearings may take even longer. In the pendency of these hearings, the status of marriage, custody of children, and financial commitments remain in a state of uncertainty. As it is, in the court, there is the intractability of pleading and arguing about the private: the family and the lives of women therein. Sexuality, housework, and issues of violence, in general, lack a cognizance in the legal processes, and thereby are subject to wide-ranging judicial discretions. In such a context, the claims of a woman who is 'diagnosed' as mentally ill become that much more complicated to become legible to the law.

Before one moves to the discussion of the actual trial, it would be important to know the specific law for securing custody of children in contested relationships. The relevant laws for this trial were: the Guardians and Wards Act 1890 (GWA); the Family Courts Act 1984; and the Hindu Minority and Guardianship Act 1956—a combination of personal and general laws that have provisions for deciding issues of custody and guardianship. Generally, these cases are filed as interim applications in larger petitions affecting the status of marriage, such as divorce and restitution of conjugal rights. Applications about the child can also be filed as independent applications under the GWA.

Analysing the contexts in which petitions are filed in the courts, Agnes (2008: 236–57) points to how petitions of restitution of conjugal rights are routinely filed by husbands to defeat the wife's complaints of domestic violence. Similarly, as counter-moves, husbands file custody cases in retaliation to the wives' claims of maintenance. In order to pressurize and manipulate the wife, a husband often threatens to separate her from her children. Such moves are common to the experiences of women who initiate legal action against the husband. Custody cases are replete with instances of one or the other spouse running away with the child to another destination, and filing cases seeking guardianship of the minor.[4]

The Hindu personal law more than adequately supports the man in such threats by stipulating that the father is the natural guardian of the child and only after him, the mother.[5] It, however, grants the mother the custody of a minor who is below the age of five years. Despite feminist critiques and case law that upholds the mothers' right to be a natural guardian, such provisions nevertheless remain in the statute books. The Hindu law offers some respite by stating that in the appointment or declaration of a guardian, the welfare of the minor shall be the paramount consideration. Similar is the case with Muslim law, which makes the father the natural guardian and grants the mother the right to custody in the early years. The GWA, while upholding the father's right to guardianship, lays down additional conditions: the welfare of the minor, preference of the child, and the personal law of the minor as conditions to be taken into account.

'Best interests of the child' (BIC) is an important term to reckon with in the legal discourse of child custody. The courts have often held that the main consideration must be welfare of the child and not the legal right of a particular party.[6] Archana Parashar, in her survey of the various High Court decisions on the interpretations of BIC, notes that judges exercise wide discretion in interpreting BIC and that the relevant statutes alone do not give them much guidance. It is left to the individual judge to resolve the contrary pulls of the welfare principle and the principles of religious personal laws (Parashar 2008: 125).

Custody battles, as a rule, are traumatic for women. The courts seldom recognize women's labour in taking care of the child. Either the scales are tilted in favour of the father as the natural guardian or there is the notion of apparent equality before law, which makes the power relations between the husband and wife opaque. Even a cursory reading of judgements shows that women have to contend with several kinds of prejudices. She has to prove that she is financially independent and, at the same time, does not put in long hours at her job. The child should be studying in a good school, and most important of all, the mother should be chaste. If she has remarried, her chances of winning the custody battle become bleak. If she happens to be 'diagnosed' as mentally ill, her capacity to claim the child will definitely come under a cloud. It is rather surprising that there is not much case law deciding the issues of the capacity of 'mentally ill' mothers. It is possible that such cases are limited to trial courts alone and do not reach the appellate courts.[7]

Now, a few words about the courtroom atmosphere where such trials take place: in the case which I recount here, the trial was conducted in a family court. Family courts are special courts to hear conflicts around marriage and marital property. Campaigning by the women's movement in the 1980s compelled the government to enact special laws and to set up special institutions. In many states, women police stations and family courts were established to provide state forums sensitive to women. Ironically, while the movement stressed on protection of women's interests in these courts, the state declared 'preservation of the family' as their primary objective.

The family court is a 'different' civil court, with emphasis on reconciliation and settlement as opposed to litigation. Here, judges are advised to adopt different approaches that include sensitivity and speedy disposal. To create a non-adversarial context of litigation, some legal procedures are relaxed and the role of lawyers is restricted. In contrast to the practices of other civil courts, litigants are expected to attend court regularly and are also encouraged to represent their own cases.

However, in practice, family courts are nowhere near this ideal picture. They are overcrowded, handling much more than they are capable of. The backlog of cases is voluminous and judges are overworked. But one can clearly see that the courtroom culture in family courts is not just determined by the fatigue of the backlog. Unlike property and other contract claims that are usually heard with great patience and perseverance, issues of the family often provoke impatience and frivolous comments from the personnel of the court. Women take the brunt of these comments and are forced to stake their claims in an indifferent atmosphere. Judges attempt to 'reconcile' in the most peremptory way, ignoring the seriousness of the distress that women suffer. That women can become seriously ill as a result of harassment in the family has no currency at all.

Pleadings: Our Facts and Their Facts

Gauri, the petitioner, came from a well-to-do middle-class family. She said that she became ill from the beginning of her marital life. During her illness, she sensed a foreign body within her and heard voices. Her husband, angry and maybe confused with her strange condition, brought her to her parents. Her parents then took her to a local baba, thinking that an evil spirit had possessed her, who advised them to take her to a psychiatrist. The latter treated her with medication and told her that she suffered from 'depression' and that her experiences were common for newly married women. Following this treatment, Gauri returned to her marital home. Despite her recovery, her husband's family was unhappy with her and taunted her that she was 'mad' and that they were cheated. Gauri's school and college certificates were examined and she was asked to go through an intelligence quotient (IQ) test. Despite succeeding in the IQ test, she was given no reprieve. Her husband stopped relating to her, humiliated her, and beat her, saying that he was saddled with a sick wife.

Gauri suffered these taunts either by being silent, or fighting back in some instances, and often confiding in her parents. Since her parents lived nearby, her only consolation was to visit them occasionally. Like most parents, they told her that 'things will settle in future'. But, very soon, even these visits were curtailed as her mother-in-law thought that she was excessively dependent on her parents. Gauri's movements were supervised, her cooking and socializing skills were criticized, and she was called 'lazy'. She was reprimanded if she woke up late, if she watched too much television, or if she did not make rotis properly. Gauri's complaint was that nothing was ever expressed to her with kindness or patience. She found her family to be always angry and dissatisfied with her. She was given no money and it was her parent's responsibility to look after her personal needs or take her to the doctor when she was ill.

Soon, Gauri gave birth to a baby girl. Now, Gauri was harassed in a different way. She was accused of being inattentive to the child's needs and that she was often sleepy and dreamy. After one year, the child was made to sleep with the mother-in-law on the ground that Gauri used to be fast asleep when the child was crying. She was not allowed to interact with her child, and thereby the child became more attached to the grandmother. Gauri was miserable that her child was being distanced from her. During the innumerable fights that ensued, Gauri was told that she was not needed, that she should leave the child behind and settle for a divorce. In the meantime, Gauri became ill again, neither eating nor sleeping for more than a week. Her husband and in-laws made no efforts to get her treated, thinking that she was sulking. Unable to take it anymore, Gauri took her daughter and ran away to her natal home; her parents had by now moved to a different town. The husband made frantic attempts to recover the child from Gauri's custody. Fearing that she would be separated from her child indefinitely, she complained to the local police station as well as moved the family court for a protection order. The court readily granted her an interim order of custody, which relieved Gauri to a great extent and gave her a respite. The interim order allowed her to settle with her parents, regain her health, and make sense of the legal proceedings.

Gauri's husband was enraged that she had not only taken away his child but also gained an interim order of custody. He pleaded, in his counter, that Gauri's petition was full of lies, that she was continuously sick and prone to hearing voices. He added that she was withdrawn, asocial, and always drowsy and inactive. He pleaded that he had taken full responsibility for the upbringing of the child, that the child had no love and affection for Gauri. He filed two dozen prescriptions issued by three psychiatrists, bills and receipts of the medicines, and records of Gauri's visits to various healing centres. He stated that Gauri was meeting her psychiatrist every month and that she had been on medication continuously all the eight years of the marriage. He also argued that her parents had deliberately concealed her illness at the time of marriage and that they had cheated him. In other words, he argued that Gauri was very ill, a patient of chronic depression, and thereby incapable. He tried his best to get the interim order vacated, but the court was not convinced and ordered that the child would remain with Gauri during the pendency of proceedings. Thus, began the trial for the guardianship of the child.

Contested Facts

The allegation that Gauri was 'chronically ill' came as a shock to me. When I asked Gauri whether she had undergone treatment all the eight years of her marital life, she said that it was true. When I enquired as to why she had not revealed the extent of her illness in the petition, she was reticent and evasive and said that she did not think it to be so serious. Gauri, however, repeatedly said that she was ill only because of her husband's ill treatment and the intolerance of his family. Gradually, she shared that during her illness, she would become withdrawn, weepy, and hear voices. The medicines made her feel very sleepy, but she regularly took them and worked hard despite the inertia that overtook her. She said that her husband's family extracted maximum labour out of her, and yet called her 'mad' because of her occasional episodes of illness. In the last instance, Gauri said that she felt lost and betrayed when she became very ill and her husband refused to take her to the psychiatrist.

Gauri's parents also confirmed the fact of her long psychiatric treatment. They said that she was always a bright and cheerful girl, but it was the marriage that brought forth this illness. They added that the psychiatrist had repeatedly asked Gauri's husband to come for counselling, but he refused to go to what he called a 'mad doctor's' clinic. Apparently, the psychiatrist told them that Gauri's recovery would be faster if her husband participated in her treatment. He also suggested that Gauri having a child now could greatly help her recovery. According to Gauri and her parents, the issue was not so much the illness but her husband's uncompromising attitude towards her that had led to the present situation.

The trial proceeded along this principal node of tension: while her married life of eight years revolved around the axis of her illness, medication, and the psychiatric clinic, her pleadings in the court had erased the issue altogether. Indeed, our petition was silent about Gauri's illness, except at the initial phase of her married life. Our petition only contained facts of general cruelty experienced in the family, rather than foreground her illness as a direct consequence of the cruelty she suffered. At this stage, we could not introduce any fresh lines of reasoning except what we had pleaded. Unwittingly, we were now forced into a difficult situation of fighting on the ground that Gauri was *never* ill, except during the initial phase of her marriage.

The trial now assumed a fictional character. There was a nagging thought that one could have pleaded that her illness was temporary or dormant, but precipitated by the cruelty of her husband. However, one was again not sure about how admission of illness would be perceived by the court. I was advised that one should not voluntarily make an admission, especially in cases of mental illness. It was up to the husband to prove that Gauri was ill and he had to execute the burden of proof.[8] There was always a chance that he may not prove it. I was also cautioned that any admission of her illness would have serious implications with regard to issues of her legal capacity; here, in this instance, the capacity to keep her child.

We expected the husband to examine the doctors who issued the prescriptions as witnesses. This was standard procedure in trials with charges of mental illness. The prescriptions produced in the court, interestingly, did not have any description of the illness or a diagnosis. They contained only a list of medicines: Trinicalm Plus, Azona (Ziprasidone) 80, Quitipin 200 mg, Oliza 10mg, Risperidon 3 mg, and Feliz S 20 mg. A brief survey on the nature of these drugs indicated that they were antipsychotic drugs, with some serious side effects. However, neither Gauri nor her husband knew much about her illness, except as depression.[9] In all probability, two or more psychiatrists could be examined, one from their side and one from our side. The prescriptions could be legally proved if the psychiatrist who prescribed the medicines would also be examined. At that point, it looked like a long trial.

In the meantime, Gauri had to change her psychiatrist. To get a better grasp of her problem, I met her new psychiatrist. He said that he had scaled down her medication considerably. He added that Gauri was in relatively good health and that living with her parents had given her a sense of security. Asked about her earlier prescriptions of heavy dosage of drugs, he said that the ill treatment by the husband could have exacerbated her illness. He hinted that some psychiatrists tended to routinely prescribe strong drugs without much thought of their side effects or about how the patient was responding to them. He advised us to suggest to the court that Gauri was open to a medical examination, a safe alternative to offset the evidence of the prescriptions. In his experience, he found courts to rely on the current status of the patient rather than past history. The psychiatrist was confident of Gauri passing the test. But he suggested that before going to the government psychiatrist for the examination, it would be better for Gauri to do some rehearsing with another psychiatrist. While the psychiatrist was confident about Gauri passing the test, I had my own fears. Should we make the first move or should we wait for the husband or the court to demand the medical examination? What if we made this move and Gauri did not fare well in the medical examination? Another round of consultations told me that one should not rush into the medical examination as the result would become legally binding.

In addition to the medical evidence, there was also the question of the preference of the child. Perhaps because of the active distancing that was practised by the husband's family, the child did not express any overt fondness for her mother and yearned more for her father. As mentioned earlier, the GWA stipulates 'preference of the child' as one of the considerations in deciding custody cases. From our point of view, the child was unpredictable. She was inconsistent, and each time behaved in a different way. It should be noted that during the trial period, Gauri had custody and the husband was given visitation rights during vacation. School required the discipline of regular meals, sleeping time, and homework. Since the mother had the custody, she was the one who disciplined her, whereas the time spent with her father was free from such everyday discipline. Each time the child was brought back from a vacation and delivered to the mother, she would weep inconsolably demanding that she be returned to her father. This added its share of complication to the case. Our anxiety was that this arrangement would make the child prefer the father to the mother. The law was disinclined to understand these specific contexts in which the preference of the child was determined.

Evidence: Facts Proved and Unproved

Quite contrary to popular notions, compiling evidence of harassment is not only challenging but sometimes nearly impossible in familial contexts. The nature of evidence expected in legal codes does not often synchronize with the processes and transactions of everyday living. In the court, evidence is counted only if there is specificity to it and a follow-up. It is often compiled in the register of *absence or lack* of a fact. Dowry and jewellery are proved if receipts and vouchers accompany them. One should retain copies of letters to friends and relatives describing one's distress. Visits to the hospital should be preserved through prescriptions and bills, children's upkeep through fees receipts and doctor's bills, husband's income in the form of pay slips, bank account passbooks, and his property in the form of the registration deed. Most often, weddings are performed and lives lived without ever keeping a record of these documents. For Gauri, except the oral testimonies of herself and her parents, there was no hard evidence to show that she had suffered in her husband's family.

Oral testimonies, again, have their share of problems. One needs to think hard to see who can best support the case. Ideally, in family cases, parents, neighbours, and relatives are lined up as witnesses. Since the legal version is different from the versions that normally circulate amongst family members and relatives, each witness requires to be 'coached' along the lines of the legal version. For instance, in Gauri's case, everyone had to affirm that she was never ill, except for the first phase of her marriage. It was crucial that all the witnesses had to remember this fact. Even if one of them forgot and fumbled, it could jeopardize our case. Witnesses have to be firm, coherent, and neither easily excitable nor unduly intimidated. Not always are family members, friends, and relatives willing to enter the witness box. Some of them may actually not be interested or even fear the prospects of entering the witness box, not to speak of the fact that becoming a witness implies several visits to the court and long hours of waiting.

All witnesses are cross-examined. Through cross-examination, the veracity of the witness is tested. A cross-examination, evidently, is a stressful exercise for the witness, and an intimidating one too. Crucial counter-evidence is collected when the witness forgets, fumbles, and slips on relevant facts. It is an exercise intended to sift through facts, to detect and expose discrepancies, and to elicit those suppressed facts which will support one's case.

Preparing Gauri for her cross-examination was the most difficult part. Her memory of early years—education, marriage, honeymoon, pregnancy, and other events—was very vague. We had to reconstruct every detail and in the process, foreground some facts but conceal others. It was important to camouflage the fact that she had discontinued her education several times. We advised her to depose that she was irregular in her studies as she was forced to take up domestic chores to prepare for her marriage. Though it is common for girls to discontinue their education, in Gauri's case, one had to be cautious. It could be read as a symptom of her illness. Similarly, she was asked to make lists of her jewellery and sets of clothes, her chores in the household, and relevant dates and places;

and to deny all knowledge about consultations with her doctors and the contents of the prescriptions. Here, we were walking on thin ice. Even during her rehearsals, if it became too stressful, she would become inattentive and start giggling. Now, this was something we had to avoid at any cost.

Gauri was cross-examined in two sessions of three hours each. She was confronted not only by the prescriptions but also with her diary and every scrap of paper that she had left behind. Apparently, Gauri had forgotten all about these papers in which she made notes on her illness, medications, and queries to the doctors. When confronted with these papers for the first time, she was so petrified that she admitted some and denied others. Some of it was damaging for the case, but she narrowly survived the sessions of cross-examination. She endured, perhaps, because the husband's lawyer was not so competent in litigating matrimonial cases. His expertise lay in property and contract cases.

Gauri's parents were also prepared for the cross-examination. Her father suffered from high blood pressure and looked wobbly and uncertain. In his confusion, instead of denying knowledge of the prescriptions, he ended up admitting one set of prescriptions. Gauri's mother similarly made mistakes and contradicted herself. We were hoping to enlist Gauri's uncle as a witness too, but had to drop him in the last minute as he was wavering in his support to Gauri. He was not convinced that Gauri had taken the right path by appealing to the law and felt that the family elders could have settled the matter.[10] He seemed to be a precarious witness and so we did not call him. With this, we closed our evidence.

In his defence, the husband examined himself as a witness and filed her diaries, prescriptions, receipts, and to be sure, also some packets of tablets. In his cross-examination, we managed to elicit from him that he pleaded no specific instances of Gauri exhibiting abnormal behaviour: pleading general instances of abnormal behaviour without a date and time do not carry much relevance as evidence. We also confronted him that the prescriptions carried no diagnosis and that the medicines could very well be prescribed for general health. He admitted that he pleaded no instances of actively seeking treatment for his wife. Such an admission, we argued, implied that he did not do so as his wife was normal and healthy.

The Unexpected Turn

The judge interviewed the child. We prepared the child too, but were very unsure. We played safe by asking the child to say that she loved both her parents and wished to live with both of them. That the child may be tutored is a common apprehension for judges. About 15 minutes prior to the examination, the eight-year-old child was asked by the judge to sit in his chambers to prevent last-minute tutoring. The child, being a minor, cannot be examined as a witness, but can only be interviewed by the judge. The child is generally asked about her likes and dislikes and loyalties to her parents.

Much to our relief, the child spoke well about her mother and even preferred to live with her. In other words, she vindicated her mother's position that given an opportunity, she could bond with the child. We filed the child's progress reports to show that she attended school regularly and did well in her studies. The child's progress cards, we hoped, were evidence of the mother's capacity to look after the child.

Following this, we were in for yet another surprise. The husband declared that he had no more witnesses. He did not examine his parents or friends, nor did he examine the three psychiatrists. The trial, in other words, abruptly came to an end. Without the evidence of the doctors, the prescriptions carried no evidentiary value. A prescription can be proved only if the doctor issuing it is examined. Examining the doctor gives the court a chance to assess the symptoms and definition of the illness in question, the medication, the chances of curability, and the risks of relapse.[11] The issue of Gauri's medical examination also did not arise. Our suggestion in the cross-examination that the medicines prescribed may well be general medicines gained validity. The strategy of not revealing Gauri's illness worked to her advantage.

Clearly, the husband's parents and uncles had declined to appear as witnesses. He had failed in summoning these crucial resources for the trial. The absence of corroborating evidence considerably weakened his case. We argued with aplomb that the husband had levelled only vague, uncorroborated, and unsubstantiated allegations against Gauri. He neither proved her illness nor could he prove that she was incapable of mothering her child. We also argued that he mounted no evidence to qualify himself as the guardian of the child. He filed no documents to show that he was financially capable, nor did he convey that his parents were interested in taking care of the child.

Our admission that Gauri was depressed in the first phases of her marriage, however, continued to be a thorny issue. Such an admission, we were aware, could give the judge a sapling of doubt that perhaps she *still* suffered the illness. He may very well say that having made such an admission, it was Gauri's duty to prove that she was well. But, again, we reassured ourselves that it was the husband's responsibility to prove that Gauri continued to be ill. The burden of proof of her illness could swing either way. The facts were unavoidably locked in a matrix leading to more than one interpretation, thereby giving wide room for the judge's discretion to operate.

In the course of the final arguments, the judge attempted another round of reconciliation and counselled Gauri and her husband in the presence of the respective lawyers. The judge insisted that Gauri should try to return to her husband, at least for sake of the child. He said that marriages are like rose bushes, thorny and flowering, and that disputes are common to all households. Gauri replied that she did not feel safe returning to him. The judge then turned to the husband. The latter promptly said that there were only petty quarrels and that he was willing to take his wife back. The husband's (male) lawyer commented that marriages are breaking up for flimsy reasons, that Gauri was like his daughter and he would like them to reconcile. The judge requested us to consider settling the matter. The complicity of interests was too conspicuous to be missed in its significance. After all, the preservation of the family was the explicit objective of family courts.

The judgement that was finally pronounced was half-hearted and quite disappointing. The judge ordered that Gauri could keep the child for two years. The trial lasted for two-and-a-half years and the respite that she got was limited custody. He was unconvinced by her accounts of cruelty, and refused to even take them into consideration. In assessing the welfare of the child, the judge stated that it was unnecessary to delve into the cruelty suffered by the mother. He also did not stress much on the allegations of her illness and declared that she was not ill. However, he used the husband's legal status as the natural guardian to set aside Gauri's prayer for permanent custody. He held that Gauri had not presented any evidence to disqualify the husband from continuing as the guardian. The judge neither dismissed her claim nor did he allow it fully, but left it inconclusive, almost expressing an inability to make up his mind.

Some Reflections

How does one reflect on the disappointment with the judgement? Can one explain it away as a misfortune that the judge who heard the case was overburdened, insensitive, and not-so-well-informed, or that our evidence perhaps was not good enough to secure full custody of the child? Or was it something inherent to the structure of the law that its outcomes are so unpredictable? Or maybe, we should not focus on the judgement and reflect more on the process of the trial and the discourse that it produced both in Gauri's life as well as the courtroom.

Let me begin by discussing the most obvious question. Why did we erase the 'illness' from the petition? It is easy to say that we misrepresented to the law that she was not ill. But, was her illness such an obvious fact? Was she really ill? Was she ill prior to her marriage? Or was she ill because of the persecution at her marital home? Who was to decide that she was ill? Could the psychiatrist's evidence be the final word on her illness? Did the medicines cure her or did they aggravate her illness? Analysing the role of the clinic in the treatment of mental illness, Davar (1999: 137) asserts that the doctor–patient relationship raises all the problems of power and exploitation. She argues that the outcomes of the clinic are determined by the clinician's knowledge about protocols for therapy, his worldview and attitude towards women, the stereotypes that would be resourced, and the communicative strategies deployed. Proving a prescription, in such cases, would press the switches of the other layers of prejudice inherent to a diagnostic setting. The trial, ideally, would then have to engage with questions of diagnosis and cure in the discipline of psychiatry, the practice of prescribing medication, and their side effects. Evidently, one was contending with a double issue, the nexus between two structures of authority— psychiatry and law. As a strategy, rather than confront this nexus, one tried to circumvent it.

Gauri's interests were pleaded using the provision of BIC; while in reality, one was actually challenging the incapacity imputed to her.

Before the law, ironically, we were forced to litigate a non-issue, that of the child. As part of this argument, we reinforced the conservative position that children of tender years should be cared only by women/mothers.[12] The child, in this instance, could have lived and developed with either of the parents. What was at issue was the ruthless way in which the husband attempted to disempower Gauri completely. He demonstrated no commitment to her recovery. Neither in the court nor with the husband was it possible to plead that the child's presence could aid Gauri in building her self-esteem. Both for the husband and the law, the child had to be protected from the mentally ill mother. The husband did not come forward with offers of support to give her a sense of security. Nor did it ever occur to the judge, during his efforts to reconcile, to propose any such measures.

The law provided Gauri a platform and an opportunity to challenge the harassment she suffered and fight the allegations of madness levied against her. It treated her as a citizen on par with her husband and gave her a much-required sense of purpose and dignity. It gave her an interim order of custody for the pendency of proceedings. But, if one looks closely, the legal process also turned out to be a limited space, elusive, tiring, and stressful, perennially fictional in its character. Before the law, as in the family, she had to contend with similar biases and limitations. Perhaps, in the case of the law, in the guise of assessing evidence, these gender biases became much sterner and unyielding in character. However, the judgement did not travel far enough to attempt any departure or rewrite equality norms in any substantive manner.[13]

The law enjoys the status of being the sole authority to offer protection to women suffering in the family. It is, therefore, imperative that every instance of injustice be brought before the law and be translated into the language of legal categories. In order to sustain its pre-eminent status, the law keeps itself alive to issues in the ethical and political domains. At the same time, it also maintains for itself a distinct identity, that of being dynamic and open.[14] From this perspective, one sees how the law has opened itself to campaigns by the women's movement, inviting demands for recognition and protection from its subjects (Agnes 1992). Selectively, the law accommodates, bringing itself in line with current demands, to include newer details of infringement, injury, and discrimination. It creates a space and provides universal languages of equality and neutrality to the victim to battle the adversary who can be a fellow citizen, the family, or the state itself. As part of its practice, it supplements the statute and constructs impressive archives of case law to be relied on as a precedent. It is through these procedures that the law conveys that it will enquire and deliver justice in an unbiased and systematic way—all this to say that its method of dispensing justice will be far superior to any other source of justice in society.

However, feminist critiques of the law have repeatedly demonstrated the intractability of petitioning the law in the domain of family (Mukhopadhyay 1998; Sunder Rajan 2003; Menon 2004), bringing into sharp relief the limits of the law. Despite three decades of negotiating with the law, one struggles to obtain even nominal successes from it. Women may either not have the accurate evidence, or the best contacts or fitting case law, or even enough public discourse to convince the law about their suffering. Any of these factors, either singly or in combination, has the potential to frustrate women's claims for recompense. Clearly, the critique sounds a note of caution about the engagement with the law and its promises of justice. Yet, many of us appeal to the rule of law with an anticipation that it will recognize and address our injuries. We do not hesitate to subject ourselves to the humiliation and uncertainty that such an appeal engenders. What could be the contents of this anticipation? It could perhaps be the optimism of having a 'good judge', or discovering a 'loophole' in the law through which one wriggles one's claims, or the sly hope that the opponent may not make the grade as a witness, or a 'settlement' that will open up halfway during the legal process. In a trial, one notices that the rigidity of the law carries its own set of fissures and crevices, opening up quite a few moments of instability in everyday legality. Even as one is aware of the limits of the law, these moments of instability nurture mild hopes of playing the game of the rule of law in our favour.

Notes

1. This case is pending appeal in the High Court. I am hence constrained to give details or quote directly from the records. All names and places have been changed accordingly.

2. On the contrary, such a narration may appear as one of the argumentative tricks that the legal profession adopts in its practice.

3. In this chapter, I often refer to Gauri's mental illness. Having been associated with her during the trial for more than two-and-a-half years, I could not know if she was ill. Neither she nor her parents spoke about the illness unless asked by me. In our conversations, her illness existed only in the past. She was energetic, focused, and highly attentive to the trial procedures. Her profile further prompted me to question the charge of mental illness that was imputed to her.

4. Section 9 of the GWA stipulates that a court can have jurisdiction to try a case for guardianship only at the place where the minor ordinarily resides.

5. The Supreme Court clarified in the famous *Gita Hariharan* case (AIR 1999 SC 1149) that the word 'after' has to be read as meaning 'in the absence of father' to make the section consistent with constitutional safeguard of gender equality. It was emphasized that the mother's right to act as the guardian does not stand obliterated during the lifetime of the father.

6. *Dr (Mrs) Veena Kapoor* v *Shri Varinder Kumar Kapoor*, (1981) 3 SCC 92 is one of the many judgements in which this point is discussed.

7. Trial court judgements are not published, unlike High Court and Supreme Court judgements.

8. I was aware of the trends in feminist lawyering that believed in pleading controversial facts proactively. A woman may get involved in an extramarital relationship, unable to bear the stress of her home front; or may suffer mental illness, unable to bear the harassment that she faced. To plead these contexts upfront would then be attempts to create new case law that would foreground the complex lives of women.

9. Gauri was asked to consume these medicines on a daily basis, often thrice a day. Yet, neither she nor her family spoke much about the side effects of the drugs, except hair fall and drowsiness. They continued with the same psychiatrist until they moved to another city. Further, they were also not surprised when the second psychiatrist reduced the medicines considerably.

10. Here, it needs to be noted that there was a parallel track to the case. Gauri's family was also trying to get the family elders and the caste panchayat involved. But the caste panchayat insisted that Gauri should withdraw her case and only then would they intervene. Having gained some positive points in the trial, Gauri's family was unwilling to take this risk. They also feared that the husband may influence the panchayat more than them.

11. *Anima Roy* v *Prabodh Mohan Roy* (AIR 1969 Cal 304); Kartik Chandra *vs* Manju Rani (AIR 1973 Cal 545).

12. Nivedita Menon (2000) makes a similar argument in her analysis of rape trials where she states that the law forces us into a language of patriarchy despite ourselves.
13. For a detailed discussion on formal and substantive equality, see Kapur and Cossman (1996: 175–80).
14. About how the law maintains itself, I refer to the extensive discussion of the crisis of legal interpretation by Michel Rosenfeld (1992).

References

Agnes, F. 1992. 'Protecting Women against Violence? Review of a Decade of Legislation', *Economic and Political Weekly*. XXVII (17): 19–33.
———. 2008. 'Hindu Conjugality', in Archana Parashar and Amita Dhanda (ed). *Redefining Family Law in India*. New Delhi: Routledge, pp. 236–57.
Davar, B. 1999. *Mental Health of Indian Women: A Feminist Agenda*. New Delhi: Sage.
Dhanda, A. 2000. *Legal Order/Mental Disorder*. New Delhi: Sage.
———. 2001. 'Women and the Law on Unsoundness of Mind', in A. Davar (ed.), *Mental Health from a Gender Perspective*, pp. 352–6. New Delhi: Sage.
Kapur, R. and B. Cossman. 1996. *Subversive Sites: Feminist Engagements with Law in India*. New Delhi: Sage.
Menon, N. 2000. 'Embodying the Self: Feminism, Sexual Violence and the Law', in P. Chatterjee and P. Jeganathan (eds), *Community, Gender and Violence: Subaltern Studies XI*, pp. 66–105. New Delhi: Permanent Black and Ravi Dayal.
———. 2004. *Recovering Subversion: Feminist Politics beyond the Law*. New Delhi: Permanent Black.
Mukhopadhyay, M. 1998. *Legally Dispossessed: Gender, Identity and the Process of Law*. Calcutta: Stree.
Parashar, A. 2008. 'Paternalistic Law, Autonomous Child and the Responsible Judges', in A. Parashar and A. Dhanda (eds), *Redefining Family Law in India*, pp. 111–40. New Delhi: Routledge.
Rosenfeld, M. 1992. 'Deconstruction and Legal Interpretation: Conflict, Indeterminacy and the Temptation of the New Legal Formalism', in D. Cornell, M. Rosenfeld, and D.G. Carlson (eds), *Deconstruction and the Possibility of Justice*, pp. 152–210. New York: Routledge.
Sunder Rajan, R. 2003. *The Scandal of the State: Women, Law and Citizenship in Postcolonial India*. New Delhi: Permanent Black.

4

Ideological Reproduction of Gender and Normality in Psychiatric Drug Advertisements

Jayasree Kalathil

...pharmaceutical citizenship entails a...friction, between citizen-as-patient who is entitled to medicines because he or she is already a full citizen, and the not-yet-citizen patient, for whom the taking of medicines becomes a practice of becoming a full citizen. In pharmaceutical citizenship, the role of civic education is replaced by medical marketing.

Stefan Ecks (2005: 241)

And if ever, by some unlucky chance, anything unpleasant should somehow happen, why, there's always soma to give you a holiday from facts. And there's always soma to calm your anger, to reconcile you to your enemies, to make you patient and long-suffering. In the past you could only accomplish these things by making a great effort and after years of hard moral training. Now, you swallow two or three half-gramme tablets, and there you are.

Aldous Huxley (1982[1932])

The influence of advertisements in the construction, consolidation, and propagation of ideologies is by now a well-researched and documented area. Drawing on a variety of disciplines, the study of gender in advertisements has engaged with consumerism and the effects of a globalized capitalist economy in our daily lives. It has pointed to the ways in which images of men and women in advertisements influence and propagate existing ideologies, and create new ideals to meet the needs of a changing world economy, thus institutionalizing these ideologies.

Previous research shows that one of the major problems that affects women's physical and mental health is gender-based stereotyping. For example, see Renu Addlakha's (2008) reading of a case history of a woman patient in an institution, her modes of understanding, coping with and analysis of her situation, and also various discussions around anorexia, bulimia, and other conditions. Stereotypes do not remain the same throughout cultures and through all times. This is quite evident in the case of advertisements. Advertisements continue to validate women's existence as mothers, wives, and daughters, and locate them firmly in realms of subservience. However, alongside these persistent images, we also encounter new representations of women who are poised at the edge of modernity—educated, conscious of their rights, and capable of asserting and demanding them. This new woman was a common protagonist in the popular culture and the media of the 1990s India, representing the globalizing processes that the country went through in that decade. The effect of such a bombardment by conflicting images on the woman of the times was the focus of many feminist studies in the 1990s. The configuration of the 'new Indian woman' has been explored in the contexts of: popular women's magazines (Srilata 1999); advertisements (Sunder Rajan 1993); the visual field (John 1998); television (Ninan 1995); and popular Hindi cinema (Kalathil 2000a).

Rajeswari Sunder Rajan's reading of advertisements featuring the figure of the 'new Indian woman' illustrates this point further. Advertisements in the 1990s (whether for cleaning products, beauty products, or *paan masala*) feature women who are elegant, confident, making choices and decisions that have financial implications, the new users and buyers of commodities, even as they continue in their roles as mothers, housewives, and daughters. Their social contexts, domesticity, housework, marriage, and so on, have been recast in the language of an upwardly mobile urban middle class that stands in for all of 'modern' India. In advertisements, the woman 'is "new" in the senses of both having evolved and arrived in response to the times, as well as being intrinsically "modern" and "liberated"...She is "Indian" in the sense of possessing a pan-Indian identity that escapes regional, communal, or linguistic specificities, but does not thereby become "westernized"' (Sunder Rajan 2004: 188).

The above-mentioned studies have all explored how ideological reconstructions happen within popular media. Is there a similar process happening in specialized media? How would such a process work in advertisements for psychiatric drugs? And if there is such an ongoing process, what are the implications for women's mental health and how women are treated by the psychiatric system? In 2000, a study was undertaken on how psychoactive drug advertisements represented women for the Women and Mental Health (India) Collective (Kalathil 2000b).[1] The study examined a random sample of advertisements published between 1991 and 1999 in the *Indian Journal of Psychiatry*, *The Journal of Clinical Psychiatry*, and *Biological Psychiatry*, and in the mainstream magazines, *India Today* and *The Week*. The main purpose was to initiate discussion in this area, from a context of increasing interest in studying and advocating for the rights of women as they interact with the mental health system in their various roles as service users, caregivers, psychiatric professionals, policy-makers, and advocates. This chapter will present some of the key findings from that study, along with a fresh look at some advertisements from the 2006 issues of the *Indian Journal of Psychiatry*.

Why Study Psychiatric Drug Advertisements?

An article in *Hindustan Times* in February 2008 reported on a bright future for pharmaceutical industries in India. The report quoted a worldwide study by IMS-Health, a global marketing research organization, which showed that India and other emerging markets would experience a 12–13 per cent growth in 2008 to reach 85–90 billion dollars. This growth would be driven by greater access to generics and innovative new medicines as primary care becomes more available in rural areas and as more people take out private health insurance. The

Indian domestic market, according to the report, was a major growth area for pharmaceutical companies, with the rural segment showing a growth of 21 per cent and the metros, a 16 per cent growth (Ghosh 2008).

There is no doubt that India is seeing a massive increase in the pharmaceutical industry. According to Medecins Sans Frontieres' campaign for 'Access to Essential Medicines' website, India manufactures 75–80 per cent of all medicines distributed by the International Dispensary Association to developing countries. Top companies in India are suppliers to the United States (US) and Europe. Whether this exponential growth is good for affordability of essential medicines within India is a matter of debate and controversy (Srinivasan 2010).

Ever-expanding markets need newer goods to sell and sophisticated strategies for marketing the new goods. There has been increasing concern about the relationship between medicines and the pharmaceutical industry. Questions have been raised about the fact that commercial interests, and not clinical needs, are driving research and development in this field (Moncrieff et al. 2005). Medical journals have been found colluding with drug companies by publishing ghostwritten articles promoting a specific drug company's interests as 'evidence' (Healy 2004). Empirical research in this field has also shown that the way in which a certain psychiatric research is reported can be influenced to promote a particular company's drugs (Melander et al. 2003). In India, specific concerns have been raised about the lack of adequate regulation structures for drug promotion (Dikshit and Dikshit 1994; Thawani 2002).

Analyses of the marketing and development strategies of drug companies have shown how the need for endless sources of marketable products results in the medicalization of everyday life (Moynihan et al. 2002; Szasz 2007). This is a concern that carries additional weight in relation to psychiatry and drug promotion within that field, given that there are no objective tests that validate psychiatric disorders. Critics have argued that this allows drug companies to reinvent 'normal' aspects of everyday life into 'disorders' that require treatment with drugs. For example, Moynihan et al. (2002) examine how, in 1997, the company Roche promoted its antidepressant, Aurorix, as a treatment for 'social phobia'. Its press release announced that more than one million Australians suffered from this 'under diagnosed', 'soul destroying condition'. It then funded a patient group and conferences raising awareness in the media and among general practitioners. By 1998, a newspaper article suggested that over two million Australians suffered from this condition. The trade journal, *Pharmaceutical Marketing*, picked up the promotion of Aurorix by Roche as a positive example of how drug marketers can shape public and medical opinion.

There are several similar stories in the annals of psychiatric drug promotion. Angell (2004) narrates how the antidepressant drug, Paxil, turned an aspect of some people's life—shyness that can sometimes be debilitating—into a psychiatric disorder called 'social anxiety disorder'. GlaxoSmithKline, the manufacturers of Paxil, saw this as a necessary step to reposition the drug as the competition from other antidepressants like Zoloft became fierce. The product director of Paxil commented: 'Every marketer's dream is to find an unidentified or unknown market and develop it. That is what we were able to do with social anxiety disorder' (Goetzl 2000). The multi-million dollar marketing and advertisement campaign that followed saw media accounts of social anxiety disorder rise from around 50 in 1997–8 to over a billion in 1999. Ninety-six per cent of these made references to Paxil as the first and only Food and Drug Administration (FDA)-approved drug for the reinvented disorder (Vedantam 2001).

In India, there has recently been increasing concern around the reinvention of trauma as the psychiatric disease category 'post-traumatic stress disorder' (PTSD). In a recent article, K.S. Jacob (2010) examines the way in which PTSD emerged as a psychiatric illness category in India by looking at psychiatric interventions for people affected by the Union Carbide factory disaster in Bhopal, the Gujarat riots, and the tsunami. The PTSD is a category that developed from the political context of the experiences of Vietnam War veterans and the anti-war activism during that time in the US. The *Diagnostic and Statistical Manual (DSM)* definition of PTSD was later broadened to include traumatic experiences arising in several contexts, including abuse, violence, and road traffic accidents. This has had welcome effects for victims in terms of taking trauma seriously, making insurance and compensation claims, and so on. However, argues Jacob, pathologizing intense but inherently human reactions to life experiences, and the blanket application of it, has its own problems. In India, the increasing recognition of PTSD has not resulted in an increase in solutions that might provide closure to the victims, including social, political, legal, and livelihood solutions. What has increased, however, is the number of medicines treating the condition and prescriptions for such medication. What is the link between translating grief, trauma, and social injustice in the contexts of natural or man-made disasters, or communal violence, into an illness category and the increasing number of pharmaceutical companies and drugs marketed to treat such a condition? How are hitherto culturally accepted phenomena reconfigured as psychiatric illnesses—for example, 'possession' as 'dissociative disorder'? The answer lies not merely in 'the development of science' but also in the pathologization and medicalization of societies, in which advertisements play a significant role.

In India, the Drugs and Magic Remedies (Objectionable Advertisements) Act 1954 (and amended in 1961, 1967, and 1992) controls the advertisement of drugs in theory, making direct-to-consumer advertising difficult. However, it has not been effective in controlling unethical marketing practices. In general, the onus of deciding what to publish lies on editors of individual journals. In effect, what is available is the hope of self-regulation, which, as argued by Thawani (2002), is not working.

Concerns around psychiatric drug advertisements in India have been largely around issues of their accuracy and the information they provide. Advertisements in Indian medical journals have been compared to those in countries like the United Kingdom (UK), and have been found wanting in terms of accurate information regarding efficacy, side effects, and dosage (Dikshit and Dikshit 1994). They have also been criticized for the usage of vague and excessive claims such as 'first choice empiric therapy' and 'assures control' (Christo and Balasubramaniam 1997). The most serious charge has been that of double standards in advertising, as found in a comparison between the *British Medical Journal* published in the UK and its Indian edition (Gitanjali *et al.* 1997).

Unlike advertisements for other consumer goods, psychiatric drug advertisements in India mostly target not the actual consumer but the doctor who prescribes it. It is important, then, to see what gendered notions of illness, treatment, doctor–patient relationships, and so on, are employed in the advertisements in order to influence prescribing practices. Studying these advertisements also provide us with clues about the ways in which the pharmaceutical industry interacts with psychiatric associations, drug control boards, and policymakers, enabling a critical evaluation of research, development, manufacture, and marketing of drugs.

More specifically, studying representations of gender may also make possible what Elizabeth Ettorre and Elianne Riska (1995: 5) have pointed out as the missing but necessary perspective in the understanding of psychiatric drugs—'the production of a feminist knowledge' on the use of these drugs. Patient behaviour studies and the insights that these can extend to a critical view of pharmacotherapy have so far remained gender-neutral. One reason for this is the focus on the 'individual' as patient, devoid of markers of identity and experience. What are the implications of how female and male patients are defined in advertisements on how drugs are prescribed?

The examination of advertisements attempted in this chapter will not address all of the issues just raised. It will, however, examine the implications of gender representations for definitions of madness and mental health in our society, and for its influence on doctors who treat people who are considered to be experiencing psychosocial disabilities. But before that, an overview of some key studies on psychiatric drug advertisements is presented to provide some context.

Gender in Psychiatric Drug Advertisements: An Overview

There has been a significant interest in the study of prescription drug advertisements in medical journals since the 1970s. One of the early studies (Prather and Fidell 1986[1973]) to analyse gendered stereotypes in advertisements for psychotropic drugs in the US medical journals found that the patients featured in these were predominantly women. Men as patients tended to feature more in advertisements for non-psychotropic drugs. This perpetuated the assumption that women tended to have emotional illnesses, while men tended to have organic ones. Further, these advertisements featured women in restricted age ranges, in provocative positions, and as irritating patients, while men were shown in serious and straightforward situations and in work-related contexts. Another important finding from this study was that the figures featuring women as patients were in proportion with the total number of psychotropic drug prescriptions given to women. No such correlation was found between the figures featuring men and the number of non-psychotropic drug prescriptions given to men. Overall, Prather and Fidell (1986[1973]) found that representations of women in psychotropic drug advertisements were very similar to the cultural stereotype of women as emotional, irrational, and complaining, and men as non-emotional, rational, and stoic.

Certain common themes emerged in studies from Europe, the US, and Australia around this time: (i) women were depicted as majority users of psychoactive drugs; (ii) women's needs for these drugs were situated in less serious and more defused contexts; (iii) women often appeared in decorative or non-serious illustrations; and (iv) women's illnesses had less legitimacy compared to that of men (see, for example, Hemminki 1975; Mant and Darroch 1975; Stimson 1975; and Thompson 1979—all these studies analysed the content of the advertisements to make their conclusions). In 1995, Ettorre and Riska explored the idea that the representation of women in psychoactive advertisements was a representation of 'gendered moods'. They examined a series of advertisements in two major medical journals in Nordic countries during 1975–85 and then again, in 1993. They argued that there was a hidden suggestion in these advertisements that Nordic women were governed by their nerves and hormones. The discourse of gendered moods, it would seem, posited an invisible femininity of the nervous system. Drug advertisements, they argued, were a part of the cultural process that assigned the body its gender attributes, which, in turn, was legitimized and confirmed by medical discourses.

Recent studies show that there has not been a great deal of shift in gender representations in these advertisements. A 2004 study that analysed psychotropic drug advertisements in the *American Journal of Psychiatry*, the *British Journal of Psychiatry*, and the *Canadian Journal of Psychiatry* found that women were over-represented in these advertisements compared to psychiatric demographic data in all three countries. Sixty-seven per cent of advertisements directed at the age groups 20– 40 years were for women, as were 90 per cent for the age group 80 years and above (Munce *et al.* 2004). Another study from the Republic of Ireland found a gendered notion of drugs and diseases in the depiction of the 'male' heart patient and the depressed 'female' patient (Curry and O'Brien 2005).

All the studies looked at so far have contributed to our understanding of the gendered nature of psychiatric drug advertisements. A logical next step is to explore what influence these advertisements have had on physicians as their primary readers, and their views on illnesses, drugs, and prescribing practices. An early study (Hemminki 1975) exploring factors that affected prescribing practices found advertisements to be one of the main influential factors (along with education, influence of colleagues, control and regulation methods, and demands from patients). Advertisements were also found to be influential in perpetuating 'the general trend of thinking of women as weaker, more sick' (McRee *et al.* 1974), and in prescribing more expensive and less effective drugs (Prosser *et al.* 2003).

Gender in Psychiatric Drug Advertisements in Indian Medical Journals

The main finding from the study on representations of women in psychiatric drug advertisements, undertaken for Women and Mental Health (India) Collective (Kalathil 2000b), was the clear differentiation between men as 'psychotic' and women as 'neurotic' that the advertisements tried to portray. Almost all advertisements for antidepressants featured women (with the exception of one which featured a man in his fifties). In most advertisements, the women portrayed were easily recognizable as 'housewives', either through direct references or through their dress, activity, and so forth. Depression was depicted through the sadness on the woman's face, her faraway gaze, or slouching position.

Interestingly, the connection made between depression and women was evident even in the advertisements that did not have an accompanying image of a woman. A good example of this was the advertisement for the antidepressant Fludac. It showed two images. The first one showed a disorderly kitchen, with dirty dishes, empty cola bottles, and cooking utensils cluttering the kitchen counter. An abandoned apron lay crumbled on a chair. In the second image, the kitchen is tidy and clean, patterned storage jars lined up, and utensils put away on racks and shelves. The caption read: 'Because depressed patients also have a life to lead'. First among a list of benefits of taking Fludac was that it 'restores normal active daily life without daytime sedation'. There will be no doubt in the reader's mind about who needs a non-sedated day to get on with the kind of normal daily life that involves clean kitchens. The idea of returning the woman to normalcy, as we shall see, was a recurring message.

The one advertisement in which depression was associated with men, as said earlier, showed a man in his fifties, looking sad and thoughtful. The caption accompanying the image tells us that he is fifty or above, has work pressures, and a chronic illness. The drug, Sedodep, the copy tells us, controls 'late life depression' and 'depression associated with cardiac disease and other organic diseases'. The text conveys a message that male depression has a causal link to organic diseases and other external causes—a message that is absent from all advertisements depicting depression in women. Women's depression remain unexplained, its causes nameless.

A similar gender-based characterization was found in advertisements for antipsychotics as well. Most of the advertisements for drugs to treat schizophrenia depicted men (with the exception of one which featured a woman from an older demographic than the women who featured in advertisements for antidepressants). These advertisements seemed to associate schizophrenia with men and with violence. These associations were made using images and/or through the accompanying text. A good example is the visual for the drug, Hexidol. The image shows a shattered mirror on which is reflected the face of a man in the 30–40 years age range, in effect showing a shattered face. His eyes are bulging, almost popping out of their sockets, his teeth bared and clenched, his whole face held in a grimace of anger, violence, and terror. The words 'excitement', 'delusion', 'hallucinations', and 'thought disorders' are scattered around the image. The strap line reads: 'Better to start with, safer to stay with'.

The advertisement plays primarily to the popular imagination of madness/schizophrenia as violent without directly using the word. It also plays on the early medical understanding of schizophrenia as 'broken' brain/self, through the depiction of the shattered face. The promise made by the drug is 'safety'.

The gendered nature of antipsychotic advertisements was further borne out by comparing two images for the same drug, Serenace: one featuring a man and the other featuring a woman. In the first one, superimposed over a milestone is the face of a man, grimacing, cracked, and indistinctive. The drug is advertised as 'a milestone in the treatment of psychiatric disorders characterized by agitation, hostility and violence, for over two decades in India and worldwide'. As in the earlier advertisement, the associations with a shattered self and violence are prominent. The other image shows the close-up of a woman's face. There is no agitation or violence in her face: it is a sad and tired face. The drug claims to 'rapidly restore the psychotic patient to an alert, accessible, compatible state'. The strap line says: 'The first move, on the road back to normalcy'. Psychosis, in these advertisements, is imagined in a clearly gendered way. Control of violence and safety were key issues to consider in men's psychosis, while in the case of women, it was the need to restore normalcy and compatibility.

Overall, in the advertisements from the 1990s, madness/mental illness in women was a deviation from 'normal' life, with the drugs promising to return them to normalcy. The associations were with the domestic realm and their duties within that realm. 'Apathy' was the primary emotion depicted in these advertisements. Men's madness, on the other hand, pointed to organic failures and did not make direct references to their sphere of activity. Aggression and violence were the prevailing emotions/moods depicted. Most of these advertisements showed solitary and isolated figures (although in the case of women, there were allusions to family and married life). The modern woman of the 1990s, a constant presence in the popular media of the time, was conspicuous by her absence.

Now, I want to look at some advertisements from the *Indian Journal of Psychiatry* in the mid-2000s. All advertisements that appeared in the issues of the journal in 2006 were examined for this purpose. Without counting the repeats, 14 distinct advertisements featured gendered notions in this year. The first striking difference that one notices is that in these advertisements (with the exception of two), men and women appeared as part of a couple or a family. Isolated figures with mental illness seemed to be a thing of the past.

The advertisement for Duvanta features a family—the quintessential nuclear family with mom, dad, son, and daughter—holding hands and running, as you might see on a beach. The drug claims to 'resolve the pains, restore the joy of life, rebuild relationships'. It is said to have benevolent properties to control emotional and physical symptoms without sexual dysfunction or sleep disorders, and in resolving symptoms like backache, headache, and shoulder pain. The text copy on the advertisement for the antidepressant Firsito (marketed as 'the first aid for depression') is minimal. The accompanying image says it all and it shows a young couple, the man feeding ice cream to the woman. Another drug, Mirtaz, shows a smiling young couple, seated on a terrace, sharing a joke in a magazine. The reader is invited to 'imagine life beyond depression'.

A similar invocation of pleasurable and companionable activities is apparent in the advertisements for antipsychotics as well. The image for the drug, AripMT, shows a young man, just back from work, lifting a little child up in the air. There are no references to aggression or violence—the drug claims to 'manage expectations' and not control or safety. Dicorate (used to treat both epilepsy and mania in bipolar disorder) features a young couple engaged in fishing with their young daughter. A modernist sensibility is invoked by juxtaposing the strap line 'control with one' and the one-child family shown in the picture.

Examining promotional materials produced by pharmaceutical companies in India, Ecks (2005: 241) argues that pharmaceutical marketing promotes a 'promise of demarginalisation'. Marginality, in relation to antidepressants in a country where most people have no access to medicines, is defined as not having access or being deprived of medication. Ecks argues that the promise that pharmaceutical marketing makes is to remove this marginality (by making antidepressants available) and bring the patient back into society, in essence conferring them citizenship. Ecks argues that this is the project of 'pharmaceutical citizenship': a biomedical promise of demarginalization that promises to redefine the sense of belonging, exclusion, duties, and rights.

Ecks observes that the images he examined in the promotional materials collected in 2003 showed no traces of marginality. He concludes that it is not just depression that the drugs claim to remove but marginality itself: 'The promise of marginalisation is not limited to mental health, but to one's social status in general. The message seems to be: "Take this medicine, and you will not only be happy, but married with children, rich, and live a Western life-style"' (Ecks 2005: 243). Ecks' arguments seem to hold true for the advertisements from 2006 as well. There is no direct reference to a gendered nature of mental illness or of characteristics defining men and women with psychiatric diagnoses. In fact, in most cases, it is impossible to say who is actually taking the medication—the man, the woman, or the child. What is being normalized is the fact of taking medication to cure mental illness. Mental illness is just another illness and taking medication is a way of joining a 'normal' world where there are no gendered or other differences.

I have, so far, discussed what is 'said' in these advertisements. Equally important is what is not said. To say that these advertisements ignore the sociocultural aspects of mental distress and refer only to a medical understanding of illness/disease is to state the obvious. Yet, the sociocultural milieu of the people in these advertisements is invoked both through direct and indirect references. The recent advertisements seem to posit a world where gender and class relations are rendered immaterial. The 'normal' human being represented here is one who is engaged with his/her family, representing a modern India of happy and well-off people. Pharmacotherapy, as offered in these advertisements, is something to aspire for— psychoactive drugs, another commodity to consume. As with the representations of 'the new women' in the popular media of the1990s, discussed at the beginning of this chapter, the 'Indian' in these advertisements have shed their regional, class, caste, or linguistic markers, and go a further step by erasing any gender markers as well.

***

There is enough evidence to show that drug advertising in medical journals is a significant factor that influences prescribing practices. The advertisements do not just sell drugs—they also sell ideological notions of mental illness and of men and women who are diagnosed with various psychiatric disorders. They are an important medium by which pharmaceutical companies control their influence over what we understand as normal life.

In India, currently, there is only a limited understanding of how these advertisements influence physicians and what effect they have on how men and women are treated within psychiatric institutions. There is a clear need to study how much influence drug advertisements in psychiatric journals have on gendered notions of illness and treatment among clinicians and how these might affect their pre-scription practices. There is also a need to study how drug companies and their promotion activities create new concepts of illnesses and how these are institutionalized. The unprecedented development of the drug industry in present-day India needs to be scrutinized to understand the creation of new narratives of illnesses and how they permeate psychiatric practice.

Although there is very little direct marketing of psychiatric drugs in India, it is possible to imagine how notions of illness and treat-ment, and consequently, what we understand as mental health and illness, is absorbed into popular cultural imagination. An example of this is the profusion of 'agony aunt' columns and other 'expert' consultations in newspapers and magazines. The concepts of mental health and illness employed in these contexts have not been studied in any detail. This is another area that needs investigating.

Note

1. The full report is available at the Centre for Advocacy in Mental Health library in Pune.

References

Addlakha, R. 2008. *Deconstructing Mental Illness: An Ethnography of Psychiatry, Women and the Family*. New Delhi: Zubaan.

Angell, M. 2004. *The Truth about the Drug Companies: How they Deceive Us and What to Do about It*. New York: Random House.

Christo, G.G. and R. Balasubramaniam. 1997. 'Commentary: Advertising adversities', *BMJ Indian Edition*, 315(7106): 460.

Curry, P. and M. O'Brien. 2005. 'The Male Heart and the Female Mind: A Study in the Gendering of Antidepressants and Cardiovascular Drugs in Advertisements in Irish Medical Publications', *Social Science and Medicine*, 62(8).

Dikshit, R.K. and N. Dikshit. 1994. 'Commercial Source of Drug Information: Comparison between the United Kingdom and India', *British Medical Journal*, 6960: 990–91.

Ecks, S. 2005. 'Pharmaceutical Citizenship: Antidepressant Marketing and the Promise of Marginalization in India', *Anthropology and Medicine*, 12(3): 239–54.

Ettorre, E. and E. Riska. 1995. 'Advertising as a Representation of Gendered Moods', in *Gendered Moods: Psychotropics and Society*, pp. 65–88. London: Routledge.

Ghosh, S. 2008. 'Drug Firms want R&D Sops to Continue', *Hindustan Times*, 13 February. Available at: http://www.hindustantimes.com/business-news/drug-firms-want-r-amp-d-sops-to-continue/article1-275609.aspx, accessed: 24 November 2014.

Gitanjali, B., C.H. Shashindran, K.D. Tripathi and K.R. Sethuraman. 1997. 'Are Drug Advertisements in Indian Edition of *BMJ* Unethical?', *British Medical Journal*, 7106: 459.

Goetzl, D. 2000. 'Paxil: Barry Brand', *'Advertising Age'*. Available at: http://adage.com/article/news/paxil/57818/, accessed: 24 November 2014.

Healy, D. 2004. *Psychiatric Drugs Explained*, 4th edition. Philadelphia: Elsevier.

Hemminki, E. 1975. 'Review of Literature on Factors affecting Drug Prescribing', *Social Science and Medicine*, 9(2): 111–15.

Huxley, A. 1932 (original) 1982 edn. *Brave New World*. Harlow: Longman.

Jacob, K.S. 2010. 'PTSD, DSM and India: A critique', in Zachariah, A., Srivatsan, R. and Tharu, S. (eds), *Toward a Critical Medical Practice: Reflections on the Dilemmas of Medicine in India Today*, pp. 57–68. Hyderabad: Orient Black Swan.

John, M. 1998. 'Globalization, Sexuality and the Visual Field: Issues and Non-issues for Cultural Critique', in M. John and J. Nair (eds), *A Question of Silence: The Sexual Economies of Modern India*, pp. 368–96. New Delhi: Kali for Women.

Kalathil, J. 2000a. 'Domesticity, Conjugality and Privacy in the Wake of Feminism: Readings in Contemporary Fiction and Cinema', Unpublished PhD dissertation, CIEFL, Hyderabad.

———. 2000b. *Representations of Women in Advertisements for Psychoactive Drugs: A Report*. Pune: Women and Mental Health (India) Collective.

Mant, A. and D. Darroch. 1975. 'Media Images and Medical Images', *Social Science and Medicine*, 9(11–12): 613–18.

McRee, C., B.F. Corder, and T. Hazlip. 1974. 'Psychiatrists' Responses to Sexual Bias in Pharmaceutical Advertising', *American Journal of Psychiatry*, 131(11): 1273–5.

Melander, H., J. Ahlqvist-Rastad, G. Meijer, and B. Beermann. 2003. 'Evidence B(i)ased Medicine—Selective Reporting from Studies Sponsored by Pharmaceutical Industry: Review of Studies in New Drug Applications', *British Medical Journal*, 326(7400): 1171–3.

Moncrieff, J., S. Hopker, and P. Thomas. 2005. 'Psychiatry and the Pharmaceutical Industry: Who Pays the Piper? A Perspective from the Critical Psychiatry Network', *Psychiatric Bulletin*, 29: 84–5.

Moynihan, R., I. Heath, and D. Henry. 2002. 'Selling Sickness: The Pharmaceutical Industry and Disease Mongering', *British Medical Journal*, 324(7342): 886–91.

Munce, S., E.K. Robertson, S.N. Sansom and D. Stewart. 2004. 'Who is Portrayed in Psychotropic Drug Advertisements?', *Journal of Nervous and Mental Disease*, 192(4): 284–8.

Ninan, S. 1995. *Through the Magic Window: Television and Change in India.* New Delhi: Penguin.

Prather, J.E. and L.S. Fidell. 1986[1973]. 'Sex Differences in the Content and Style of Medical Advertisements', in J. Gabe and P. Williams (eds), *Tranquillisers: Social, Psychological and Clinical Perspectives*, pp. 90–9. London and New York: Tavistock.

Prosser, H., S. Almond, and T. Walley. 2003. 'Influences on GPs Decision to Prescribe New Drugs—The Importance of Who Says What', *Family Practice*, 20(1): 61–8.

Srilata, K. 1999. 'The Story of the "Up-market" Reader: *Femina*'s "New Woman" and the Normative Feminist Subject', *Journal of Arts and Ideas*, April, 32–33: 61–72.

Srinivasan, S. 2010. 'Drug prices and access to health care: some issues and options', in Zachariah, A., Srivatsan, R., and Tharu, S. (eds), *Toward a Critical Medical Practice: Reflections on the Dilemmas of Medicine in India Today*, pp. 201–19. Hyderabad: Orient Black Swan.

Stimson, G. V. 1975. 'The message of psychotropic drug ads', *Journal of Communications*, 25(3): 153–60.

Sunder Rajan, R. 1993. *Real and Imagined Women: Gender, Culture and Post-colonialism.* New York: Routledge.

———. 2004. 'Real and Imagined Women: Politics and/or Representation', in L.F. Rakow and L.A. Wackwitz (eds), *Feminist Communication Theory: Selections in Context*, pp.187–202. London: Sage.

Szasz, T. 2007. *The Medicalization of Everyday Life: Selected Essays.* New York: Syracuse University Press.

Thawani, V. 2002. 'Drug Promotion: Can Self-regulation Work?', *Indian Journal of Pharmacology*, 34: 227–8.

Thompson, E.L. 1979. 'Sexual Bias in Drug Advertisements', *Social Science and Medicine*, 13(A2): 187–91.

Vedantam, S. 2001. 'Drug Ads Hyping Anxiety Make Some Uneasy', *The Washington Post*, 16 July, p. A01.

5

Mining Marginalities and Mainstreaming Differences

The Disability Paradigm in Perspective

Renu Addlakha[1]

Impairment, Disability, and Feminism

The periodic pendulum-like swings in the biology–culture or nature–nurture debate do not detract from the common-sense perception that body, mind, and society are inextricably linked, a finding for which contemporary neurobiological and psychosocial research provides formidable evidence, that is, for a recursive interaction between biological, psychological, and social factors (Luyten and Blatt 2007). While socioculturally oriented perspectives like the biopsychosocial model (Engel 1977) and the psychosomatic approach sought to challenge the hegemony of the medical model in softer medical specialities like psychiatry, genetic research has consistently prioritized biological factors and processes. The impact of the latter in the social and human sciences is typified by the sub-disciplines of sociobiology and neurolinguistics. The nature–nurture controversy is a sterile exercise if its aim is to privilege one over the other; its productivity lies in its capacity to explore the multiple patterns of their interaction in specific geographical, historical, and sociocultural contexts. While biological universalism and cultural relativism are themselves open to interrogation, interactions between soma and psyche, biology and culture, organicity and society are not. To my mind, individual experiences of illness, disease, and disability constitute a rich context to highlight the differential patterns of the intertwining of the somatic, the psychic, and the social at the micro level.

Due to the confusion created by the interchangeable usage of related terms such as handicap, impairment, and disability, the World Health Organization (WHO) has sought to develop standardized definitions. Impairment was defined as a loss of or abnormality of physical bodily structure or function, of logic–psychic origin, or physiological anatomical origin. Impairment as bodily or psychic anomaly was distinguished from disability, which was defined as a consequence of impairment that prevents the performance of an activity in the time lapse considered normal for a human being. Handicap was defined as the disadvantaged condition deriving from an impairment and/or disability preventing a person from performing a role considered normal in respect of her sex, age, and sociocultural context (WHO 1976). This tripartite classification was standardized in 1980. Table 5.1 shows the analytical interconnections between these three terms.

According to the International Classification of Impairments, Disabilities and Handicaps (ICIDH), a single impairment may lead to a number of disabilities and imply several handicaps. For instance, a person with a psychological impairment may have a behavioural disability, a disability of communication, a disability caring for herself, a disability of circumstance, among others. The corresponding handicaps might include handicap of orientation, occupational handicap, handicap in social integration, handicap in economic self-sufficiency, etc. Similarly, a particular handicap may be tied to a number of disabilities, which, in turn, may derive from one or more impairments. So, impairment is a more permanent aspect subject to correction, by the level of medical knowledge and intervention. Disability is inextricably linked with activities that an individual has to (for example, walk) or wants to (for example,

Table 5.1 Impairment, Disability, and Handicap

Impairment	Disability	Handicap
Impairment of intellectual ability, other psychological impairments.	Behavioural disability.	Handicap of orientation.
Impairment of language and wording.	Disability of communication.	Handicap of physical independence.
Hearing impairment.	Disability within specific activities.	Handicap in social integration.
Visual impairment.	Disability of movement.	Handicap of mobility.
Organ impairment.	Disability due to body assets, disability of dexterity.	Occupational handicaps.
Bone impairment.	Disability in caring of oneself.	Handicap in economic self-sufficiency.
Scarring and aesthetic impairments.	Disability of circumstance.	Other handicaps.

Source: Derived from WHO (1980).

dance) undertake. It is a situation-dependant phenomenon. Handicap emphasizes the inequality with non-disabled persons and the disadvantages thereof. This classification not only postulates multiple associations between structures and functions of the human body, but it also links activities and participation in the social life of an individual.

In their critique of the WHO definition, members of the disability movement underscored that while impairment referred to physical, sensory, or cognitive limitations like the inability to walk or see, 'disability refers to the specific social restrictions imposed on persons with impairments through the discriminatory practices and attitudes of society'. For instance, the Union of the Physically Impaired against Segregation (UPIAS 1976: 3–4) stated: 'Impairment is the functional limitation within the individual caused by physical, mental or sensory impairment'; and 'Disability is the loss or limitation of opportunities to take part in the normal life of the community on an equal level with others due to physical and social barriers'.

Accordingly, disabled people are persons with impairments who experience disability on account of socially imposed restrictions that are, more often than not, discriminatory. Consequently, the concept of disability includes environmental barriers and not only the impairment(s) *per se*. While a useful heuristic tool in the areas of special education and rehabilitation, the ICIDH is grounded in the medical model and is too centred on the individual. It does not adequately clarify or highlight the interaction between societal conditions and expectations and the capabilities of individuals.

In 2001, the International Classification of Functioning Disability and Health (ICF) was endorsed by WHO member states for measuring health and disability at both individual and population levels. Framing the concepts of health and disability in a universal human perspective, the ICF acknowledges that every person experiences a decrement in health and hence, some degree of disability during the life course. By challenging the notion that disability is the experience of a minority of the population, it mainstreams the disability experience and validates the notion of the temporarily able-bodied person. By shifting the focus from cause to impact, the ICF places all health conditions on an equal footing, allowing them to be compared using a common metric—the ruler of health and disability. The emphasis on contextual factors allows for a spectrum approach to health and disability. Another important difference between the ICIDH and the ICF is the abandonment of the term 'handicap' altogether, which is accompanied by an expansion of the term 'disability' to cover both the restrictions of activity as well as limitations to participation. The ICF is a multi-axial classification that codes an individual's present level of functioning in terms of bodily functions, bodily structures, participation and activity (including mobility, care of self, domestic and social life), and environmental factors (inclusive of the human environment, technology, and social attitudes). By universalizing illness and disability as germane to the human condition, the ICF helps in at least conceptually challenging the commonly associated negativity and stigmatization.

Underlying the recently enacted United Nations Convention on the Rights of Persons with Disabilities (UNCRPD) is a conception of disability that is very much in keeping with the definitions contained in the ICF and the social construction perspective of the social model (Oliver 1996). The Preamble of the UNCRPD states: '(e) Recognizing that disability is an evolving concept and that disability results from the interaction between persons with impairments and attitudinal and environmental barriers that hinders their full and effective participation in society on an equal basis with others.'[2] Then, Article 1 clearly specifies: 'Persons with disabilities include those who have long term physical, mental, intellectual and sensory impairments which in interaction with various barriers may hinder their full and effective participation in society on an equal footing with others.'[3]

In light of the biological grounding and the social construction of disablement, disability may be defined, at core, 'as a deviation from biomedical norms that is statistically grounded and socially reinforced'. The reality of impairment and the biological limitations that it entails are not disputed in the above-mentioned classifications: what is at stake is the role of society and culture in creating the disadvantages that bedevil the lives of persons with disabilities. Contesting the biological primacy of impairment, Abberley (1996: 61) says: '…(I)mpairment is not a natural, but a historically changing category', adding that '(T)o recognize the inevitable historicity of impairment is not to deny its materiality'. Historians of medicine and medical anthropologists have highlighted the social construction of many 'diseases' and 'impairments'. For instance, Robert Barrett (1988: 364) opposes the idea of schizophrenia as 'an uncontested unproblematic fact of nature proved beyond reasonable doubt by psychiatric science' and regards it, on the contrary, as 'a historically and culturally contingent category of psychiatric discourse'. Similarly, Peter Barham (1986) places the origin of this psychiatric syndrome squarely within the free market liberalism and social Darwinism prevailing in Europe during the nineteenth century. The imperative of productive efficiency necessitated an equally imperative response to the problems posed by the poor, the unemployed, the infirm, and the 'dangerous' classes (including the 'insane'). The creation of the 'schizophrenic' social type as the embodiment of a natural and inexorable disease process gave scientific legitimacy to the bourgeois ideals of unremitting and efficient productivity. In a diametrically opposite context of present-day rural Haryana (India), Mehrotra and Vaidya (2008) highlight the conceptualization of intellectual disability as constitutive of the person's intrinsic nature, rather than a deficiency in mental capacity. In fact, there is more a feminization than medicalization of the intellectually disabled male in such a scenario. But if the category of impairment is as socio-historically embedded as disability, then differences between the two become blurred. So, for purposes of the present discussion, I would subscribe to the UPIAS distinction, which clearly demarcates the biological and social disjunctions that impairment and disability bring to bear on the lives of individuals.

Feminist discourses on the body have overwhelmingly focused around issues of reproduction, sexuality, and violence. It is ironic that while the body has been a major site of contestation in feminist theory, yet the disabled body has been, until recently, marked by its absence in such debates. This is partly due to the hegemony of the medical model, which naturalized disability, thereby taking it out of the realm of socio-economic, political, and cultural configura-tions. Deriving from the conventional feminist principle that the body is a site of ideological contestation, disability scholars and activists enunciated the premise that experience of impairment is central in women's lives. As a logical corollary, the imperfect body comes to signify absence of femininity and social unacceptability, since female subjectivity is so deeply intertwined with embodiment in patriarchal society. There is the simplistic chain of association that, since disabled women do not look like normal women and their bodies do not function like normal bodies in some respects, they cannot take on the roles of normal women, and hence they are less than women. According to Michele Fine and Adrienne Asch (1988), this situation turns conventional feminist wisdom on its head in three striking ways. First, at an experiential level, the social obscurity and annulment of femininity signalled by a defective body prompts disabled women to long for the roles of wives and mothers that their able-bodied feminists decry and critique as oppressive. Second, sexual objectification gives way to asexual objectification, frustrating normal sexual needs and aspirations and consigning the affected woman to a life of social isolation. Lastly, a core component of the normative construction of femininity is a woman in caregiver, procreative, and maternal roles, but the woman with a disability is herself in need of care. Men with disabilities do not become victims of such total emptying of roles that is the fate of their female counterparts, though disabled masculinity also poses challenges for men with disabilities (Shakespeare 2000). Thus, asexual objectification and pervasive rolelessness differentiate the operations of patriarchy on disabled female bodies, creating unique oppressive practices of exclusion and personal devaluation.

Just as gender is socially constructed from the biological differences between men and women, disability is similarly constructed from the biological differences between disabled and non-disabled persons. Wendell (1996) situates the marginalization and low self-esteem of women with disabilities on the disabled or what she calls 'rejected body'. She argues that the celebration of the female body by a feminist like Adrienne Rich (1976) as a source of pleasure and empowerment has strengthened processes of idealization and objectification of women's bodies. There is an underestimation of bodily frustration and suffering engendered by difference. Consequently, women with disabilities may consider themselves an embarrassment to feminism (Wendell 1996). Corker (1999) highlights the dangers of applying a universalizing disability norm or discourse overwriting the diversity among persons with disabilities. She critiques the categorization of disability into sensory, physical, and mental impairments leading to a certain essentialization of disabled identity. People with different disabilities have 'different notions of efficacy and limitation'. There is a need for exploring different forms of anomalous embodiments in the project of emancipation from oppression. Similarly, Meekosha (1990) feels that impairment is a variable process and challenges the fixity and permanence of a socially constructed corporeality. Like Wendell, she questions the notion of an unproblematic normal female body and in this process, highlights the constant change and flux of the body in negotiating the disabled identity. Bringing a strongly post-modernist perspective, Price and Shildrick (1998) argue that the experience and knowledge of disability are situated and positional. We need to move beyond simple binaries of health/illness, normal/abnormal, and disabled/non-disabled, because silencing the categories that do not fit '...(M)ay acquire in their dislocation an accumulative force that comes to inhabit the moments of fracture' (Price and Shildrick 1998: 241).

The logical clarity of theoretical perspectives is put to the test when we move to empirical reality, and especially when that reality involves understanding human behaviour. In the following two case studies, I highlight the similarities underlying the life world of Neena and Priya. Even though one is a clinical narrative from a general hospital psychiatry ward and the other is the story of a college student living in an integrated hostel, other common variables such as gender, socio-economic status, marital status, and a certain north Indian cultural ethos combine to create very similar experiences of selfhood, relationship with the material and social worlds, and perspectives on family life, marriage, and the future in general. The two case studies were part of two different earlier studies: one was developed as part of an ethnographic research conducted in the psychiatry department of the Lady Hardinge Medical College and Hospital, a government hospital in New Delhi; and the other was a detailed interview in a study conducted with young college students on sexuality and reproductive health in Delhi University.

Neena: 'Who Told Her to Eat the Samosa?'

Neena is a 26-year-old unmarried Punjabi woman living with her widowed mother in a self-owned flat in Kalkaji, a middle-class locality in Delhi. Her father, a clerk in the government, died of cancer three years earlier, and her mother is a primary schoolteacher employed in a government school. Neena dropped out of school in the ninth standard. According to Neena's mother, her daughter's illness history is of five years duration. Initially, she developed feelings of loneliness and helplessness when her elder sister got married. Neena's symptoms surfaced in a more concrete fashion when her father passed away. She stopped doing housework, would bang her head against the wall, and sit quietly for hours. At that time, she felt that the police would take her away and their neighbours would beat her. She also felt someone was trying to kill her, but would not elaborate. She received treatment for this from a nearby government dispensary and improved within a few months with medication. She remained all right for the following two years. Subsequently, during the third episode, Neena claimed she was a goddess and began to distribute personal belongings to neighbours, inviting strangers home, and making food for them. She again improved with allopathic treatment. Thereafter, her mother stopped her medicines because she felt they made her daughter weak. However, after discontinuing allopathic treatment, she took Tibetan medicines for some time before the onset of the current episode.

The present episode began 15 days earlier (to the time of my meeting her), for which she was admitted for a month in the psychiatry department at the Lady Hardinge Medical College and Hospital in New Delhi. The initial complaints recorded in her case sheet were violent behaviour, hearing voices, seeing things, muttering to self, excessive spending, using make-up, giving away household articles, and so forth. This was the fourth episode with 'acute onset' and 'progressive deterioration' of an illness trajectory of several years duration. The case sheet concluded with a differential diagnosis of 'bipolar disorder (currently manic)', 'chronic schizophrenia', or 'psychosis not otherwise specified (NOS)'.

She was very restless during her stay in the ward, striking up conversations with other patients and their attendants, and repeatedly telling them: 'My mind is out of order (*Mera dimaag kharaab hogaya hai*). I am mad (*main mental hoon*). I am abusive (*main gaali galoch karthi hoon*), and I also beat people (*main maar peet bhi karti hoon*). My illness began after I ate a samosa in the ninth class.' An apparently insignificant incident like eating a samosa at school without paying for it becomes the opening line of Neena's illness narrative. She said that her friends made fun of her when she was caught, and she was too fearful to tell her mother about it.

She also said she was weak at housework. She felt bad that she could not serve tea and food to relatives properly. One day, she started eating soap in the ward, and when asked the reason, she said that since she had not bathed properly on that day, she was eating soap. On another occasion, she rubbed kerosene on her face. Her mother said that Neena did not know whether she was eating in the room or in the toilet. In addition to abusing and beating people, Neena's case sheet recorded a variety of somatic complaints such as dizziness, darkness before her eyes, palpitations, anxiety and restlessness, diarrhoea, breathlessness, sinking heart, weakness, sleepiness, and not being able to engage in any work due to lack of energy.

Working on the popular misconception that equates mental illness and mental subnormality, her mother, who was the only informant and attendant, said that Neena was clever (*hoshyaar*) and understanding (*samajdaar*). Before she became ill, she used to do a lot of work: she said that her daughter used to visit her sister by commuting alone on the bus, used to purchase rations, could withdraw money from the bank, and pay the monthly instalment for the flat, water, and electricity bills. Yet, almost in the same breath, her mother also recounted how Neena had earlier started a lending library at home, but due to her credulity, many books had not been returned. Her mother said: 'People would take one book and steal another without her knowledge, she is so simple (*seedhi*).'

A conflict-ridden, co-dependant mother–daughter relationship characterized their interactions. Neena was not just a victim and her mother not just an aggressor. But both women engaged in mutually consuming behaviour patterns. Feelings of helplessness and insecurity took the form of mutual recriminations. For instance, Neena's mother said about her daughter: 'She has gone mad (*Iski mumdi ghum gayi hai*). We also think a lot, but why haven't we broken down?' Tiring of hearing the samosa story for the umpteenth time, one day her mother burst forth saying: 'Why don't you die? Go jump in the Yamuna (river). Who told you to eat the samosa? You have ruined my life!'

According to her, the main reason for her daughter falling ill was that she was not given a government job after the death of her father on compassionate grounds, a practice found in some government departments. But the office found out that she (the mother) already had a government job, so they did not give it to Neena: 'That really upset her and she went out of her mind.'

Both mother and daughter are connected in a symbiotic relationship going beyond a common living arrangement and consanguine ties. A patriarchal world that consigns single women to the periphery of the social order stalks their every move and utterance, a situation poignantly captured in the refrain of both: 'We are all alone. People can cheat us.' Neena's mother's anxiety is highlighted in the following:

I'm also alone. I also need some support. I can't even get her married. It is not that I have not looked around for a boy. It would also help economically, but how can I get her married in her present condition? My husband died, my son died, but I did not lose my head. Who told her to eat the samosa?

Commenting on the supportive role of her son-in-law in her life, she said: 'He is very good. He brings lunch for me everyday. Apart from him, she (Neena) is as much my support as I am hers.' A deep, underlying gender-based insecurity echoed in the utterances of both mother and daughter. Neena kept asking her mother if she had locked the house. Earlier, she would give her address to everyone, but then her mother told her that she should not do that because they were alone and something terrible could happen to them. The sense of danger and desolation was highlighted in the refrain that there was no one to help them.

As in the case of other female psychiatric patients (Addlakha 2008), a critical criterion for assessing improvement in Neena's condition was her level of acceptance of gender-based role expectations and behaviours. So, when she evinced a desire to go home and take up household chores like sweeping, mopping, and washing dishes and clothes, it was interpreted as sufficient grounds for discharge from the hospital. In addition to the disappearance of overt manifestations of unruly behaviour and speech, the articulation of desires and motivations that highlighted an unquestioning commitment to the family played an overriding role in her psychiatric evaluation.

Priya: You Wait Until She Becomes *Kaabil*...

Priya is an 18-year-old first year, visually challenged undergraduate student staying in the hostel of Indraprastha College, Delhi University. Her family lives in Saharanpur, a small town in the state of Uttar Pradesh, where her father is a manager in a factory. Her mother is a housewife and she has a younger school-going brother. Priya has total congenital visual loss for which she was taken to major hospitals in the cities of Delhi, Mumbai, Kolkata, and Baroda. She said that because there was internal damage (*androoni nukhsaan*) in the eyes, there was no treatment for her condition. She began formal schooling at the age of six years, when she was enrolled in the National Institute for the Visually Handicapped (NIVH) in Dehradun, also located in

Uttar Pradesh. She completed her schooling at this residential institution before coming to Indraprastha College.

I encountered Priya at a time in her life when she was making a transition from a sheltered residential school life to living in an integrated college hostel. With the exception of periodic visits to her home during her schooling, this was her first exposure to the non-disabled world, and she was still in the process of adjusting to her new life situation. One of her main goals was to go out alone on her own. She told me that whenever she expressed this wish to her friends, they said in shock: 'Are you mad? You will go out alone?' To add to this, her mother had strictly forbidden her from venturing out on her own. As she said: 'I have heard "cases" where the person has a cane in hand but the rickshaw passed over the person's feet. I am scared of something like that happening. Then, what will Mummy say?' But she added: 'I feel I should be "independent" as one can't have someone around all the time.'

When in the course of a conversation, I asked which hostel she would prefer to be in, the one for blind girls in Rohini or in the Indraprastha College Hostel, she opted for the latter saying: 'One should have all kinds of experiences. So, I should have experience to live with "normals" also. If we stay only with "blinds", then what will we do in future? If tomorrow we go out to do a job, we won't get only blind people.' Then, treading on the thin line between necessary assistance and overmuch help, Priya said:

> I am very lucky. All girls co-operate with me here. In the welcome function last week, they dressed me up and insisted that I participate. I also danced the dandia, and everyone appreciated it. I felt very good also. I know that I can't dance. I don't know any actions nor have I seen anything, but why should I remain behind in anything?

But in the course of the same interview, she also said: 'Some people are such that they do not show any sympathy towards you. They say you need to do your work and walk on your own. I like such people. Those trying to be "helpful", they are also, however, doing the right thing from their side.'

In Priya's perception, there was a clear demarcation between the world of blind/disabled persons and their non-disabled counterparts.

She highlighted this difference in a variety of experiential contexts in her life. She explained:

> There are a lot of things that 'normal' people talk about, which we have not experienced. It is not possible that among 'normal' people, we feel that we are like them. I have never walked alone much. When I am walking alone, I wonder what other people are thinking, looking at me. Maybe I am not looking very 'active' while walking.

Priya dwelt at length on the negative perceptions of even family members. She lamented some relatives' negative attitude towards blindness. She said that someone in her native village had said that it would have been better if she (Priya) had some deformity of the feet or hands or was deaf. That would have been better than being totally blind. 'Is this a thing to say?', she wondered angrily. Then, another relative had told her mother that now that her daughter had grown into a young woman, she should find a groom of a lower socio-economic stratum and get her married. Her mother was also advised to deposit some money in her name in the bank. Priya said that her mother was very angry at such comments, and told the relative: 'You wait until she becomes established (kaabil), then people will come on their own and want to marry her.' Priya felt that even educated people could have the same ideas about disability as illiterate people, like some of her relatives, if they had not been actually exposed to interactions with disabled persons.

Regarding marriage, she said:

> I will do whatever my mom and dad tell me to do. Whatever they like, I will go according to that. He should be someone with whom my thinking matches, and who can make me happy. But he must be blind or he can be partially sighted. His nature should be good. He should be a friend to me. He should have a good 'job'. If the other person is sighted, it can't be 'maintained' in the long run. I have heard of some cases.

She said even in those cases where a blind person had married a sighted person, it was never a totally 'normal' person. The other person has some disability other than visual. Priya's fondest memories are of her schoolmates at the NIVH. She told me nostalgically: 'We all lived like a family. There was so much love between us. Among my group of friends, we used to share everything. We took turns at fetching breakfast for the group, which we then ate in our room. Those were such good times. I still keep in touch with them through "letters" and "phone".'

Although Priya identified, by name, a large network of 'friends' in college among her classmates and the hostellers, she said she did not have any close friends with whom she could talk about anything and everything. And unlike others in the college, she did not go out much because 'no one will take that much responsibility'. Furthermore, she said:

> They ask things like: 'Are you blind since birth? How do you find your way around? Are your brothers and sisters also like this? Do your parents love you?' I feel really bad when they ask about my brother. That really hurts me because I have a very sweet little brother. We got him after a long time with great difficulty. He is our diamond.

She told me that she liked to mimic dialogues from movies, sing, and dance. She likes to record her voice on her cassette recorder and then listen to it. Her talents are recognized by her college friends, and she is often prevailed upon to sing popular songs and mouth excerpts from the latest movies. So, while on the one hand Priya said she was praised for her talents, on the other hand, the same persons in another context would ask her uncomfortable questions or ignore her completely, particularly when she was the single visually challenged girl in a group of non-disabled girls. She gave a graphic illustration of the latter situation:

> Actually, it is the way they talk. I am there listening to them but in reality they are talking among themselves. They are not paying any attention to me. They are conversing among themselves, as if they consider me different, or as if I am not there at all. So, one girl is talking about her 'boyfriend' with others and I am there. Then, when I ask her who he is, she says it is her brother. First, she was saying he is her 'boyfriend' and now she is saying he is her brother. They don't know that I am not a fool. I know everything. I ask one question and I get another answer, but that does not happen when someone else in the group asks the same question, then she gives the right answer. I

ask the question because I feel I am also a friend, but when this happens, I feel that I am different from them. They don't want to 'share' their things with me.

And, in conclusion, Priya said: 'If I look at it from their point of view, I can see why "normal" people have such ideas, that is, that disabled people can't wash their clothes or cook or have sex. Then, such thoughts appear natural to me, because our life is different. We have our own set of experiences and they have their own.'

Neena and Priya: Sharing a Common Discourse of Experience

Any wholesome understanding of disability must encompass chronic illness. That is the first strand that links psychosocial disability with physical disability. Women are more likely than men to be disabled by chronic illness (Morris 1993), and women suffer more ill health than men in general (Carroll and Niven 1993). The relationship between disability and illness is complex: disability may be caused by chronic or life-threatening illnesses, for example, tuberculosis, leprosy, cancer, and human immunodeficiency virus (HIV)/acquired immunodeficiency syndrome (AIDS). Then, persons with disabilities may have chronic health problems as a consequence of the disability, for example, muscular atrophies, chronic constipation, and obesity. Disability activists have fought against the identification of disability with illness because it feeds into the medical model: disability is projected as an individual problem or misfortune, which can be managed by medical intervention, ignoring the role of social and cultural factors (Morris 1991; Amundson 1992; Oliver 1996). Nonetheless, this denial does not annul the reality of impairment that requires interventions at the level of the individual as patient.

Despite different spatial sites, living arrangements, medical problems, and even personality traits, Neena and Priya, to my reading, share a common matrix of experience arising out of a range of ground realities that structure not only their lives but also their self conceptions. For instance, in both the narratives, the capacity to negotiate with the outside world, be it paying bills, or shopping, or just walking out on the street unescorted, is perceived as a major measure of overcoming the problem, be it mental illness or visual impairment. And both women regard this as a test of their approximation of a socially constructed normality. But while being able to go out alone is being perceived by both the young women as a sign of being well/abled, there is also the gendered reality that women's access to the public space is highly restricted. How is one to understand this gendered prohibition/disability-related incapacity? Are the two women challenging patriarchal norms of confinement of women within the domestic space? Or are they responding to emerging constructions of femininity that endorse women's presence in the public sphere for legitimate reasons or in the absence of a male figure? In my view, there is no definite response.

One of the major findings of my research on women and psychiatry in India is the dovetailing of psychiatric and gender norms in the mental status examination and subsequent treatment (Addlakha 2008). This is one of the manifestations of a wider process of construction of selfhood and otherness that pervades patrifocal social systems. Similar inferences may be drawn from the articulations of Neena and Priya regarding themselves, family, and marriage. While Neena demonstrates her return to normality by expressing the desire to engage in the routine chores of domesticity, for Priya, unquestioning filial dutifulness is the ultimate measure of her actions and aspirations. Among other things, she wanted to fulfil her father's aspiration of seeing her become a college lecturer in the future. In a society that regards marriage as the sole route to successful womanhood, it is not difficult to empathize with Neena's mother's lament about her daughter's bleak prospects in that regard. From another perspective, Priya feels that her visual disability circumscribes her marriage options within the ambit of her own kind, that is, other visually challenged persons. Whether Neena or her mother would endorse a similar possibility in the domain of marriage is a thought worth pondering.

The sociological literature describes the strong bond between mother and daughter as one inhibiting the daughter from establishing her own identity. The first bonding in infancy is with the mother. Although this initial bonding is true for both sexes, boys break away at an early age to identify with their fathers. Many studies have highlighted the conflicted nature of the mother–daughter relationship, especially during adolescence. Flax (1978) and Fischer (1981) reported that adolescent daughters hold the most negative attitudes towards their mothers and that the daughter's quest for autonomy, often manifested sexually, is not commended by the mothers. Fischer feels that daughters struggle all their lives to separate from their mothers. Ironically, the mother plays the main role in her daughter's socialization into a docile subject of patriarchy, inculcating in her the template of a subjugated femininity.

The emotionally charged and highly co-dependent relationship between Neena and her mother has already been discussed. A similar, if less emotionally tumultuous, relationship also appears to characterize Priya's life. While on the one hand, her mother was very protective of her in the face of the extended family's negative comments, she also evoked fear in her daughter. Priya said that her mother had warned her that if there were any 'complaints' against her, she would be taken out of school and would have to remain at home. She had also told Priya not to go out on her own, not to interact with 'wrong' people, and to focus on her studies. One may speculate that the relationship between Priya and her mother could take on the same contours as that of Neena and her mother under similar circumstances.

Son preference and the indispensability of a male figure as essential to the conduct of a normal life configure the narratives of both Neena and Priya. Neena's mother's reliance on her son-in-law as the main family support has been mentioned. In addition, her distress was multiplied by the birth of a fourth granddaughter around the time of Neena's hospitalization. She said in a choked voice: 'She has given birth to the fourth girl. She is still in the medical centre. She (Neena) is mad, and now, that one has also gone mad. Now what shall I do?' Then, Priya's comparison of her younger brother to a diamond highlights the extent to which the male presence is perceived to be absolutely essential for the conduct of the everyday life of a woman.

An attempt has been made to show that despite apparent differences, psychosocial and physical disabilities entail very similar consequences for affected women and their families. The daughter represents family honour in the Indian context, which means that disability is not just a problem in terms of treatment and management, but a taint for the entire family entailing a range of negative social outcomes. In their development of the concept of domestic citizenship, Das and Addlakha (2001) extend the notion of disability beyond individual bodies into body selves and family systems. While visible physical disabilities may appear to have a more harmful impact on the life chances of individuals, psychosocial disability (which appears invisible at a superficial level), especially one of a long-term nature, may actually be more damaging to the self in the long run. The chapter ends with some observations on how an emerging paradigm of disability may be used not only to arrive at a better understanding of physical and psychosocial disabilities, but may equally be applied to a range of other conditions like HIV/AIDS, infertility, and the whole gamut of lifestyle diseases.

***

Is disability a master status, infecting all other status a person has in the eyes of society, as writers like Barnartt (2001) would propound, or is it a contingent and variable status affecting an individual during her lifetime? Obviously, there are limitations to social interventions to alleviate medical problems at any given point of time, and yet, social factors play an overwhelming role in definitions, experiences of, and reactions to impairments and disabilities. Then, medical problems cannot be separated from the social context as they are themselves closely linked to existing knowledge systems, distribution of resources, and the wider natural and sociocultural environments. The purpose of this chapter has been to view disability in a holistic perspective with equal emphasis on its biological and social dimensions.

Some readers may question the methodological basis of this chapter in drawing upon different types of narratives from different experiential contexts. This choice was deliberate; and an attempt has been made to substantiate the category of disability as a viable frame to capture different impairments that configure a range of common experiences of exclusion, marginalization, discrimination, and violence.

Empowerment, autonomy, difference with dignity, valorization of vulnerability, and the inherent meaningfulness of lived experiences are some key features of the contemporary disability paradigm. The paradigm derives from the minority rights/social model of disability that bridges the gap between physical disabilities like visual disability and the emerging category of psychosocial disability. The spectrum approach to health and illness, impairment, and disability, embodied in the WHO classifications and in the UNCRPD, also does not conflict with the overarching category of disability as the interface between personhood, biology, culture, and society. It is only in the context of this multi-factorial analytical frame that the differential impact of biological, personality, sociocultural factors on a case-by-case basis can be assessed and similarities and differences marked. For instance, Priya's discomfort at not looking 'active' in the eyes of sighted persons is linked to certain social norms of appearance that her visual impairment rendered her difficult to understand, let alone follow. Similarly, there are far more disadvantages associated with psychiatric impairment than the actual needs linked to the impairment would warrant. Disqualification from litigation and political participation of a person with mental illness as a blanket rule in many parts of the world derives from social constructions of mental illness and the mentally ill individual that are historically and culturally embedded.

Among all the social variables that frame experience, gender plays perhaps the most critical role. In the context of disability, patriarchy imposes multiple burdens on the woman with a disability. She is at a disadvantage in comparison to non-disabled women and disabled men, throwing her into a socially residual category that is yet to be clearly articulated. It has been the purpose of this chapter to give voice to this group, which has been marginalized both by mainstream women's and disability movements.

Notes

1. I am grateful to Neena, and her mother, and Priya for discussing intimate details of their lives with me. I also acknowledge the cooperation of the staff of the psychiatry department at the Lady Hardinge Medical College and Hospital, New Delhi, and for financial support from the MacArthur Foundation in India.
2. Available at: http://www.un.org/disabilities/documents/convention/convoptprot-e.pdf, accessed 27 May 2009.
3. Ibid.

References

Abberley, P. 1996. 'Work, Utopia and Impairment', in L. Barton (ed.), *Disability and Society*, pp. 61–80. London: Longman.

Addlakha, R. 2008. *Deconstructing Mental Illness: An Ethnography of Psychiatry, Women and the Family*. New Delhi: Zubaan Books.

Amundson, R. 1992. 'Disability, Handicap and the Environment', *Journal of Social Philosophy*, 23(1): 105–18.

Barham, P. 1986. *Schizophrenia and Human Value: Chronic Schizophrenia, Science and Society*. London: Basil Blackwell.

Barnartt, S. 2001. 'Using Role Theory to Describe Disability', in S.N. Barnartt and B.M. Altman (eds), *Exploring Theories and Expanding Methodologies: Where We Are and Where We Need to Go*, pp. 53–75. London: JAI Press.

Barrett, R.J. 1988. 'Interpretations of Schizophrenia', *Culture, Medicine and Psychiatry*, 12(3): 357–89.

Corker, M. 1999. 'Differences, Conflations and Foundations: The Limits to Accurate Theoretical Representations of Disabled People's Experience', *Disability and Society*, 14(5): 627–42.

Carroll, D. and C.A. Niven. 1993. 'Gender Health and Stress', in C.A. Niven and D. Carroll (eds), *The Health Psychology of Women*, pp. 1–13. Chur (Switzerland): Harwood Academic Publishers.

Das, V. and R. Addlakha. 2001. 'Disability and Domestic Citizenship: Stigma, Contagion and the Making of the Subject', *Public Culture*, 13(3): 511–31.

Engel, G.L. 1977. 'The Need for a New Medical Model: A Challenge to Biomedicine', *Science*, 196(4286): 129–36.

Fine, M. and A. Asch. 1988. 'Introduction: Beyond Pedestals', in M. Fine and A. Asch (eds), *Women with Disabilities: Essays in Psychology, Culture and Politics*, pp. 1–37. Philadelphia: Temple University Press.

Fischer, L.R. 1981. 'Transitions in the Mother–Daughter Relationship', *Journal of Marriage and the Family*, 43: 613–16.

Flax, J. 1978. 'The Conflict between Nurturance and Autonomy in Mother–Daughter Relationships and within Feminism', *Feminist Studies*, 4(2): 171–89.

Luyten, P. and S.J. Blatt. 2007. 'Looking Back towards the Future: Is it Time to Change the DSM Approach to Psychiatric Disorders? The Case of Depression', *Psychiatry*, 70(2): 85–99.

Meekosha, H. 1990. 'Is Feminism Able Bodied? Reflections from between the Trenches', *Refractory Girl*, August: 34–42.

Mehrotra, N. and S. Vaidya. 2008. 'Exploring Constructs of Intellectual Disability and Personhood in Haryana and Delhi', *Indian Journal of Gender Studies*, 15(2): 317–40.

Morris, J. 1991. *Pride and Prejudice: Transforming Attitudes to Disability*. London: The Women's Press.

————. 1993. 'Feminism and Disability', *The Feminist Review*, 43: 57–70.

Oliver, M. 1996. *Understanding Disability: From Theory to Practice*. London: Macmillan.

Price, J. and M. Shildrick. 1998. 'Uncertain Thoughts on the Dis/abled Body', in J. Price and M. Shildrick (eds), *Vital Signs: Feminist Reconfigurations of the Bio/logical Body*, pp. 224–49. Edinburgh: University of Edinburgh Press.

Rich, A. 1976. *Of Woman Born: Motherhood as Experience and Institution*. New York: Norton.

Shakespeare, T. 2000. 'Disabled Sexuality: Towards Rights and Recognition', *Disability and Sexuality*, 18(3): 159–67.

Union of the Physically Impaired against Segregation (UPIAS). 1976. *Fundamental Principles of Disability*. London: Union of the Physically Impaired Against Segregation. Available at: www.leeds.ac.uk/disability-tudies/archiveuk/index, accessed 11 November 2008.

Wendell, S. 1996. *The Rejected Body: Feminist Philosophical Reflections on Disability*. London: Routledge and Kegan Paul.

World Health Organization (WHO). 1976. *Document A29/INFDOCI/1*. Geneva: WHO Press.

————. 1980. *International Classification of Impairments, Disabilities and Handicaps* (ICIDH). Geneva: WHO Press.

————. 2001. *International Classification of Functioning, Disability and Health* (ICF). Geneva: WHO Press. Available at: http://www.who.int/classifications/icf/zh/index.html, accessed 11 November 2008.

6

Growing Up and Sexual Identity Formation

Mental Health Concerns of Lesbian Women

Ketki Ranade and *Yogita Hastak*[1]

Visibility to issues of sexual minorities is greater today than ever before. Lesbian, gay, bisexual, trans[2], and queer (LGBTQ) activists in India have been raising a number of issues, including decriminalization of homosexuality; non-discrimination based on gender and sexual orientation; ending silence associated with same-sex sexuality; right to an informed and healthy sexuality, especially in the context of the human immunodeficiency virus (HIV)/acquired immunodeficiency syndrome (AIDS) epidemic; raising questions about violence faced by LGBTQ in families, on streets, at the hands of police, doctors; and so on. Print media has seen a revolution in the twenty-first century with more books, newsletters, newspaper articles, and editorials being written about queer lives. These have included books and articles on the history of same-sex love, narratives of gay and lesbian individuals and couples from urban and rural parts of India describing their lived experiences, gay persons, views on gay parenting and adoption, and fiction, short stories, poetry, and films with gay themes (for details, see Sukthankar 1999; Vanita and Kidwai 2000; Sharma 2006; Chandran 2008; *Bombay Dost* 2009 and Nandy-Joshi 2009).

However, there exists sparse academic literature on the mental health concerns of sexual minorities. Except for reports of lesbian suicides and a few writings on violence faced by lesbian women (Khaitan 2004; Voices against 377 2005), there exists no substantive material on lesbian and bisexual women's mental health. In this chapter, we bring forth themes that emerged from an analysis of narratives of lesbian women about their growing up experiences. The themes covered in the chapter include: questions about sexual desire and identity; sense of isolation and being different; gender atypicality; correction of this from self, family, and peers; and stressors due to sexual orientation and choices. We do not propose any model of same-sex sexual identity development; nor do we claim generalizability of these narratives. It is a step towards building a knowledge base on the various processes, barriers, challenges, tasks, and stressors that lesbian women go through in the process of growing up in a predominantly heterocentric world. Here, we have focused only on growing up issues of lesbian-identified women through childhood and adolescence.

Developmental Perspective and Mental Health of Lesbian Women[3]

A developmental perspective on human growth and behaviour is concerned with studying the progressive series of changes and maturational processes that occur among human beings throughout the lifespan and are influenced by both genetic endowments as well as environmental phenomena. Being gay/lesbian or becoming gay/lesbian is an area shrouded in controversy. There is a position that claims that sexuality, and homosexuality in particular, is inborn and a result of biological or natural influences; and then there are theorists, academics, and activists that claim sexuality to be socially constructed. These theorists put forth the argument that there is nothing natural about heterosexuality or homosexuality and that several social processes interact in complex ways to construct normative notions of sexuality. Rubin (1992) uses the term 'charmed circle' to refer to the socially constructed notion of the most accepted, pure, blessed, and healthy form of sexuality between adults, that is, monogamous, heterosexual sex, within wedlock, for procreation based on the Victorian notion of 'pure, forever, romantic love'. This charmed circle then becomes the reference point for creating a range of sexualities, choices, and behaviours that fall outside of the charmed circle and that can be judged as inappropriate, bad, sinful, unhealthy, abnormal, unnatural, and damned. According to this argument of the social constructionists, homosexuality is thus socially created (not biologically) in opposition to the 'natural' and 'virtuous' 'within-marriage, heterosexuality'.

Whether seen as the product of biology or social construction, it is clear that the emergence of sexual identity is not an event that occurs at a given moment during adolescence or adulthood. It is a process of consolidation of one's sexual identity along with development and consolidation of one's overall identity as a human being. Erickson (1968) states that identity development is a process that starts from infancy and may continue throughout the life course of an individual and hence, should not be viewed as static or immutable. This process of identity development is not merely the journey of an individual in isolation, but rather mediated by several social processes as described earlier. Personal life and collective social arrangements are linked in a fundamental and constitutive way, and hence to study one without attention to the other would provide us with only a partial picture. Social structures that dictate norms of sexuality and gender are constituted by practice of the same. Similarly, the practice of normative gender or sexuality expressed in, for instance, rules about marriage in a given society—who marries whom?, what is the gender, caste, class, age of the two parties entering into a marriage?—cannot float free, but is responsive to and constrained by the circumstances which those social structures constitute (Connell 1987).

Applying tools of human development research to study lesbian women's mental health implies that sexual orientation is considered to be a significant context that affects the childhood, adolescence, and life course of an individual with same-sex desires. This chapter has been written with the underlying assumption that being attracted to individuals of the same sex can have an impact on all aspects of living across the lifespan. It describes the complex processes and challenges that a woman with same-sex attractions goes through during her childhood, adolescence, and all through her growing up years. It also highlights, from her perspective, responses from her immediate environment to these internal processes.

Discrimination based on sexual orientation is known to impact many areas of life, including education and employment (D'Augelli 2006; Sandfort *et al.* 2006), romantic relationships (Herek 2006), and family concerns (Patterson 2006a, 2006b). Research focused on sexual orientation across the lifespan—childhood, adolescence, adulthood, and ageing—has made some interesting progress and provides significant learnings. For instance, Green (1986) reported that boys who showed substantial gender-variant behaviour in childhood were likely to adopt gay identities as adults. Drummond *et al.* (2008) reported in a 12-year follow-up study of gender dysphoric girls that they, too, were more likely than average to report same-sex sexual behaviour in adulthood. Adolescents and youth who identify as non-heterosexual are more likely than their peers to experience a variety of mental health problems (Cochran and Mays 2006), most serious among which is the elevated tendency for suicidality (Russell 2006). Safren and Heimberg (1999) state that lesbian and gay (LG) youth face a greater number of stressful events and have access to less social support than their heterosexual peers, which could at least partially explain LG youth being more at risk for mental health problems.

Research on gay, lesbian, and bisexual adults has mostly focused on adult romantic relationships, which is often challenging in the absence of legal recognition for same-sex couples (Balsam *et al.* 2008; Roisman *et al.* 2008). Research has included gay/lesbian parenting (Patterson 2006a) and ageing (Kimmel *et al.* 2006).

In the Indian context, most models of human growth and development that continue to be used for training of mental health professionals and that inform mental health practice are heterocentric. They focus on stereotypical descriptions of development processes, tasks, and goals to be achieved by human beings in different stages of the life cycle. For instance, most of these models in their description of adolescence state that it is a developmental stage where adolescents will 'develop an interest in the opposite sex, finding information about sexual intercourse, contraception use, unwanted pregnancy', and so on (Hurlock 1981). Experiences of the internal processes of adolescence who may not 'fit' into the above-mentioned description and who may have non-heterosexual fantasies, attractions, crushes, or who may not fit into the gender binaries of 'man' and 'woman', do not find any space in these development models. As mental health professionals who work with adults in distress from a developmental perspective,[4] we find this silence about the growing up years of individuals with non-heterosexual orientation to be a serious form of invisibility. This is also one of the contributors to the lack of awareness, general sense of apathy, and resulting homophobia often seen among mental health professionals, who are primarily exposed to heterocentric ideas and models of practice during their training.

Alternatively, Western scholars have proposed many developmental models of identity formation. These describe the complex process of LG identity formation, barriers, challenges, and the role of internalized and external homophobia in identity development. A six-stage model of Cass (in Ritter and Terndrup 2002: 90–7) describes stages such as identity confusion, comparison, tolerance, acceptance, identity pride, and identity synthesis. Each stage in this model is characterized by various developmental tasks, such as beginning to question socio-familial heterosexist assumptions about oneself, developing an awareness about same-sex thoughts, feelings, and fantasies, and admitting to oneself the possibility of being gay. Troiden's (1984) model is one more such model that views LG development as mediated by both external factors (heterocentrism and sexual prejudice) and internal factors (such as one's internalized homophobia and character strengths). More spiral than linear, Troiden's model suggests that individuals move back and forth between stages and that not all will experience all stages or sub-stages.

Even these LG identity models have limitations in describing developmental phenomena fully. This is because most of them rest on assumptions of linearity, universality, and the uniform nature of growth and development, which compromise the fluidity and diversity that is the essence of human sexuality. In addition, most of these models are proposed in the Western context and are often based on white, gay men's experiences. Hence, their applicability to the context of lesbian women in India and in the Asian, Southeast Asian regions is questionable. Developmental psychologists or mental health workers working with sexual minorities would have to evolve new culturally relevant frameworks to better conceptualize the lived experiences of sexual minorities.

Another reason for using a lens of growth and development to understand mental health issues of lesbian women is that research (mostly done in the Western context) on LG health and mental health issues focuses primarily on morbidity, prevalence of illnesses, risk reduction, and so on. This is the case with research focusing on health issues such as HIV or sexually transmitted infections (STIs), as well as mental health research focusing on prevalence of mental illness, depression, or suicide in the community. In the Indian context, this focus on morbidity increases the risk of double discrimination. In the history of psychiatry, homosexuality was classified as mental illness until 1973, and some of the Indian practitioners continue to hold the same belief till date. The widely prevalent social attitudes, regressive laws, lack of a psychosocial discourse on sexual minority health issues, and commonly prevalent health provider views of 'homosexuality' being 'unnatural' and 'deviant' form a fertile background for the risk of a further discrimination. Given these attitudes and practices, any research with the community that primarily occupies itself with morbidity runs a risk of further pathologizing this community. Meyer (2001) describes this risk of pathologizing in his article titled, 'Why Lesbian, Gay, Bisexual and Transgender Public Health?' Meyer observes that placing sexuality, sexual orientation, and gender under a public health lens may lead to their 'medicalization and public healthification'.

Research done from a development lens focusing on growth, development, and the unfolding of an individual's life story within their social and psychological context is, therefore, of relevance in the Indian context. Also, in the absence of a systematic body of literature on sexual minority and mental health concerns in India, exploratory studies such as the one presented in this chapter are a suitable starting point.

Focusing on the growing up experiences of homosexual people does not imply that adolescents or young people from this community are a different group altogether and have nothing in common with heterosexual teenagers; nor is it an attempt to establish aetiology of same-sex desires. It is only to underscore that, while such individuals struggle with the same issues as straight people do, they may have some additional developmental tasks to carry out that could be linked with their sexual minority status. Allport (1958) points to some fundamental differences. Most LG persons grow up in heterosexual families and hence, they are not instilled with a gay identity at birth. They must discover it on their own, while they may have no role models in parents to help consolidate a minority identity. Often, they cannot count on parental support for protection from discrimination from the outside world (Allport 1958; Martin 1982). These tasks are further complex for a lesbian woman who, in addition to dealing with heterosexism, has to also fight sexism that all women face in our society (Greene 2003).

Methodology

This chapter is based on a research project on understanding health/mental health needs of lesbian and gay individuals and the nature of health services provided to this community. The study was carried out in two metropolitan cities of Mumbai and Pune, Maharashtra, India. The current chapter is focused on growing up experiences of lesbian women, which is based on life history interviews with 15 self-identified lesbian women.

Among the 15 lesbian women interviewed, 12 women were from Mumbai and three were from Pune. The age range of the respondents was between 21–42 years, with most respondents (n = 13) falling in the age range of 21–30 years. Of the 15 women interviewed, two were married (one continues to be in a heterosexual marriage and the other is separated). Six women identified as being single and nine were in a relationship with a woman. Eight women had studied up to graduation, six had completed their postgraduate degrees, and one had studied up to Class 12. Four women were living by themselves, four with partners, and seven others with family. Twelve women were working and three were currently not in any kind of employment.

An interview guide and a timeline were used to collect data regarding the process of sexual identity development and growing up in a sequential manner. All the interviews were tape recorded, transcribed, and entered into the computer, which were analysed as user-coded text segments using a computer package. A purposive sampling method was used and respondents were contacted through LG support groups and e-groups in both cities as well as through informal networks and contacts of consenting respondents. All the necessary protocols that need to be followed while working with an invisible and marginalized group were followed: maintaining confidentiality; restricting access to raw data; masking identities; seeking oral consent from research participants; sensitizing the research team to issues of sexual minorities; and providing referrals of support organizations to those participants who needed them.

The data were collected along a timeline from earliest memories in childhood till date, and information in 10 different domains was generated, including family relationships, childhood friends, school/college experiences, first knowledge about sex/sexuality, same-sex relationships, coming out, and so on. Common themes relevant to experiences of growing up of lesbian women were derived from these information domains. The themes with implications for growth and development as well as the overall mental health of lesbian women have been presented here.

It is important to note that the average age of the respondents ranges between 21 to 30 years and when they describe their childhood experiences, they are describing a time approximately of the early 1990s in urban India. In the early 1990s, even in urban India, the campaign against Indian Penal Code (IPC) Section 377 for decriminalization, non-governmental organizations (NGOs) working on gay rights, and media covering issues of gay persons was largely unheard of. Also, the HIV/AIDS epidemic that eventually played a pivotal role in visibility and collectivization among men who have sex with men (MSM), gay men, and trans persons, including *hijra*s and *kothi*s, as well as in getting a state response to marginalized sexualities, had just begun to throw up challenges and questions related to sexuality in the 1990s. Similarly, women's rights groups talking and demonstrating openly about lesbian women's issues in India after the controversy following release of the film, *Fire* (Campaign for Lesbian Rights [CALERI] 1999), had not yet taken place. Thus, the following findings have to be viewed in light of these social circumstances of public silence about issues of sexuality.

Questions about Identity: Feelings of Confusion and Isolation

A lesbian woman growing up in a predominately heterosexual world faces confusion and several questions about herself, her body, her identity, her attraction to other girls, and acceptance by society. Some of the respondents in the study talked about having questions about their identity, such as: 'Is it normal to be attracted to the same-sex?'; 'Will I be accepted in society for who I am?'; 'Will I be heterosexual some day?'; and 'Why am I different?'

> Many a times I felt that I should stop thinking about girls, I should never behave like this. I mean I used to feel, why I am thinking this way, why I am attracted to girls? Why don't I get attracted to guys? I used to feel that it is only me who thinks that way and it's a problem with me. (30 years, married, Pune, when in Classes 8–9)

> I thought I was the only idiot who was like that and I didn't know the term and I didn't know how this works and I didn't know whether it would be accepted and I was scared as a kid. So I never spoke to anybody about it until much later, when I met my first girlfriend! (30 years, Mumbai, when in Class 6)

Both these respondents, in addition to confusion, describe a sense of isolation and a belief that they are 'the only one!' In most of these respondents, the isolation continued till they met others from the lesbian community. Quite a few respondents talked about these feelings as being a great source of stress in their formative years.

> 'I was like at that time isolated…I was the only woman in Bombay who feels this way', I would think. There is not a single woman in Bombay who feels this way…And where do I find them? And I was under real stress…(42 years, married, Mumbai, when, at 35 years, she was getting out of a 10-year-long heterosexual marriage)

Sexual Attraction

For a few respondents, questions about their sexual orientation arose primarily in the context of attraction towards another girl or through sexual exploration. For some, this attraction was not articulated at that time as sexual, and therefore, was connected with sexual identity or preference only later. However, most of the respondents mentioned at some point on the timeline that being attracted to someone as well as expressing it were significant markers in personal journeys of self-identification.

> I knew about my sexuality when I was very little, maybe in 6th or 7th standard...I was attracted to my head teacher; she was Catholic and very sexy. She had something about her...I would feel very uncomfortable if I wouldn't see her. I used to go to school just to see her first thing in the morning. I didn't know what was going on with me, but that's how my childhood was. And I had my first girlfriend when I was 16... She initiated the coming closer, being physical. First I was like, 'Hold on, what the hell is going on?' She was like, 'No it's fine, why are you scared?' So it started from there. And then I was pretty much out. I was like, cool! (30 years, Mumbai, describes the time between Classes 6–7 in school till age 16)

> In my childhood at the age of 12 when I had my dad's friend's family living with us...They were, like, 4 daughters. Out of them, one was very close to me. In fact, she started sharing my bedroom. She was the first one who started making moves on me. So, the first ever sexual interaction that I had with a person was with this girl. And that was a very significant one. We grew very close, even emotionally, and that was when I first found out that I was attracted to a girl. (42 years, Mumbai, at age 12)

Most adult lesbian and bisexual women would describe memories of first attraction in terms of intense and strong emotional bonds. Similarly, for most of them, significant factors that contributed to questioning about sexual identity were feelings of attraction and developing an emotional crush on or attachment to another woman (Savin-Williams 2005).

Lacking a Language

Throughout the interviews, most of the respondents repeatedly talked about the lack of language to articulate what they were feeling about their sexuality and the confusion that followed because of the same.

You know until you have learnt the word gay, you are always wondering what's going on with you and then you see that 'Oh! this is a normal thing. There are other people like me...' (24 years, Mumbai, at age 16)

I mean, we didn't even have the language to kind of understand what we were doing...Because apart from that, we would do a lot of other things like talk, get along, fight so bitterly, cry and be there for each other...all the things that best friends do. Except that we also shared this, but we never talked about it. The thing is that everything is in a heterosexual context. So somehow, when I was doing it with this woman, I didn't think of it as sex! I didn't think I was having sex with her, because for me the image of what sex was, was something between a man and a woman. (26 years, Mumbai, at age 17)

One respondent talked about the significance of knowing that there exists a word in English language for her sexual desires. She described that this helped her to look for more information and become comfortable with herself.

When I went to college, I had this friend, who told me about this thing; That it is called homosexual and lesbian and knowing that there was a name for it, I was eager to know more...Around this time only, star movies was a new thing and once I saw a movie, in which for the first time, I saw two girls kissing... And from that day, I started realising what I am. (29, Mumbai, at age 17)

The role of imagery in facilitating a sense of self-identification has been described here as well as in the following quote of a 26-year-old lesbian activist:

Yeah, not having the language, not having the vocabulary and the words that you know have such a derogatory connotation to it. Not just language, images also! I mean I was 23 and I had had sex with three women, but it was only at 23 that I finally saw on screen what it looks like: So just no images, nothing positive, no role models. Newspaper articles about lesbians running away and all also have come out now: When I was, say, in college nothing on same sex ever in sex education; No visible images, no visible people, no language. (26 years, Mumbai)

Feelings of Alienation—Being 'Different'

Linked with questions about sexuality were feelings of being different, alienation, and exclusion, especially from peer groups. Eight out of 15 respondents in our study said that one of the activities that formed a large part of peer socialization during school and college was sitting around in groups and discussing sex and boys. They would often ignore such discussions or participate minimally. Most of them said that they would never even think of disclosing their sexual interest in other girls due to fear, stigma, and the possibility of exclusion or being misunderstood. Often, these conversations led to a sense of being different from their friends.

> See, I don't know, but I just felt (pause)... I never identified with lesbianism or gayness at that time but I just thought, I am different and that's all...Yeah, I could feel that I was different, even when I was in St. Peters (name of school changed) and I was liking the girls a lot and I was seeing that all these girls are attracted to boys... (34 years, Mumbai, when in Classes 8–9)

> Yeah, I did feel different as all my friends were ultra girly and all they had to talk about was guys and all their crushes. I was no doubt attracted to that girl in my class, but I just couldn't share it with anyone. (26 years, Mumbai, at age 13)

This sense of being different from friends, lack of spaces to talk about one's desires, and invisibility to same-sex sexuality were significant stressors for most respondents. Perhaps, the best early predictor of a same-sex orientation is a child's subjective feeling of being different from peers (Savin-Williams 2005). It is noted that 'pre-homosexual' children already experience a sense of being different from peers and usually, the experience of childhood is marked by themes of marginality, alienation, and estrangement (Troiden 1979, 1989). This estrangement from the surroundings and lack of awareness of other homosexual teens can lead to not just isolation, invisibility, and silencing, but also self-invalidating attempts to fit in and 'pass' as heterosexual.

Ordinarily, some of the developmental tasks that individuals have to achieve during 'adolescence' include individuating from parents, socializing with peers, forming an identity, exploring intimate relationships, and orienting themselves to the future (Coleman and Remafedi 1989). Peer influences and relationships in this context are very significant as these interactions help the adolescent practise and learn new social behaviours and develop new values in friendship selection, social acceptance, and rejection. It is these social interactions that help the adolescent to achieve the goal of learning adult patterns of socialization (Hurlock 1981). Unfortunately, the primary task for the LG youth is entry into a stigmatized role and the major developmental task for them includes passage into that social identity. Since so much of the psychic energies of these youth are consumed with stigma management, they may have difficulty with normative developmental concerns of adolescents and this may impact their emotional well-being (Ritter and Terndrup 2002: 115).

Internalized Normative Ideas—Shame and Homophobia

A few of the respondents, while talking about their identity, described being in complete denial of their sexuality. Some said that, while they knew that they were gay, they did not want to acknowledge it at all, due to shameful messages from the environment around them, and preferred to be silent about their desires.

> You know how these hostels are, one day we were having a late night session in the hostel and someone said something about lesbians and I remember cringing because by then I knew, that probably what I am doing with this woman is what would make me lesbian and I just didn't want it! So I remember cringing at the word and saying, 'I hope I am not lesbian', though somewhere I knew it but I was like, 'I hope I am not lesbian! Or then I am different'. You know that what I am doing with this woman is not dirty and not what lesbians do (laughing). Yeah, I remember that embarrassment, that cringing, that fear so clearly! I was so traumatized that I might just be lesbian. You know it was very bad. (26 years, Mumbai, at 18–19 years, during undergraduate studies)

The given narrative is an example of the manner in which the invisibility of same-sex desire in the immediate environment and experiencing a lack of safety by the LG individual leads to silencing an important aspect of selfhood. O'Brien (2005) describes silence around sexual orientation as a form of psychological death that perpetuates a sense of shame about oneself.

Lesbian women, like many other marginalized groups, suffer wide-ranging effects of stigma and one such effect is that of internalized shame. Being seen as different from family and friends is one potent source of shame. Shame is deeply connected with self-esteem and identity. Feelings of internalized shame often lead to a desire to hide and become distrustful of others (Wells and Hansen 2003)

While elaborating on the theme of denial of sexuality, one respondent, who now identifies as a lesbian and who was in a heterosexual marriage for over 10 years, said:

> I was too scared to look at what I was feeling. I was this complete *darpoke* (one who is easily scared). There was this girl in my group and I was really attracted to her but I never ever had the guts to tell her, 'I like you'. I didn't know what she would say if I told her. So, till I got married, all my fantasies were only about women... Yeah, and yet the marriage happened; Because I was too scared to admit it or look at it or address it in any way. Had I had an inkling that this is what's happening to me, I would not have got married! (42 years, Mumbai, describes the time between Classes 9–10 in school till 24 years of age when she got married)

Models of LG identity have described the theme of denial of same-sex sexuality. Most of these models state that in the initial stages of identity development, individuals, while privately labelling their emotions, fantasies, and thoughts, often continue to maintain a heterosexual social image. It is usually during this time that LG people are evaluating the acceptability of their desires in their immediate environment and many mediating factors, such as peer influences, family environment, and their general visibility to same-sex sexuality, play an important role in the individual's process of self-labelling. Often, if same-sex desires are viewed as undesirable and unacceptable, the person may adopt 'inhibition strategies' such as restricting information about homosexuality, deny its personal relevance, become celibate, or seek a cure. This might lead to identity foreclosure, which may or may not be revisited by the individual in later life (Ritter and Terndrup 2002: 90–7).

Gender Atypicality in Childhood

The childhood of same-sex attracted people has often been ignored, possibly because of the presumption that sexual behaviours and attractions develop only at the stage of puberty. However, childhood behaviour might be a clue to adult homosexuality. Perhaps the best early predictor of a same-sex orientation is a child's subjective feeling of being different from peers. Objectively, this is usually linked to atypical gender expression (Savin-Williams 2005). There are suggestions of developmental uniqueness during childhood for those who later identify as gay or lesbian. Boys and girls who showed substantial amounts of gender-variant behaviour in childhood were later likely to adopt gay/lesbian identities as adults (Bailey and Zucker 1995; Drummond *et al.* 2008; Rieger *et al.* 2008).

In the present study, non-conformity of traditional gender roles during childhood emerged primarily in two main domains: play and clothes/grooming. Most of the respondents (n = 13) described their preference for playing with their brothers or other boys, games like football or cricket, when they were younger. Some of them also mentioned that they did not get along with girls their age and did not like to play girly games like dolls or *bhatukli* (kitchen game).

> ...People used to take me for a boy because I would always be playing with the boys, I would have short hair, I would be on my bike...always sporting some kind of a wound or the other...In my family, my dad was the fun guy. I would do all the fun stuff with him; We would go riding on bikes. He never stopped me at all, *bahut maza atha tha* (It used to be a lot of fun). He would teach me how to play *gillidanda* (ball and stick), marbles...I used to play all the boys games!! Hated playing that girl doll thing, dolls *ko main ek dam ganja kar deti thi* (I used to shave off the doll's head). I couldn't deal with all the suffocation of girly girly!! (laughing)...pushing girls around, tying their shoelaces together, tying their plaits together, everything that boys do at that age, I used to do that. (34 years, Mumbai, during Class 4 in school)

Quite a few of the women interviewed (n = 6) talked about preferring to keep their hair short, wearing their brothers' clothes, having a dislike for feminine dresses, and hating to wear jewellery and flowers in their hair during their growing up years.

...I felt that I wanted my hair to be short. Also piercing my nose and all, I didn't like it, but that was forced on me. And even earrings and all, I didn't like them much...I didn't like things like *gajra* (string of flowers often worn in the hair). I liked to wear only shirt pant. (30 years, married, Pune, when in Classes 7–8 in school)

There were a lot of things I did as a child which were not acceptable. When I was very very young, in the 2nd standard or so, I used to take clothes from my brother's cupboard and wear them and pretend to be a guy! (25 years, Mumbai, when in Class 2)

One of the respondent stated that her gender non-confirming behaviour often got her unwanted attention in public spaces:

...That gets me into a lot of trouble because when I climb into a ladies compartment on the train, I am constantly stared at, I am constantly asked '*mulgaahey, mulgiahey*' (is it a boy, is it a girl?). If I am walking on the streets, this comment is passed. Whenever there is any kind of checking going on in public places, if I am standing in the ladies line...In fact just yesterday at the station, there were these lines and this guy reached out for me and kind of pulled me by my collar and I had to put my hand out and say, 'Ladies *hai*' (I am a woman). And you know then he looks you up and down...If I am sitting at the station in the ladies seat, the policeman will come and tap the chair with his stick and say, '*Porga* (Lad), get up'. So I have to constantly explain myself and say that I am a girl, but I look like this, and that can be a little annoying. (26 years, Mumbai)

According to Cook and Pawlowski, 'By the time most individuals reach early adolescence, they have been deeply enculturated in the sexual attitudes and values of their family, the larger culture and their particular sub-cultures' (quoted in Ritter and Terndrup 2002: 114). Rigid messages about gender-appropriate behaviours and heterosexist images are bombarded from almost all sources of socialization, including family, school, media, peers, and so on. Significant to the implications of gender atypicality in an adolescent's life is the question of how rigidly the culture in which an individual is growing up views gender roles and deviation from the same (Savin-Williams 2005).

Some respondents described that they would be comfortable with both kinds of clothing: that which was considered more feminine as well as what was considered masculine. They also described changes in preferences about clothes and grooming over a period of time. A 42-year-old lesbian woman, who was earlier in a heterosexual marriage, after separating from her husband and coming out to herself as a lesbian, said that she began to give up girly things like wearing lipstick and skirts after she started realizing who she was: '...By then, I slowly started changing my appearance. I stopped wearing lipstick and I used to not really like it...I started wearing shoes that were comfortable. Not very feminine shoes and things like that. Mostly in trousers...' (42 years, Mumbai, said around the age of 37).

Corrective Responses to Being Different

Since most of the women described themselves as having some degree of gender atypical behaviours, especially around gender roles and expectations, they also stated that this non-conformity was met with some form of correction efforts. During childhood, most of the corrective responses were targeted towards gender atypicality, but during and after adolescence, corrective behaviours were often linked with sexual orientation and preference. These corrective behaviours were usually in the form of taunts, scolding, subtle forms of disapproval, or even physical abuse. In a few cases, it also led to more extreme measures of seeking medical treatment for this 'different' behaviour. The correction would be self-initiated at times and, in some cases, from family members, elders, teachers, peers, and friends.

A few respondents described their attempts to 'fit in', as well as attempts to develop an interest in the opposite sex. Some talked of exploring relationships with boys, whereas others talked of pretending to be interested in boys. Some also tried out relationships with boys as a way of coping with rejection from their girlfriends.

> When I was 12, all the girls in school would like guys and I didn't really like guys, but I would sometimes fool around and tell them, 'Oh! There is this guy and he's cute and all', just to mask it, just to fit in you know... Some people thought I was just a late bloomer and that maybe after some time, I would find guys... (21 years, Mumbai, at age 12)

Childhood experiences of departing from family/peer norms in concrete ways, such as atypical gender expression and traits and sexual interest in individuals of the same-sex, may be experienced by the child as not good difference, but a 'bad' one. This could cause feelings of being misunderstood, isolated, shamed, suppressed, and internally repressed. A number of efforts at self-correction or masking and passing as heterosexual can be viewed as coping with this sense of isolation (Savin-Williams 2005).

Two of the respondents spoke about their close relationship with their mothers. They both mentioned that they knew at some level that their mothers would have never approved of their same-sex desires. This may have been a motivation for them to try to conform to societal norms and not embrace their sexuality initially.

> …My mom said that, 'I think you just stick to this particular friend a lot'. I think the Marathi word, which I remember is, *khoop anga anga shi kartes* ('you stick to her too much'). I remember thinking at that time, 'Does she know? What does she mean by saying that?' Another incident I remember was, once my mother unexpectedly came to the hostel and I was sleeping in bed with this other girl. So my mom came and woke me up and it was a single bed…And my mom was like 'Why is she in your bed?' And I was like, 'Oh my god'…I think I sensed that my mom would be highly uncomfortable. Maybe she didn't give me any overt messages, but, maybe that sentence about sticking to that girl too much might have stayed with me. I still remember the words. I still remember the expression when she saw that woman and me get out of bed. Subtle things like disapproval of my special friends…a little bit of coldness… I haven't articulated this before. It's probably that thing of I don't want to hurt my mother. That must have played a really severe role, now that I am thinking about it. (26 years, Mumbai, first incident at 15 years of age and second at 21 years)

Regarding relationships between lesbians and their mothers, Ritter and Terndrup (2002: 302–4) note that relationships with mothers are more strained for lesbian women than for gay men. With gay men, a mother stepping in to rescue the gay son from rejection was more common. The traditional role expectations from the mother are to pass on the baton of womanhood and traditional roles of a woman to her daughter (Ritter and Terndrup 2002: 305). It is the power of this precept that may cause a sense of 'personal failure' in the mother and make it challenging for her to be receptive of a gender role-discordant daughter, possibly causing a lack of mutual empathy between a heterosexual mother and a lesbian daughter.

Most of the respondents (n = 10), while growing up, were rebuked by parents, and in some cases other elders, about their choices. For some respondents, it was only a one-off incident, but in some cases, the parents vehemently disapproved of certain things like 'tomboyish dressing' or relationships with other girls and punished such behaviours.

> I remember that once I really wanted to cut my hair, I made a big fuss over it but I was not allowed to…I liked to wear shirt–pant but I was not allowed only. Whatever girls could wear I wore, like skirts, midi, Punjabi dress, etc. Also piercing my nose and all, I didn't like it, but that was also forced on me. (30 years, married, Pune, when in Class 7)

One of the respondent talked of disapproving messages from her mother, 'Actually my mother saw us once and she just said, "What the hell are you doing?" We didn't have anything to say and she said, "No! no! It's dirty, you shouldn't do it…God will punish us"' (25 years, Mumbai, at age 13). In the case of one of our respondents, when her father and brother came to know about her orientation, they resorted to physical abuse.

> …I had seen lots of guys for marriage and I was saying 'No' to all of them. In one case, it was too much because from the boy's side, they wanted to go ahead with the marriage. I was so angry! And I didn't even want to spoil his life and so then I called him and told him that I cannot get married. I told him to say that he didn't like me. But he went and told my father everything. Then my father had hit me a lot…And my older brother, he also hit me lots. He said that girls don't have this kind of thing and all! (26 years, Pune, when at 24)

Rejection from family, fear of rejection, or the need to 'hide' is a significant stressor during growing up for many gay youth (D'Augelli and Hershberger 1993). Research indicates that most lesbian, gay, or bisexual individuals place the family of origin among the last group of people to whom they would come out and from whom they would expect any support (Ritter and Terndrup 2002: 295). In the Indian context as well, reports and testimonials of lesbian women indicate that family is rated as most oppressive and least supportive of lesbian relationships (Fernandez *et al.* 2001; People's Union for Civil Liberties [Karnataka] [PUCL-K] 2001), as well as a major source of violence in the lives of sexual and gender minorities (Ghosh *et al.* 2011; Lesbians and Bisexuals in Action [LABIA] 2013). Pressures for marriage (often seen as a social duty of every adult person in India) and forced marriages are a common source of stress and violence from families in India (Creating Resources for Empowerment and Action [CREA] 2012; Joseph 2005).

The developmental impact of this kind of a relationship with one's family of origin, characterized by a need to hide and be secretive, anticipating rejection and even violence from them, can be severe. It is certain that a lesbian teen who has come out to every member of her family and who has received praise and acceptance from each (a highly improbable outcome) will develop in a very different manner from a lesbian teen who has told no one at all, or a lesbian who tells only carefully selected friends because she expects abuse at the hands of her family during the years that she must live at home.

Some respondents (n = 5) said that their friends, knowing about their orientation, asked them to try having a sexual relationship with a man or expressed the opinion that being gay is wrong and needs to be treated or changed. One of the respondents talked about a girlfriend who wanted the respondent to 'improve' and get married.

> My senior said to me one day, 'I think you are a lesbian and I think you should go see a doctor'. So I said, 'My father is a doctor, why should I go see another doctor?' So then all these friends ganged up and they wrote a letter to the agony aunt in *Femina*, it was very humiliating... (28 years, Mumbai, when in Class 8)
>
> Many of my friends say, 'Have you ever tried a male?' I say 'No!' They always advise me to try a male and I am, like, why are you telling me to? I am happy with what I have, but they are, like, you will know what you are missing only then... (29 years, Pune)

For respondents (n = 3) attending 'all-girls' schools or staying in hostel, these corrective behaviours came from teachers and other figures of authority too. These figures of authority were constantly giving the message that 'liking a girl in that way' is dirty and wrong.

One of the respondents talked about an incidence of physical abuse and public humiliation at her residential school as a response to knowledge about her same-sex desires and relationship with a girl. The respondent described her fragile state of mind and her suicide attempt when her girlfriend was married off. The suicide attempt occurred in the residential school where the respondent was staying and she said:

> I made a suicide attempt. I cut my nerve, I was unconscious and was hospitalised. I had a dorm matron who was like a Hitler...When I came back from the hospital she said, 'How can you say something like this, how can you fall in love with a woman, are you freaking out of your mind? This doesn't happen, it is not there in the Bible and the Gita and the Koran...' She beat me up real bad. Real bad! She beat me with a belt, with a chair...everything!...Later, when I joined the school back, I was humiliated in front of the entire hostel during the prayer meeting, where I was asked to confess that I was in love with a girl and to promise that this would never happen again... (30 years, Mumbai, when at 16)

Hunter and Schaecher (1987) highlighted social isolation, harassment, and violence as the most serious problems among school issues faced by LG teens. Schools are the primary institutional context in which adolescents are housed, where administrators, teachers, counsellors, and coaches can convey messages about homoerotic development explicitly and implicitly. Schools are also the site for enactment of peer cultural norms, which can be deeply heterosexist in adolescence. Thus, LG youth are highly vulnerable in school settings (Ross-Reynolds and Hardy 1985).

A few respondents, when their family got to know or where the respondent told family members about her same-sex sexual preference, were taken to a psychiatrist for changing their orientation. The intensity of this form of correction varied, with some parents actually taking their daughter against her will to a psychiatrist and some others suggesting that the daughter see a psychologist to bring about a change in her preference.

> So what my father wanted then was that no matter what happens, I should be better and he was ready to do whatever it takes. He told the

doctor, 'Pills or operation or whatever it is, we will do it, but she should become alright and she should get married' (26 years, Pune, when 24)

I had a painful coming out with my mother. My dad called later and said, 'Mamma told me and I am upset of course but don't worry, we still love you, its not that we blame you, but I read up on this...' He was very sweet, I remember his words...'I read up that it is a learned behaviour and I am sure you can unlearn it so do you want to meet a good psychologist? We don't want to push you but I'm sure one can do something about it...' (26 years, Mumbai, when 25)

Conversion treatments for homosexuality have been critiqued on two main grounds: lack of any sound efficacy studies; and ethics of this form of treatment (Haldeman 1994; Serovich 2008). It has been noted that the practice of sexual reorientation therapies socially devalues homosexuality and bisexuality (Haldeman 2002). Shidlo and Schroeder (2002) state that a majority of those who sought these forms of reparative or conversion therapies perceived psychological harm in the form of depression, suicidal ideation and attempts, social and interpersonal harm, loss of social support, and spiritual harm as a direct result of these interventions. Also, the recent international human rights document on sexual and gender identity (*Yogyakarta Principles*, United Nations 2006) includes a clause (Principle 18) listing conversion treatment or any form of medical treatment aimed at change of homosexual orientation under medical abuse.

***

This chapter highlights the complex processes and challenges that young lesbian women face, while bridging the disconnect between sociocultural expectations placed on them and their internal processes of recognizing and identifying with their same-sex desires. Isolation, invisibility, internalized shame, and lack of a language to talk about one's sexual desires in a predominantly heterosexual world have been common themes running through most of the narratives presented here.

The chapter highlights the need for sensitizing schools, teachers, NGOs working with children, and other professionals such as doctors and educationists who work primarily with children and adolescents, on issues of diversity in child development, specifically sexual identity development. Life skills programmes as well as sex education programmes in schools and colleges need to incorporate such diverse information.

Mental health professionals in India continue to consider homosexuality to be a form of mental illness that needs to be cured (Ranade 2009). There is a dire need for advocacy with professional bodies of mental health professionals to ensure a ban on reparative/conversion treatments for homosexuality. There is also a need to start a dialogue with teaching institutes and associations of mental health professionals regarding what would constitute affirmative care with sexual minorities in the Indian context.

Most of the LG activism in the country currently focuses on legal reform, collective action against human rights violations in the form of police atrocities, discrimination at the workplace, within families, and so on. In the context of health, a great deal of work in the area of HIV/AIDS prevention, awareness, access to quality care has taken place in the last two decades. However, mental health concerns of individuals often leading double or secret lives, facing social ostracism and stigma, seem to have slipped the agenda of LGBTQ activism in India. One hears of anecdotal evidence, newspaper articles carrying reports on lesbian suicides, violence against lesbian women, and so on. However, we know very little about the mental health impact of such adverse events or even day-to-day gay-related stressors on the lives of lesbian women in India. There is a need for research to build a comprehensive understanding on these issues. Such an understanding would inform both practice and policy.

Finally, it is important to note that while this chapter attempts to highlight some significant themes around growing up 'lesbian', it does so from the recalled childhood memories of adults who currently identify as lesbian. This form of retrospective data gathering has limitations because these accounts can be distorted by many intervening events, memory lapses, changes in the individual's belief systems, and so on. However, most importantly, growing up gay today would be different (if not drastically) from what it was a decade ago and these differences in the lives of today's children and adolescents with same-sex desires do not get reflected in the findings of this study.[5]

Notes

1. The study has been supported under the Health and Population Innovations Fellowship Programme of the Population Council, India (2006–8), awarded to the first author. We wish to sincerely thank all the respondents for openly sharing their life experiences with us. We are grateful to Pertti J. Pelto for his inputs in research methods throughout the study; to Meera Oke for training the research team in the use of computer package for data analysis; and to Shireen Jejeebhoy at the Population Council for her guidance throughout the study. Finally, we are thankful to Sudeep J. Joseph, who dedicatedly worked as a research assistant for this study; and to the Bapu Trust for Research on Mind and Discourse, Pune, for housing this research project and for library and administrative support throughout.

2. Trans is an umbrella term used in gender studies to refer to individuals, who fall outside of the rigid gender binary of 'man' and 'woman'. They may include persons who identify as transgender, gender fluid, gender queer, and so on.

3. Childhood narratives of same-sex attractions can be seen as problematic, politically, because they may be viewed as being motivated by or even used to identify 'pre-homosexual' children, who can then be discouraged or prevented from 'becoming' homosexual. Also, sometimes such narratives could be used to establish an aetiology of homosexuality in childhood experiences, such as childhood sexual abuse, family pathology, and so on. The authors are aware of this dimension to doing lesbian and gay (LG) growth and development research in India where homosexuality commonly gets looked upon as deviation, and would, therefore, like to underscore that the current study is motivated by the intent of creating a knowledge base on development issues of LG individuals that would inform affirmative practices and policies in working with this community.

4. That is, seeing linkages between experiences of growing up years and adult emotional life.

5. Some of the other limitations of the study include use of an exploratory design, purposive sampling, and a small sample size that limit the generalizability of the study findings.

References

Allport, G.W. 1958. *The Nature of Prejudice*. Garden City: Doubleday.

Bailey, J.M. and K.J. Zucker. 1995. 'Childhood sex-typed behaviour and sexual orientation: A conceptual analysis and quantitative review', *Developmental Psychology*, 31: 43–55.

Balsam, K., T. Beauchaine, E. Rothblum, and S. Solomon. 2008. 'Three Year Follow-up of Same-sex Couples Who had Civil Unions in Vermont, Same-sex Couples not in Civil Unions, and Heterosexual Married Siblings', *Developmental Psychology*, 44: 102–16.

Bombay Dost. 2009. Vol. No. 1. Mumbai: Centre for Excellence and Research, Humsafar Trust.

Campaign for Lesbian Rights (CALERI). 1999. *A Citizen's Report—Khamosh! Emergency Jari Hai! Lesbian Emergence*. New Delhi: CALERI.

Chandran, V. 2008. *Tehelka*, 5(4), 18 October. 'Homosexuality Does Not Preclude Paternity'. Available at: http://archive.tehelka.com/story_main40.asp?filename=Ne181008homosexuality_does.asp, accessed, November 2014.

Cochran, S. and V. Mays. 2006. 'Estimating Prevalence of Mental and Substance-using Disorders among Lesbians and Gay Men from Existing National Health Data', in A. Omoto and H. Kurtzman (eds), *Sexual Orientation and Mental Health*, pp. 143–65. Washington, DC: American Psychological Association.

Coleman, E. and G. Remafedi. 1989. 'Gay, Lesbian and Bisexual Adolescents: A Critical Challenge to Counsellors', *Journal of Counselling and Development*, 68(1): 36–40.

Connell, R.W. 1987. *Gender and Power*. Cambridge: Polity Press with Blackwell Publishers.

D'Augelli, A. 2006. 'Developmental and Contextual Factors and Mental Health among Lesbian, Gay and Bisexual Adolescents', in A. Omoto and H. Kurtzman (eds), *Sexual Orientation and Mental Health*, pp. 37–53. Washington, DC: American Psychological Association.

D'Augelli, A. and S. Hershberger. 1993. 'Lesbian, Gay, Bisexual Youth in Community Settings: Personal Challenges and Mental Health Problems', *American Journal of Community Psychology*, 21(4): 421–46.

Drummond, K.D., S.J. Bradley, M. Peterson-Badali, and K.J. Zucker. 2008. 'A Follow-up Study of Girls with Gender Identity Disorder', *Developmental Psychology*, 44: 34–45.

Dutta, D., M. Weston, J. Bhattacharji, S. Mukherji, and S.J. Kurien. 2012 (eds). *Count Me In! Research Report on Violence against Disabled, Lesbian and Sex-Working Women in Bangladesh, India and Nepal*. New Delhi: CREA Publications.

Erickson, E.H. 1968. *Identity: Youth and Crisis*. New York: Norton.

Fernandez, B. and Gomathy N.B. 2001. *The Nature of Violence Faced by Lesbian Women in India*, Report of Research Center on Violence Against Women. Mumbai: Tata Institute of Social Sciences.

Ghosh, S., B.S. Bandyopadhyay, and R. Biswas. 2011. *Vio-map: Documenting and Mapping Violence and Rights Violation Taking Place in the Lives of Sexually Marginalized Women to Chart Out Effective Advocacy Strategies*. Kolkata: SAPPHO for Equality (copies can be ordered from sappho1999@gmail.com).

Greene, R. 1986. *The 'Sissy Boy Syndrome' and the Development of Homosexuality*, pp. *xiii–iv*. New Haven, CT: Yale University Press.

Greene, B. 2003. 'Foreword: Lesbian and Bisexual Women's Mental Health', in R.M. Mathy and S.K. Kerr (eds), *Lesbian and Bisexual Women's Mental Health*. NY: Haworth Press.

Haldeman, D.C. 1994. 'The Practise and Ethics of Sexual Orientation Conversion Therapy', *Journal of Consulting and Clinical Psychology*, 62(2): 221–7.

———. 2002. 'Gay Rights, Patient Rights: The Implications of Sexual Orientation Conversion Therapy', *Professional Psychology: Research and Practice*, 33(3): 260–4.

Herek, G. 2006. 'Legal Recognition of Same-sex Relationships in the United States: A Social Science Perspective', *American Psychologist*, 61: 607–21.

Hunter, J. and R. Schaecher. 1987. 'Stresses on Lesbian and Gay Adolescents in Schools', *Social Work in Education*, 9(3): 180–90.

Hurlock, E. 1981. *Developmental Psychology—A Life Span Approach*, 5th edition. Delhi: Tata McGraw Hill.

Joseph , S. 2005. *Social Work Practice and Men Who have Sex with Men*. New Delhi: Sage.

Khaitan, T. 2004. 'Violence against Lesbians in India'. Available at: http://www.altlawforum.org/Resources/lexlib/document.2004-12-21, accessed 5 December 2007.

Kimmel, D., T. Rose, and S. David (eds). 2006. *Lesbian, Gay, Bisexual, and Transgender Aging: Research and Clinical Perspectives*. New York: Columbia University Press.

Lesbians and Bisexuals in Action (LABIA). 2013. *Breaking the Binary: Understanding Concerns and Realities of Queer Persons Assigned Gender Female at Birth across a Spectrum of Lived Gender Identities*. Mumbai: LABIA.

Martin, A.D. 1982. 'Learning to Hide: The Socialisation of the Gay Adolescent', *Adolescent Psychiatry*, 10: 52–65.

Meyer, I.H. 2001. 'Why Lesbian, Gay, Bisexual and Transgender Public Health?', *American Journal of Public Health*, 91(6): 856–9.

Nandy-Joshi, A. 2009. 'Quilts of Love', *Tehelka*, 6(26), 4 July. Available at: http://www.tehelka.com/quilts-of-love/, accessed November 2014.

O'Brien, J.M. 2005. 'Sexual Orientation, Shame and Silence', in J.M. Croteau, J.S. Lark, M.A. Lidderdale, and Y.B. Chung (eds), *Deconstructing Heterosexism in the Counselling Professions—A Narrative Approach*, pp. 97–102. California: Sage.

Patterson, C.J. 2006a. 'Children of Lesbian and Gay Parents', *Current Directions in Psychological Science*, 15: 241–4.

————. 2006b. 'Lesbian and Gay Family Issues in the Context of Changing Legal and Social Policy Environments', in K.J. Bieschke, R.M. Perez, and K.A. DeBord (eds), *Handbook of Counseling and Psychotherapy with Lesbian, Gay, Bisexual and Transgender Clients*, 2nd edition, pp. 103–33. Washington, DC: American Psychological Association.

People's Union for Civil Liberties (Karnataka) (PUCL-K). 2001. *Human Rights Violations against Sexuality Minorities in India. A fact-finding report about Bangalore*. PUCL-Karnataka.

Ranade, K. 2009. 'Medical Response to Male Same-sex Sexuality in Western India: An Exploration of "Conversion Treatments" for Homosexuality', Health and Population Innovation Fellowship Programme Working Paper No. 8, Population Council, New Delhi.

Rieger, G., J.A.W. Linsenmeier, L. Gygax, and J.M. Bailey. 2008. 'Sexual Orientation and Childhood Gender Nonconformity: Evidence from Home Videos', *Developmental Psychology*, 44: 46–58.

Ritter, K.Y. and A.I. Terndrup. 2002. *Handbook of Affirmative Psychotherapy with Lesbians and Gay Men*. New York: Guilford Press.

Roisman, G.I., E. Clausell, A. Holland, K. Fortuna, C.H. Hu, and C. Elieff. 2008. 'Adult Romantic Relationships as Contexts of Human Development: A Multi-method Comparison of Same-sex Couples with Opposite-sex Dating, Engaged, and Married Dyads', *Developmental Psychology*, 44: 91–101.

Ross-Reynolds, G. and B.S. Hardy. 1985. 'Crisis Counselling for Disparate Adolescent Sexual Dilemmas: Pregnancy and Homosexuality', *School Psychology Review*, 14: 300–12.

Rubin, G. 1992. 'Thinking Sex: Notes for a Radical Theory of the Politics of Sexuality', in C.S. Vance (ed.), *Pleasure and Danger: Exploring Female Sexuality*, pp. 267–93. London: Pandora.

Russell, S. 2006. 'Substance Use and Abuse and Mental Health among Sexual Minority Youths: Evidence from Add Health', in A. Omoto and H. Kurtzman (eds), *Sexual Orientation and Mental Health*, pp. 13–35. Washington, DC: American Psychological Association.

Safren, S.A. and R.G. Heimberg. 1999. 'Depression, Hopelessness, Suicidality and Related Factors in Sexual Minority and Heterosexual Adolescents', *Journal of Consulting and Clinical Psychology*, 62(2): 261–9.

Sandfort, T., H. Bos, and X. Vet. 2006. 'Lesbians and Gay Men at Work: Consequences of Being Out', in A. Omoto and H. Kurtzman (eds), *Sexual Orientation and Mental Health*, pp. 225–44. Washington, DC: American Psychological Association.

Savin-Williams, R.C. 2005. *The New Gay Teenager*, London: Harvard University Press.

Serovich, J.M., S.M Craft, P. Toviessi, R. Gangamma, T. McDowell and E.L. Grafsky. 2008. 'A Systematic Review of the Research Base on Sexual Reorientation Therapies', *Journal of Family and Marital Therapy*, 34(2): 227–38.

Sharma, M. 2006. *Loving Women, Being Lesbian in Unprivileged India*. New Delhi: Yoda Press.

Shidlo, A., and M. Schroeder. 2002. 'Changing Sexual Orientation: A Consumers' Report', *Professional Psychology: Research and Practice*, 33: 249–59.

Sukthankar, A. 1999. *Facing the Mirror—Lesbian Writing from India*. New Delhi: Penguin Books.

Troiden, R.R. 1979. 'Becoming Homosexual: A Model of Gay Identity Acquisition', *Psychiatry*, 42: 362–73.

———. 1984. 'Self, Self Concept, Identity and Homosexual Identity: Constructs in Need of Definition and Differentiation', *Journal of Homosexuality*, 10: 97–109.

———. 1989. 'The Formation of Homosexual Identities', *Journal of Homosexuality*, 17(1–4): 43–73.

United Nations. 2006. *Yogyakarta Principles—Principles on the Application of International Human Rights Law in Relation to Sexual Orientation and Gender Identity*. Geneva: United Nations.

Vanita, R. and S. Kidwai. 2000. *Same-sex Love in India*. New Delhi: Macmillan India Ltd.

Voices against 377. 2005. *Rights for All: Ending Discrimination against Queer Desire Under Section 377*. Delhi: A compilation by Voices against 377.

Wells, G.B. and N. Hansen. 2003. 'Lesbian Shame: Its Relationship to Identity Integration and Attachment', *Journal of Homosexuality*, 45(1): 93–110.

7

A Researcher's Tale

Shazneen Limjerwala (née Commissariat)

This study is about choreographing a dance between theory and practice, as one works in harmony with the other. In doing so, it recognizes the need to be open to witnessing, observing, listening, and feeling. It highlights the potential of permeable boundaries between the experiencer, the researcher, and the reader—boundaries that facilitate realization of commonalities in experience, a realization that could be the beginning of change.

Dear Reader

I'm Shazneen. A woman. In my thirties. Researcher and practitioner with professionals and experiencers of sexual violence. This is my story.

A Bit about Me

I was born in an upper middle-class Parsi,[1] Indian joint family in Ahmedabad, Gujarat. The younger of two sisters, I was intelligent, loving, and questioning. My mother died when I was 11. She encouraged me to question accepted norms and conventions. My *kaki* (paternal aunt), who mothered me, inculcated in me an acceptance of social hierarchy and encouraged me to pursue education. I was taught not to argue or 'speak up' against persons in authority, my father and uncle/s, in the immediate family. It was considered disrespectful, even futile. I studied abnormal psychology, trained as a psychotherapist, was an Academic Associate at Indian Institute of Management (IIM), and later joined Oxfam[2] as a project officer.

'My' Fear of Rape

I enjoyed reading, interacting with people, practising therapy, undergoing psychoanalytic therapy, and spontaneous writing. Engaging in these activities facilitated one realization. I feared rape. I believe that given our socialization, we were programmed for the fear. We were not to go out alone at night or be alone in secluded areas; to avoid confrontation with authority (usually adult males in positions of power professionally and socially); and sometimes remain silent even when we wanted to speak. The underlying message, though not always verbally articulated, was: 'Don't cross your boundaries. You may be punished/violated.' By boundaries, I mean modes of dress, demeanour, and most important for me, expression, agency, and instrumentality.[3]

Whilst my immediate and extended family was responsible for my upbringing, my friends and community played an important role in my socialization as well. They were protective: so, for example, they would accompany me whenever I travelled beyond a certain hour. Additionally, Hindi movies were replete with scenes of the heroine being raped or molested by the villain and then rescued by the hero.[4] Such storylines sent the message that women, unless accompanied by men, were vulnerable and devoid of agency. No wonder, I harboured a strong distaste for Hindi movies. These were some of the precipitates of my fear of rape.

'Our' Fear of Rape...

However, whilst I acknowledge the personal nature of this fear, studies support the view that it is a common (if not universal) fear amongst women (Pain 1991). Nearly half the rural women in Batliwala *et al.*'s (1998) study in the Indian state of Karnataka reported a sense of insecurity and fear of sexual assault. Gordon and Riger's (1988) study suggests that six out of every 10 women in the United States (US) feel 'very unsafe' or 'somewhat unsafe' being out alone in their neighbourhoods at night. In the United Kingdom (UK), women are five times more likely than men to worry extensively about their personal safety (Hough and Mayhew 1983, 1985; Mayhew *et al.* 1989). Such differences, which hold regardless of age, place of residence, and experience of victimization (Smith 1989), can largely be accounted for by the fear of rape and other forms of sexual violence (Riger and Gordon 1981; Warr 1985; Stanko 1987).

To be fair, our fears are to some extent grounded in reality. Studies show that women of all classes, races, ages, and backgrounds are potential victims of rape (Russell 1975; Schwendinger and Schwendinger 1983; Stanko 1985; Kelly 1988; Koss 1988; Warshaw 1988). Sexual violence is found to be more pervasive and widespread in location than any other type of crime (Hanmer and Saunders 1984; Hall 1985), and in the light of this, it is women who are most likely to experience physical assault (Stanko 1991).[5]

Feminists have forwarded explanations for the (almost universal) fear of rape. According to them, rape and the fear of rape is a patriarchal tool to intimidate all women, irrespective of whether they have been raped or not. It shapes women's behaviour, restricts their mobility, and exerts controls over their lives (Griffin 1971, 1979; Medea and Thompson 1974; Brownmiller 1975; Russell 1975; Riger and Gordon 1981; Gordon and Riger 1988; Nordstorm and Robben 1995).

Challenging the Fear…

I was aware of my fear of rape. It seemed acceptable to fear rape in the wider culture, almost a given in women's life. However, this fear or its harmful consequences were neither discussed nor articulated. Given my focus on personal growth and belief in agency, at a personal level, I was unwilling to 'accept' this fear, even though I had 'acknowledged' it.[6] I considered it a hindrance to my personal growth, and was not ready to 'live with' it. It disallowed me from doing things I valued:

'raise voice' when wronged, and experience closeness with nature in a solitary place. I wanted to challenge this fear. I believe this fear and my questioning of it is beautifully encapsulated in the following short story I wrote as a teenager.

The Fire

She sat there, praying. Or maybe just sitting. That's what she'd come there for: the ambience. No, that's too crude a word for the sacred place. And sacred it was. Sacred in its quiescence, in its darkness, and the tiny diyas[7] that illuminated it in some places, in the fire that glowed, a symbol of her faith.

There was no one around; or was there? She didn't know. She was too caught up in her thoughts, her memories and the sundry contents of her mind. Trying to experience the spirituality of the place and yet never quite defeating the distractions. The world outside was just that: outside. Far away, except for its images in her mind. She didn't want to reach out. Rather, she wanted the warmth of the Fire to reach within her. She so badly wanted it to be a religious experience, if not spiritual—one that transcends the mundane experiences of everyday living.

She sat there savouring those moments, savouring the experience, the first of its kind in her life. Time stood still. And then the bell tolled, signifying the change of the 'Geh'. It was time to leave. She bowed down before the Fire and communed with God one last time.

She retraced her steps slowly, the experience still lingering in her mind. And then she became aware of the darkness and stillness of the night. Her pace quickened, as vague apprehensions beset her mind. And then she heard the dogs bark, gripping her by that tangible fear. Where would she run? What would she do?

And just as she began to run, she saw a figure come towards her. Before she could think any further, she recognized the form. It was He. A frown on his forehead. That's all she had time to notice before he descended on her with a volley of outbursts. 'How could you go out alone in this dark place with its lonely lanes and stray dogs?'

She said nothing. Too meek to react to what had been her fears as well. She shouldn't have gone out alone in the dark. She had felt scared. And yet she had craved for the experience. The darkness, the stillness, the glimmer of the tiny diyas, the warmth of the fire, the solitude…

And now, she realized the reality of his concerns. But then, is reality always right? She wondered as she followed him through the dark.

When I shared this story with my English professor, she read more into it than 'just a creative outburst'. I vaguely remember her commenting on the feminist nature of the story. Unexposed to feminist literature at the time, I felt that she had 'over-interpreted' it.

I was introduced to women-centred literature at the IIM library where I worked as an Academic Associate. Amongst the thousands of books available, I found myself drawn to those that reflected women's lives and multiple experiential realities. I read almost all the books on the 'Women's Studies' rack; some of them more than once. One was *Off the Beaten Track* by Madhu Kishwar (1999). It was a collection of essays based on her experiences in fighting for women's rights in India. These struck me as well argued based on the data, and almost 'atheoretical'. I appreciated the 'unacademic' scholarship in them. Papers on qualitative and narrative research too influenced me deeply. These include Denzin and Lincoln's *Handbook of Qualitative Research* (2000); and *The Narrative Study of Lives* by Amia Lieblich and Ruthellen Josselson (1993). I found the papers in these edited collections very interesting, engaging, and evocative of the people, places, and experiences they wrote about. I realized that research need not be dry and clinical. It could absorb the multifarious nuances of lived experiences. The meaningfulness of these methodologies touched me.

Along with these readings, my training in and experience of psychoanalytic psychotherapy influenced me deeply. It stemmed from a deep desire to understand myself and facilitate healing of others. It encouraged introspection, a looking within at one's own self and actions. This was also advocated in 'countertransference', a technique wherein a therapist analyses her feelings during therapy, to give clues to the mental state of the analysand.

Writing has been and continues to be an abiding strain in my life. As a child, I wrote letters to my loved ones. Ever since I was a teenager, I have had a book in which I write whatever I want to. I write anything that comes to mind. I can write things I cannot speak of. Having written for many years, I have experienced it as healing, empowering, and most importantly, allowing me to let go of my losses in life. It has allowed me to express myself uninhibitedly. And I love it.

Each of the above-mentioned strands—my understanding of Indian women's experiences of violence; qualitative methodology; experience of writing; healing; my desire to challenge rape (and its fear) and seek healing from it—was woven together to create a research proposal, 'Using Storytelling to Heal Trauma of Rape Victims'. I wanted to engage with rape victims as a therapist to learn how to do therapy with them. I explored the prospect of studying at some universities in India. However, I found that there was a dearth of faculty trained in psychotherapy. At the time, I laid emphasis on this aspect of training, and therefore decided to go abroad to study. I joined the Institute for Health Research at Lancaster University, UK.

Exploring Rape

During my first year of training, I credited courses on research methodology, read on subjects of interest, framed different research designs, and explored their viability. With a view to recruit participants for my research, I published a write-up in a local magazine asking if persons who had experienced sexual violence would be interested in sharing their experience/s. One day, I received an email from a gentleman who revealed that he had been sexually abused as a child. As part of his healing, he had written a letter to the 'rapist', which he attached with his mail. For him, it was an act of letting go. By sharing it with me, he was inviting me to engage in this intensely personal journey.

I was slightly unnerved by his letter. It showed the vulnerability of a male rape victim and its influence over his life. He had been abused as a child and yet, this experience continued to haunt him decades later. Reading his email, never having been 'exposed' to an acknowledged[8] rape victim[9] before and yet empathic to his experience, I wished to respond. However, I needed to wait for my supervisors' guidance. This took a couple of days, by which time he expressed his anger at not having received a response. Meanwhile, in discussion with my supervisors, we concluded that since I had decided to do research with women and he was a man, his experience was beyond the purview of my research. However, communicating this decision was challenging. First, I had asked for research participation, and he had been kind enough to share his letter with me. I had delayed my response for a few days, and as a novice, had waited for my supervisors' guidance before even acknowledging it. This had (perhaps rightly) angered him. And following this, I was turning down his offer. Given the aim and scope of my research, this was the best course of action. I was also aware of the limitations of email, devoid of facial expressions, as a medium to communicate this message. Aware of this context, I carefully worded my email to avoid any further disgruntlement. This was my first direct communication with an acknowledged rape victim, albeit written.

Eager to learn about the support systems available to rape victims in the UK, I undertook a pilot study exploring the experiences of counsellors of rape victims.[10] Some rape counsellors worked independently or in voluntary organizations. Their 'clinics' had an informal, homely feel to them. One of my interviewees was Carla, a middle-aged counsellor. The interview was conducted in her office, a warm, comfortable place. We sat on sofas facing each other. I found her quite forthright, almost piercing in her responses. During the interview, she revealed, rather abruptly (to me), that she had been raped. I was taken aback by this 'exposure'. I had been mentally prepared to meet a rape counsellor, a person who facilitated healing from the trauma of rape, and therefore (in my view) 'mastered' it. I was shocked when told that she was a victim herself. I realized that this was the first time I had come 'face-to-face' with the vulnerability of rape.

I met with a similar revelation during my brief meeting with Gillie Bolton in London, an exponent of writing therapy (Bolton 1999, 2010). I had read her work and wanted to explore the possibility of collaborating for research. As I was about to leave, she revealed that she had been sexually abused as a child. She mentioned that she had revealed this in her writing, but I had not come across it. I found it difficult to digest this information and yet pretend to appear unaffected by it. These two experiences afforded some personal insight. I was very scared of rape. Meeting someone who had been raped was like coming closer to it. I felt I needed some preparation for such meetings (Coles *et al.* 2010).

I was afforded a different exposure to rape in the Sexual Assault and Forensic Examination (SAFE) centres. These were a joint initiative of the police and the hospital.[11] They aimed to examine and treat rape victims in a safe and supportive atmosphere. They were equipped to collect evidence and preserve it for years, in case the victim decided to prosecute the rapist later. However, the choice regarding whether to register a case with the police lay with the victim. Her access to treatment was independent of this decision. I found the facility very well planned, mindful of the needs of victims. There was room for seating, resting, and even an additional set of clothes as victims' clothes would be collected as evidence.[12] Nurses were trained to conduct the physical examination as well as give counselling.

As I was being shown around the centre, we came close to the 'examination table'. This was where the victim was asked to lie on her back, whilst swab samples of semen and other evidence were collected from her body. There were also provisions to record this evidence through body charts[13] and video recording. I felt very uncomfortable, almost anxious in that space. It felt as if I had suddenly come close to 'being' a rape victim: the intensity of her/their pain and bodily trauma struck me. I felt an urgent need to escape. However, I was conscious of my professional role as a researcher and hid my feelings.

Here, being in the same physical space as has been inhabited by rape victims generates fear. I remember a similar experience when being pointed out a place where one of the victims had been raped during fieldwork. It had dawned on me that I was 'coming close to' rape and this generated a degree of anxiety.

Meanwhile, I continued to be influenced by my reading on sexual violence. During my research, I read a document containing the recorded testimonies of women rape victims during the war in Darfur, Sudan. These were recorded in the International Criminal Court:[14] they recorded, in excruciating detail, the gruesome acts of sexual violence perpetrated on them. These included women being tortured with weapons and objects thrust into their vaginas. These struck my core as a woman. It drew home the reality that sexual violence is more about violence than sex. I felt overwhelmed, numbed sometimes by the range and frequency of sexual violence used 'strategically' to silence individuals and groups.[15]

Retrospectively, I also realized that I had grown partially tolerant of anger, anxiety, and helplessness evoked by reading and listening about sexual violence. Prior to beginning the research, I had borrowed *Aruna's Story* by Pinki Virani (1998). This was an account of the rape of a nurse, Aruna Shanbaug, and its aftermath. On the first page itself, there was a gruesome account of the rape and violence. The book lay in my locker for a month, and was later returned, unread. It was read a year later, after I had done a bit of reading around rape. The same happened with another book, *The Other Side of Silence*, by Urvashi Butalia (2000). This is a beautiful book where Butalia revisits the history of the Partition of India. It includes accounts of women avoiding sexual violence by committing suicide and those who had borne the children of their rapists and had chosen to continue living with them.[16]

This shows that 'engaged' reading and listening about rape, forms of exposure to it, require a tolerance of feelings they evoke. They are, however, crucial in the training of a researcher, or practitioner, as these are relatively muted forms of engagement. Engaging in person with those who have been violated, a prerequisite as a researcher or practitioner, would arouse more intense feelings (Coles *et al.* 2010).

Besides reading, acting too allowed me to enter the life worlds of rape victims. The play, *Vagina Monologues*, was being staged by a group at Lancaster University (1996). This is a collection of monologues, based on Eve Ensler's interviews with 200 women around the world about their views on sex, relationships, and violence against women. I chose to enact 'My Vagina was My Village', based on the experience of women in rape camps in Bosnia.[17] It was a gut-wrenching piece. 'She' spoke of her vagina, before, and after, she had been raped. I momentarily identified with her. I repeatedly rehearsed in the presence of trees, and a duck pond, imagining them as my audience. They allowed me to raise my voice sharply, and listened quietly. Theirs was a soothing presence. They 'contained'[18] me. Later, enacting the play in a city theatre was very satisfying. The acoustics allowed me to lower my voice and yet be heard. Through the audience's response, I believe, in those few dark moments, they sensed what it was like to be sexually violated.

By September 2004, a year into my research training, I had framed several research designs to get access to rape victims. However, none of these were feasible in the UK. Since I was adamant on engaging meaningfully with victims to understand their experiences, I moved to India for my fieldwork. In the initial stages, I had extended conversations with non-governmental organization (NGO) professionals who had supported victims of violence. They encouraged me to have an open mind, to have questions in mind, rather than follow an interview schedule. The fieldwork was carried out in a phased manner. Each phase involved exposure to a particular system. I began with the NGO (voluntary organization)[19] phase, followed by the medico-legal and social phase. It involved interviews, observations, and conversations with doctors, lawyers, the police, family members, and most importantly, the victims themselves.[20] Broadly, I learnt how these systems function. The procedure involved registering a First Information Report (FIR),[21] conducting a rape case in court, and medical examination of a rape victim. I also learnt about the attitudes and behaviours rape victims are exposed to in these systems. Additionally, through interaction with victims in their homes, I learnt about family dynamics and their relationships with NGO fieldworkers. The norms or 'rules' of these social systems, that is, the family, caste, and community, more commonly referred to as *samaj*, were not written. However, they were heavily influenced by social custom and tradition, and resistant to change. Additionally, they exerted a powerful influence on the victim and her readiness to take a stand against the violence.

One of my relatively early field visits was to meet Fatima,[22] a 16-year-old who had been raped by boys of a different community two weeks ago. Her case[23] was being handled by Salma, a lawyer NGO professional working for the minority community and Dalits. She and her co-workers had apprised me of Fatima's case. Eager to meet Fatima and listen to her story, I felt that since Salma had supported her, it would be good to have her present during our meeting. It was also necessary since being an outsider, it would have been impossible to locate her home in a remote village. It was advisable in the interests of my personal safety too.[24]

I was also aware that in most rural Indian communities, there are stringent norms governing interaction between the genders and opportunities to express oneself in conversations. These mostly favour men, the elderly, and the rich. Their opinions are voiced, and followed. I was most keen to listen to Fatima. Given the norms, in an attempt to subvert them to facilitate Fatima to talk, I asked Salma that we meet her with her female relatives, in the absence of her male relatives. I assumed that we were the only ones from the NGO going to meet her. However, as we readied ourselves for an hour-long drive to meet Fatima, I realized that we were being accompanied by her male co-workers. I deemed this inappropriate, as I wanted our meeting to be discreet. But, before I could express my reservations, there was a rather heated argument between them with regards to 'ownership' of the case; and so, I meekly accompanied them to the site.

We reached the outskirts of the village where Fatima lived: her *masi* (mother's sister) met us and took us to the house where she lived. The villagers knew the NGO workers; so, it was obvious that we had gone to meet her. They were curious to learn the purpose of our visit. As we entered the house, the men stood outside, talking to each other. This increased my discomfort as it highlighted the purpose of our visit even more.

In the house, her mother, *bhabhi* (brother's wife), Salma, Fatima, and myself sat on the ground. Fatima and I were sitting close, facing each other, her head covered with an *odhni* (long scarf worn on top of shirt [kurta] of women) and a scarf, her face slightly bent. We looked at each other when we talked, or rather when I asked questions and she answered them. She seemed open to talking to me and smiled on some occasions.

I painfully realized that I had not been given any time or space to 'warm up'. I was expected to ask questions about the rape, questions that she had probably been asked about a dozen times before. I felt strangely uncomfortable, not because of the setting but because of the impressions they had about me, and the expectations this had given rise to. Despite my best attempts, I had not been able to communicate the 'differentness' of my 'interview' or conversation.

Given this setting, I asked Fatima and her relatives a few questions about her day-to-day life. I learnt that she used to go to the local religious place to make chapatis earlier, but now she was restricted to staying within the home. I also asked her questions like, 'Do you eat?' and 'Do you sleep at night?' In retrospect, these were vague, or perhaps too specific and downright clinical. I had felt unhinged by the unexpectedness of the situation, and perhaps, yielded slightly to the pressure. I also suggested that we walk to the pond where they washed clothes. But this suggestion was not taken up.

In a few minutes, her father and brother entered. Her father related his story. They made mattresses for a living. He was suffering from a disease and was physically disabled. He had two sons, one was married, the other mentally challenged. Fatima's rape by members of a different community had taken on communal hues; so, their lives were in danger, and they had to relocate to a different village for security. This had affected their livelihood: they had to depend on a co-religionist for shelter and support. Having narrated his tale, looking at us, rather despondent, he said, '*Enea mari maya nathi rahi*' (She does not love us anymore).[25] Fatima, quiet so far, had tears in her eyes.

Unnerved by this situation, and feeling somewhat guilty and responsible for it, I deemed it judicious to end the meeting. We bid each other goodbye. I briefly held Fatima's hands in mine. The sense of touch evoked closeness.[26] Also, because she was a younger girl, I might have felt protective of her like an 'elder sister'.

Before I left, for some reason, I almost had tears in my eyes; She got up when I was leaving, there was one question I wanted to ask her, 'what did she want?' But somehow I felt it was to be asked at a later date. I said bye to her. Her father asked her to shake hands with me; we shook hands.[27]

Later, away from the research site and following in-depth conversations with Salma, who herself belonged to the same community as Fatima and had spent considerable time with her family, I tried to understand the situation she was in. It occurred to me that the rape was one motif in a pattern of poverty, dejection, and isolation. Fatima, even in 'normal' circumstances, belonged to a poor family. She had been minimally educated as she had to be removed from school every time they moved home in search of livelihood. Even before her rape, her family was grappling with poverty, debilitating illness, disability, and lack of livelihood. Her rape was seen as having brought dishonour to the family. Since persons of a different community had raped her, her rape had taken on communal connotations and, as related by the NGO members, could have caused riots.

This had caused the family to fear for their lives, and they had been relocated to another place. They were now living in a house owned by a benevolent man of their community and depended on him for their survival.

Fatima may have taken responsibility for the condition of her family and felt guilty about it. Additionally, her parents overtly expressed their fears that since she had been raped, no one would marry her. This caused them considerable anxiety and worry. This can be better understood within the backdrop of their social reality whereby marriage is seen as the only viable option for survival for women in most communities in rural areas. There, to be unmarried is seen as to be unprotected and vulnerable to exploitation for life.

Additionally, she was not allowed to go out to do her daily work. Confined within the home, her interaction with other girls her age was probably minimized. This again, in my view, would have worsened the situation by not allowing for normalizing. Rape, in my view, 'abnormalizes' a person's life and it is important to 're-normalize' it.

Fatima would also have been aware that her neighbours and villagers knew of her rape. This might have caused intense exposure to her and her family. Also, because of its negative connotations, it would have been perceived as inviting dishonour. Additionally, relocation, dependence, poverty, incapacitating illness, insecurity, and fear had rendered the family vulnerable. She might have felt guilty for having 'invited' this misfortune on her family through her rape. Her silence might have been an expression of guilt, shame, fear, or a complex intermingling of these emotions.

Her father, aware of the traditional male role of protecting the women in his family—wife, sisters, and daughters—would have felt guilty and perhaps emasculated.[28] He interpreted his daughter's silence as her aloofness, a departure from her earlier loving relationship with him. This hurt him immensely. This 'misunderstanding' could have been furthered by the lack of verbal communication between father and daughter, typical in these social settings.[29]

In my opinion, the inter-communal nature of the rape had hijacked all attention to the exclusion of the victim's experience.

Experiences with other rape victims were touching and insightful, too. Durga was a rural, married woman, a mother, in her twenties. She was found lying unconscious, burnt from waist down, partially uncovered, by the roadside. A local person found her in this condition and informed an NGO. The NGO contacted her family, took her to a local hospital, and tried to register an FIR with the police. At the time, Durga was in deep pain and her speech was incoherent. The police, according to the NGO fieldworker, refused to lodge a complaint of rape despite Durga telling her mother twice that she had been forcefully made to drink alcohol, eat non-vegetarian food, and taken to unknown places by her abductors. She also described actions that could have pointed to anal penetration.

The NGO members, whose work focused on the welfare of tribals, provided her and her family with material and physical support. They were eager that the police lodge a complaint of rape. Aware of my experience as a therapist, and research on rape, they contacted me with the 'brief' of evaluating whether she was 'mentally prepared' to record her statement with the police. At the time, since she did not get adequate medical treatment in the district hospital, she had to be moved to another city hospital.

At the hospital, I managed to get access to her at the burns ward after considerable effort lasting a few hours.[30] The sight of burnt bodies lying partly covered, some of them covered by a big iron frame, was appalling. I tried talking to Durga and her mother. Durga barely spoke; her speech was incoherent. Her mother told me that she rarely ate, and her neck and legs ached. She herself was feeling claustrophobic in this closed place as she was used to being in the open. Our conversation focused on Durga and her needs. When she wanted to urinate, we asked for a bedpan. But the nurses said there wasn't one. So, we held her tight and took her to the nearby bathroom. There, in the absence of any English-styled toilet,[31] she was made to sit on her haunches and urinate. This must have been painful for her. When she complained of pain in the neck, we had to make several attempts to get her a pillow. My concern, at the time, was to get some relief for her, and perhaps even her mother.

A few weeks later, eager to meet her, I accompanied an NGO fieldworker to her home. She lived in a remote rural area surrounded by hills and open fields. There were two thatched houses at a distance from each other. There was also an open well. It was evening by the time we reached. Eager to meet her, I went over to where she was 'kept'. There she was, tied to a bed with ropes, shouting abuses in the dark. Her grandfather kept watch over her with a stick, and hit it on the ground at regular intervals to control her. Aware of our presence, she thrashed her legs as we spoke. I felt helpless. And despondent.

The NGO professionals believed that she needed to be shown to a psychiatrist to alleviate her suffering. However, the family, particularly her father, was not open to this. They lived in a remote rural area, a couple of hours away from where the NGO was based. There had been a death in the family recently, and they were trying to cope with it. They believed in a *bhua*, a traditional healer, and were trying 'treatments' suggested by him, such as tying threads around her arm. Later, reflecting on this experience, I realized the family was doing what it felt was in her best interests.

Challenging Rape

In July 2009, I presented at an international conference of Sexual Violence Research Initiative (SVRI) in Johannesburg. It was heartening to share my experiences and feel a sense of solidarity with other professionals committed to similar issues. During one of the presentations, I realized midway that the speaker had survived rape and was talking of her own experience. Now, her 'speech' took on a different meaning. Here was a woman, in the midst of 200 people, mostly professionals, from across the globe, sharing that she had been raped. I understood this as a very challenging experience. She continued to work on this issue. When she finished, some of us stood up in appreciation. When the session ended, I went up to her, took both her hands in mine, looked at her, and smiled. In that unspoken moment, I felt, we both had come a long way.

I have continued to work in this area. I have made presentations; conducted workshops; given lectures at various educational institutions (schools, colleges, higher education institutions); written papers and articles on sexual violence, women's empowerment and research methodology; and used audio-visual media to generate awareness, raise questions, and motivate action[32] (*Parsiana* 2008; *Satyamev*

Jayate 2008; Sharma 2008). I have also researched and conducted interventions in the area of vicarious trauma in India and South Africa (Coles *et al.* 2010).

The Path Ahead

I strongly believe, in the wake of people's reactions to the Nirbhaya rape case in December 2012, that we need to create a multipronged strategy involving various stakeholders to address the malaise of sexual violence. I am working towards creating such a programme.

Dear Reader,

Its been a struggle writing this chapter. The struggle has been as much with 'rationalizing' the style of writing, as with the writing per se. In an attempt to hone my writing and make it more reader friendly, I shared it with persons at different stages for review. Invariably, it stimulated a series of questions, often asking for specific answers. I often grappled with these, trying hard to answer them. And I did. Only differently.

So, here's my 'different' answer to these questions. I'm aware that the style of this chapter is somewhat different from standard academic practice. I must admit that I have deliberately created it. This is because I believe that genuine change is possible through immersion in an experience/series of experiences. Here, the change I was seeking was towards an understanding of rape victims' lives. Also, perhaps less consciously at the time, but more conscious of it retrospectively, I was confronting and challenging my fear of rape. This was never an explicit aim of my research. However, looking back, I am aware of its role in its genesis.

I am telling you my story because I believe it is important to be told. And heard. It is important to see the human: emotional, physical, and cognitive involvement of the researcher in her research. Then we can appreciate its impact. It is also important to learn of how we sometimes change as a result of being immersed in our research. I'd like to articulate the change. Before beginning the research, I was asked one question: 'what would you prefer, being raped or killed?' I had chosen 'killed'.

I could not even entertain the possibility that a woman could or would want to survive after being raped.[33]

Today, I can.

I know that life after rape is fraught with countless obstacles: guilt, stigma, and frustrating encounters with the medico-legal systems. I also know that some victims, had it not been for their faith in their fight, and their children, might have taken their own lives.

However, there have been women who have chosen to expose rapists at grave personal cost. And those who have supported them. This gave me a sense of hope. And faith.

I'd like to share the story of this hope and faith. I began my exposure to rape through reading. Reading encapsulated theoretical, empirical pieces and first-person narratives. I listened to and viewed some audio and video cassettes on rape. During my first year of research, I read the letter of a rape victim to his rapist. I enacted the role of a rape victim in the *Vagina Monologues*. This required partial identification. I interviewed rape crisis counsellors, some of whom had been violated themselves.

During the fieldwork, I listened to men and women who had come in contact with rape victims, personally and/or professionally. I travelled to places where they lived, and traversed the corridors of courts and hospitals, spent time in hospital wards, police stations, courtrooms, NGO offices, and perhaps, most importantly, their homes. I travelled through the public, semi-public, and sometimes, private modes of transport they must have used. Most importantly, I spent time with rape victims, listening to them, sharing with them, trying to understand their experiences.

Each of these activities involved an exposure to rape. It also involved a potential for identification. Linked as it was/is with a fear, I experienced anxiety in each of these exposures. However, as I view it, it was graded. It increased in intensity: by the closeness it held with rape and rape victims, by the breath of exposure they evoked. So, for example, reading about rape probably evoked the least exposure, and therefore anxiety, whereas meeting a rape victim, and listening to her trauma, evoked the most. This is an arbitrary delineation, as at times, when the writing was powerful and in first person, it evoked a considerable degree of 'identification'.

Each of these exposures, coupled with my keenness for learning, evoked a degree of anxiety. With increased and repeated exposure in/to the field, and with constant and almost continuous writing to document as well as express my feelings and through regular supervision, I was able to process the feelings the research evoked. This allowed for continued exposure to the field and involvement in often exhausting fieldwork.[34]

In my view, along with the 'degree' of exposure, which was graded, the 'nature' of exposure, which was physical, cognitive, and emotional, also played a role. I'll explain. Embodying the spaces inhabited or traversed by rape victims was a physical exposure. Understanding their experience from several sources of information and different viewpoints was a cognitive exposure. It required considerable skill and constant questioning to understand their realities. The emotional involvement required was considerably demanding. It required a fine-tuning—I needed to be involved and attuned to their feelings; however, I could not afford to be overpowered by them. This is a skill that required continuous working at; I had to continuously work through the feelings evoked through and during this research.

My exposure was thus graded as well as varied. It allowed me to slowly get attuned to and work through the anxieties evoked by a minimal exposure, and then move on to more challenging exposure/s.

These were some of the processes I underwent as a researcher. They worked to create a deeper understanding of rape. Now that I have described the interface between the researched and me, the researcher, I move on to you, my reader.

With hope and faith,
Dr Shazneen Limjerwalla (née Commissariat)

Notes

1. Parsis are an ethnic group originally from Iran, some of whom migrated to India. They practise the Zoroastrian religion.
2. Oxfam is an international non-governmental organization (NGO) working on a range of social issues. I worked on the Kutch earthquake project and violence against women. The job involved travelling to rural

areas to learn about women's problems and programmes to empower them.

3. Agency has been variously conceptualized in Indian women's writing. See Chakravarti (1983); Butalia (1993); Sangari (1993); Thapan (1997) and Gedalof (1999). I use it to mean the potential to make a difference by one's words or actions.

4. Examples are *Ram Teri Ganga Meli* (1985) and *Meri Jung* (1985).

5. For a detailed discussion and understanding on the 'female fear of rape' refer to Hanmer and Saunders (1984); Warr (1984, 1985); Koss *et al.* (1987); Ferraro (1995, 1996); Stanko (1995) and Jackson (2009).

6. I would like to make a distinction between acknowledgement and acceptance here. To acknowledge is to be 'aware of'. However, it need not include acceptance. So, in my case, I acknowledged that I harboured the fear of rape. However, I did not accept it as part of my personality. It was a foreign, alien idea that had been injected into me, rather than received happily and consciously. I do not know when it began, but I could sense its presence.

7. *Diya*s is plural for *diya* (Hindi). It refers to small lights in containers filled with oil.

8. I have used the word 'acknowledged' to establish a distinction between those persons who evaluate their experiences as sexual violence and those who do not. The most common example of this could be forced sex within marriage, or sexual acts performed by godmen condoned by the victim and her family and therefore, not recognized or labelled as sexual violence. *Nithyananda's disciple seeks police protection,* Times News Network, Mar 7, 2010. Available at: http://timesofindia.indiatimes.com/city/chennai/Nithyanandas-disciple-seeks-police-protection/articleshow/5652671.cm, accessed November 2014.

9. Social science literature uses the term 'survivor' rather than 'victim'. The rationale is that it accords agency to the person and celebrates her raising her voice and taking action. I have used the word 'victim' because I found that their experiential and material realities resonated more with the word 'victim', than 'survivor'. This was to retain the emphasis on their treatment in social, legal, and medical systems. I tried alternative terms, but each seemed problematic. The term 'raped woman' is problematic as it seems to stamp the woman as raped and ignores other aspects of her identity.

10. One of the participants counselled rapists. It was an interesting experience to try to understand the 'whys' behind counselling rapists.

11. I have done exposure visits of SAFE in Preston and Manchester. Both these were housed in hospitals. They were managed by sexual assault

nurse examiners (SANEs). A SANE is a registered nurse (RN) who has advanced education and clinical preparation in forensic examination of sexual assault victims. The SANEs offer victims prompt, compassionate care and comprehensive forensic evidence collection. In addition to helping preserve the victim's dignity and reduce psychological trauma, SANE programmes are enhancing evidence collection for more effective investigations and better prosecutions. See https://www.ncjrs.gov/ovc_archives/bulletins/sane_4_2001/1.html, and also, SAFE, St Mary's Hospital, Manchester. Available at: http://www.cmft.nhs.uk/directorates/smc/links.asp.

12. This was in stark contrast to the experiences of rape victims in Gujarat, who had to sometimes trudge long distances, and travel by overcrowded public transport, to get to a police station or hospital. Often, they did not anticipate that their clothes would be needed as evidence. So, when the police asked for their clothes, the NGO workers accompanying them had to arrange for a 'fresh' set.

13. Body charts are outlines of the female/male body. The examining nurse is required to draw and mark on the chart, the injuries sustained by the victim. These are included in sexual violence examinations and they work as evidence to indicate the extent and nature of the injuries sustained.

14. The International Criminal Tribunal for Rwanda (ICTR) is an international court established in November 1994 by the United Nations Security Council in order to judge people responsible for the Rwandan genocide in 1994. The trial of Jean-Paul Akayesu established precedent that rape is a crime of genocide. The Trial Chamber held that 'sexual assault formed an integral part of the process of destroying the Tutsi ethnic group and that the rape was systematic and had been perpetrated against Tutsi women only, manifesting the specific intent required for those acts to constitute genocide'. Presiding judge, Navanethem Pillay, said in a statement after the verdict: 'From time immemorial, rape has been regarded as spoils of war. Now it will be considered a war crime. We want to send out a strong message that rape is no longer a trophy of war.' Available at: http://en.wikipedia.org/wiki/International_Criminal_Tribunal_for_Rwanda, accessed November 2014.

15. Rape has been perpetrated in inter-group conflicts in Yugoslavia (Drakulic 1994), during the partition in India (Butalia 2000), Gujarat in India (Women's Panel 2002), Darfur in Sudan (Gingerich and Leaning 2004). See Chakravarti (1993), Agarwal (1995), Kannabiran (1996), Menon and Bhasin (1998), and Mookherjee (2003) for a theoretical understanding of group rape.

16. This brings out the complexity of rape victims' lives. When teaching a class at Lancaster, I invited students to respond to whether it was possible for rape victims to 'choose' to live with their rapists. It elicited a variety of interesting responses.

17. Bosnian women were raped by Serbians in the ethnic war that lasted from 1992 to 1995. They were kept in detention centres, later known as rape camps. *Bosnian 'Rape Camp' Survivors Testify in The Hague*, WEnews, 19 July 2000. Available at: http://www.womensenews.org/story/rape/000719/bosnian-rape-camp-survivors-testify-the-hague.

18. Here, I invoke Bion's concept of containment whereby a person's feelings are absorbed by another entity (Bion 1970).

19. An organization that has been set up for some social cause. Its objective is not to create profit.

20. The fieldwork lasted 10 months. It involved interviews and conversations, lasting a few minutes to several hours, with 23 NGO professionals, six medical-cum-forensic professionals, five legal–judicial professionals, three police officers, and 17 rape victims. It also included observations lasting a few hours to several days in the common sites in each of these systems: police stations, hospitals, courts, lawyers' chambers, NGO offices, fieldwork sites, homes, amongst others.

21. This is the description of the complaint, the crime as related by the complainant and taken down by the police.

22. Names of victims have been changed.

23. The word 'case' is used differently in different set-ups. So, within the legal system, each complainant and the legal proceedings arising thereof is referred to as a case. In the hospital, each patient and her file is referred to as a case. In NGOs, the history and problems of each individual are written up in a case file and referred to as a case.

24. Researchers who study sensitive topics, such as sexual violence, are at risk of physical harm (see Liamputtong 2007: 76–9). In this case, I perceived risk of danger since the incident had sparked off communal strife. Also, I had never been to that area, and was a complete stranger. There have been other experiences where I have felt insecure. However, these have not been discussed in detail here due to lack of space.

25. I would like to emphasize here that in several places in my thesis, I have retained the original quote of the participant, in her own language. I have done this when the original quote retains a unique essence that is compromised by translation. It is in keeping with my endeavour to retain the original voices of the researched.

26. I have experienced a closeness, intimacy, with women in several research encounters because of the sense of touch. For example, I had felt a similar closeness, when Ranna, a victim with whom I had spent several hours in her homestead, helped put the haversack bag onto my back and bid me goodbye with both hands. This has been an unconscious learning, as sometimes when I counsel or support girls/women in distress, I unconsciously hold/touch them. This goes contrary to training in psychoanalysis wherein one must abstain from touching the analysand at all costs.

27. Here, shaking hands is a gesture that involves 'holding' both hands momentarily. It is different from a businesslike handshake.

28. According to feminist analyses, the women of a group represent its honour and thereby, by defiling them, one is humiliating the group: first, through the defilement of its women; and second, through the underlying message that its men were not 'potent' enough to protect them (Agarwal 1995; Mookherjee 2003).

29. According to Lau (1990), in the traditional Asian or Oriental family, relationships are hierarchical between the sexes as well as between the generations. Authority is invested in the most senior male member of the extended family.

30. Her case had received media attention and being a police case, the hospital authorities were wary. There was no air-conditioning in the ward despite the temperature being about 35 degrees Celsius, at least. I had been oblivious of the tormenting influence of the heat on the burns' victims, until it was pointed out to me by my friend. This, and muteness on my part to reacting to certain situations commonly found in the hospital, led me to believe that I was probably suffering from 'acclimatization', that is, being less sensitized to the nuances of the field, due to extended immersion in the field.

31. An English toilet is designed like a seat, whereas an Indian toilet is like a hole and has to be squatted on. I have included this detail to show the extent of inconvenience, amounting to pain, that patients in public hospitals are forced to tolerate.

32. These include Mt Carmel School, IIM, St Xavier's College, Behavioural Science Centre, Ahmedabad Women's Action Group (AWAG) , Indian Institute of Technology (IIT), Centre for Enquiry into Health and Allied Themes (CEHAT), Mumbai and Sophia College, Mumbai. Through these presentations, I must have reached out to more than 2,000 persons.

33. Here, of course, I mean survival in a broader sense, as going beyond the mere act of breathing, eating, and sleeping.

34. I have noted in my field notes that on some days, I have called up almost 30 people, such was the extent of heavy networking the field-work required.

References

Agarwal, P. 1995. 'Savarkar, Surat and Draupadi: Legitimizing Rape as a Political Weapon', in T. Sarkar and U. Butalia (eds), *Women and Right-wing Movements: Indian Experiences*, pp. 29–57. London and New Jersey: Zed Books.

Batliwala, S., B. Anitha, A. Gurumurthy, and C. Wali. 1998. *Status of Rural Women in Karnataka*. Bangalore: National Institute for Advanced Studies.

Bion, W. 1970. *Attention and Interpretation*. London: Tavistock.

Bolton, G. 1999. *The Therapeutic Potential of Creative Writing: Writing Myself*. London: Jessica Kingsley Publishers.

———. 2010. *Reflective Practice: Writing and Professional Development*. UK: Sage Publications.

Brownmiller, S. 1975. *Against Our Will: Men, Women and Rape*. London: Secker & Warburg.

Butalia, U. 1993. 'Community, State and Gender: On Women's Agency during Partition', *Economic and Political Weekly*, 28(17): WS12–24.

———. 2000. *The Other Side of Silence: Voices from the Partition of India*. London: Hurst and Company.

Chakravarti, U. 1983. 'The Development of the Sita Myth: A Case Study of Women in Myth and Literature', *Saumya Shakti*, 1(1): 67–72.

———. 1993. 'Conceptualizing Brahmanical Patriarchy in Early India: Gender, Caste, Class and State', *Economic and Political Weekly*, 28(14): 579–85.

Coles, J., E. Dartnell, S. Limjerwala, and J. Astbury. 2010. 'Researcher Trauma, Safety and Sexual Violence Research'. Available at: http://www.svri.org/traumabooklet.pdf, accessed November 2014.

Denzin, N. and Y. Lincoln. 2000. *The Handbook of Qualitative Research*, 2nd edition. London: Sage.

Drakulic, S. 1994. 'The Rape of Women in Bosnia', in M. Davies (ed.), *Women and Peace*, pp. 176–81. London: Zed.

Ferraro, K. 1995. *Fear of Crime: Interpreting Victimization Risk*. New York: SUNY Press.

Ferraro, K. 1996. 'Women's Fear of Victimization: Shadow of Sexual Assault?', *Social Forces*, 75: 667–90.

Gedalof, I. 1999. *Against Purity: Rethinking Identity with Western and Indian Feminisms*. London: Routledge.

Gingerich, T. and J. Leaning. 2004. 'The Use of Rape as a Weapon of War in the Conflict in Darfur, Sudan', Prepared for the US Agency for International Development/OTI, under the auspices of the Harvard School of Public Health and the Francois-Xavier Bagnoud Center for Health and Human Rights. Available at: http://www.hsph.harvard.edu/fxbcenter/HSPH-PHR_Report_on_Rape_in_Darfur.pdf, accessed 11 November 2006.

Gordon, M. and S. Riger. 1988. *The Female Fear*. New York: Free Press.

Griffin, S. 1971. 'Rape: The All-American Crime', *Ramparts*, 10(3): 21–35.

————. 1979. *Rape: The Power of Consciousness*. San Francisco: Harper and Row.

Hall, R. 1985. *Ask Any Woman: A London Enquiry into Rape and Sexual Assault*. Bristol: Falling Wall Press.

Hanmer, J. and S. Saunders. 1984. *Well Founded Fear: A Community Study of Violence to Women*. London: Hutchinson.

Hough, M. and P. Mayhew. 1983. *British Crime Survey: First Report*. London: Her Majesty's Stationery Office (HMSO).

————. 1985. *Taking Account of Crime: Key Findings from the British Crime Survey*. London: HMSO.

Jackson J. 2009. 'A Psychological Perspective on Vulnerability in the Fear of Crime', *Psychology, Crime and Law*. 15: 365–90.

Kannabiran, K. 1996. 'Rape and the Construction of Communal Identity', in K. Jayawardena and M. De Alwis (eds), *Embodied Violence: Communalising Women's Identity in South Asia*, pp. 32–41. New Delhi: Kali for Women.

Kelly, L. 1988. *Surviving Sexual Violence*. Minneapolis: University of Minnesota Press.

Kishwar, M. 1999. *Off the Beaten Track: Rethinking Gender Justice for Indian Women*. New Delhi: Oxford University Press.

Koss, Mary P., A. Christine Gidycz and N. Wisniewski. 1987. 'The Scope of Rape: Incidence and Prevalence of Sexual Aggression and Victimization in a National Sample of Higher Education Students', *Journal of Consulting and Clinical Psychology*, 55(2): 162–70.

Koss, M. 1988. 'Hidden Rape: Sexual Aggression and Victimization in the National Sample of Students in Higher Education', in M. Pirog-Good and J. Stets (eds), *Violence in Dating Relationships: Emerging Social Issues*, pp. 145–68. New York, NY: Praeger.

Lau, A. 1990. 'Gender, Power and Relationships: Ethno-cultural and Religious Issues', in C. Burck and B. Speed (ed.), pp. 120–35. London: Routledge.

Liamputtong, P. 2007. *Researching the Vulnerable: A Guide to Sensitive Research Methods*. London: Sage.

Lieblich, A. and R. Josselson (eds). 1993. *The Narrative Study of Lives*. London: Sage.

Mayhew, P., D. Elliot, and L. Dowds. 1989. *The 1988 British Crime Survey*. London: HMSO.

Medea, A. and K. Thompson. 1974. *Against Rape*. New York: Farrar, Straus, and Gironi.

Menon, R. and K. Bhasin. 1998. *Borders and Boundaries: Women in India's Partition*. New Brunswick: Rutgers University Press.

Meri Jung. 1985. Hindi movie directed by Subhash Ghai and produced by N.N. Sippy.

Mookherjee, N. 2003. 'My *Man* (honour) is Lost but I Still Have my *Iman* (principle): Sexual Violence and Articulations of Masculinity', in R. Chopra, C. Osetia, and F. Osetia (eds), *South Asian Masculinities: Context of Change, Sites of Continuity*, pp. 131–59. New Delhi: Women Unlimited.

Nordstorm, C. and A. Robben (eds). 1995. *Fieldwork under Fire: Studies of Survival and Violence*. Berkeley, CA: California University Press.

Pain, R. 1991. 'Space, Social Violence and Social Control: Integrating Geographical and Feminist Analyses of Women's Fear of Crime', *Progress in Human Geography*, 15(4): 415–31.

Parsiana. 'Fight Rape Intellectually. Zoroastrians Abroad'. 21 January 2008. Patel, Jehangir (editor). pp. 20–1. Mumbai, India.

Ram Teri Ganga Meli. 1985. Hindi movie directed by Raj Kapoor and produced by Randhir Kapoor.

Riger, S. and M. Gordon. 1981. 'The Fear of Rape: A Study in Social Control', *Journal of Social Issues*, 37(4): 71–92.

Russell, D. 1975. *The Politics of Rape: The Victim's Perspective*. New York: Stein and Dey.

Sangari, K. 1993. 'Consent, Agency and Rhetorics of Incitement', *Economic and Political Weekly*, 28(18): 867–82.

Satyamev Jayate. 2014. 'Fighting Rape'. Aamir Khan Productions.

Schwendinger, J. and H. Schwendinger. 1983. *Rape and Inequality*. Beverly Hills: Sage.

Sharma, R. 2008. 'Why don't rape victims speak up?', *The Times of India*. Ahmedabad edition.

Smith, S. 1989. 'Social Relations, Neighbourhood Structure, and the Fear of Crime in Britain', in D. Evans and D. Herbert (eds), *The Geography of Crime*, pp. 193–227. London: Routledge.

Stanko, E. 1985. *Intimate Intrusions*. London: Unwin Hyman.

————. 1987. 'Typical Violence, Normal Precaution: Men, Women, and Interpersonal Violence in England, Wales, Scotland and the USA', in J. Hanmer and M. Maynard (eds), *Women, Violence and Social Control*, pp. 122–34. London: Macmillan.

————. 1991. 'Challenging Orthodoxies: Women and Crime Prevention', Paper presented at the Preventing Crime against Women National Conference, Hammersmith Town Hall.

————.1995. 'The case of fearful women: Gender, personal safety, and fear of crime.' *Women & Criminal Justice*, 4:117–35.

Thapan, M. 1997. *Embodiment: Essays in Gender and Identity*. New Delhi: Oxford University Press.

Virani, P. 1998. *Aruna's Story: The True Account of a Rape and its Aftermath*. India: Viking Penguin.

Warr M. 1984. 'Fear of Victimization: Why Are Women and the Elderly More Afraid?', *Social Science Quarterly*, 65: 681–702.

————. 1985. 'Fear of Rape amongst Urban Women', *Social Problems*, 32(3): 238–50.

Warshaw, R. 1988. *I Never Called it Rape*. New York: Harper & Row.

Women's Panel. 2002. *The Survivors Speak: How has the Gujarat Massacre Affected Minority Women?* Ahmedabad: Citizen's Initiative.

8

Women's Rights, Human Rights, and the State

Reconfiguring Gender and Mental Health Concerns in India

Anubha Sood[1]

In August 2001, a tragic accident in the small south Indian town of Erwadi led to a series of events and actions that would reverberate across India's mental health sector for years to come and conclusively shape public discourse and future policies in the field. The tragedy occurred in the vicinity of a Sufi shrine (*dargah*), a 'faith healing' centre for sufferers of mental afflictions, when a fire caused by an oil lamp led to the death of 28 people. The deceased, 'mentally ill' persons, who had allegedly sought healing in the dargah, had been tied with iron chains to their cots and to trees in the night when the fire broke out. Media reports recounted vivid, disturbing details of the tragedy.[2] News stories related how the victims had struggled to free themselves from the chains to escape the fire, and how distraught town residents were when they had heard their cries for help late into the night. Investigations revealed that the site where the tragedy occurred was one of the numerous shelters that had operated in the area as profit-making businesses, housing mentally ill persons abandoned by their kin and left to the mercy of the shelter owners for small sums of money. The mentally ill had been kept in abysmal conditions in these shelters, fettered in iron chains, restrained, and unattended for the most part. The existence of such 'zones of social abandonment' as the Erwadi shelters in the country, where the mentally ill were meted out such a wretched existence devoid of basic human rights, was a revelation that shook the nation and beyond (Biehl 2008).[3]

In ensuing days and months, the tragedy acquired the status of a 'critical event', gaining deep rhetorical significance in public memory and imagination (Das 1996). Not only did the incident bring to light the plight of mentally ill people and the lack of humane mental health care in the country, it challenged India's self-image as a modernizing, progressing nation. If Indians still resorted to 'superstitious beliefs' about mental illnesses, lamented those who fashioned public discourse, and sought 'faith healing' instead of going to doctors, what claim could India make to its commitment to development? And if people with mental illnesses were still subjected to such inhuman treatment as chaining and other gross human rights violations in these traditional healing sites, should these errant spaces not be clamped shut? In the build-up of public reaction to the incident, anger against the malpractices committed in the garb of traditional healing around the Erwadi dargah turned into censure of all such modes of healing. In subsequent days and months, traditional healing centres across the country became salient reminders of the shameful Erwadi episode, and their popularity, an indication of the state's failure to provide modern, 'scientific' mental health services to the country.

Implicated in the heated debates, though nowhere in popular deliberation, were the millions of Indian women who frequent places such as the ill-reputed Sufi dargah. For the dargah belonged among a diverse range of religiously based folk healing systems—Hindu temples, Christian churches, and Islamic shrines—that constitute the single-most popular pathway to mental health care for women in the country. Working alongside state-driven psychiatry, these indigenous systems occupy a huge segment of the total mental health care delivery system (Weiss *et al.* 1986; Raguram *et al.* 2002; Pakaslahti 2009; Sebastia 2009).[4] Even so, women are heavily over-represented as healing seekers at these sites (Bellamy 2011; Dwyer 2003; Skultans 1991; Varma *et al.* 1992). In contrast, women tend to be largely missing in public health psychiatric facilities (Davar 1995). In fact, it would be right to claim that these traditional healing centres serve essentially as female healing spaces.

This chapter addresses the implications of a transitioning mental health policy scenario after Erwadi for the mental health needs of Indian women. Following the incident and the wide national and international attention it received, a series of legal and policy actions were initiated with the express aim to 'reform' India's mental health system. These legal actions involved, barring any other corrective measure, the aggressive surveillance and policing of traditional healing centres across the country. Serious malpractices that plague the country's psychiatric set-up were, paradoxically, left out of the reform initiative.[5] In a seminal judgement dated February 2002, the Supreme Court (SC) of India directed state governments to ensure that 'mental patients should be sent to doctors and not to religious places such as temples or *dargahs*' (vide Writ Petition Civil 334 (1); see Government of India 2003). The SC directive was a precursor to what may be considered an unprecedented shift in attitudes towards traditional healing over the past decade. Benign disapproval of traditional healing practices in the years preceding the Erwadi episode turned into aggressive 'witch-hunting' of traditional healing sites in the years following it (Davar and Lohokare 2009). Today, these indigenous modes of healing face a tough challenge for their survival in the face of vehement opposition by an Indian state that espouses psychiatry as the only legitimate mental health system for the country. Indian women's affinity for these healing traditions, in such a policy milieu, sets the aims of the Indian state in direct conflict with the women's health-seeking strategies.

What is the state's rationale for denouncing traditional healing practices with such fervour? How were the policies resulting from these 'anti- traditional healing' sentiments executed on the ground in the aftermath of the Erwadi tragedy, and more importantly, what might the consequences of such policies be for women who are the primary users of these systems? This chapter attempts to situate

Indian women's mental health concerns squarely and firmly in the centre of the policy debates and legal actions that mark a changing mental health scenario in the country. The central argument of the chapter is that the legal responses and policy developments building against traditional healing practices in present-day India hold grave significance for the mental health concerns of Indian women who are the primary users of these alternative systems.

Religiously based healing traditions offer women especially, creative and possibly efficacious means of expressing and addressing the psychological and social distress they experience in gender-inequitable societies, as much research from around the world indicates (Boddy 1994; Keller 2002; Bourguignon 2004). The expulsion of these practices from India's medically plural mental health landscape might foreclose access to a vital resource for women seeking mental healing and well-being. Echoing Davar and Lohokare's (2009) argument regarding the need to better understand the role of traditional healing in mental health care delivery, I propose that women's affinity for traditional healing needs to be examined in greater depth for the positive role it plays in addressing their mental health needs before declaring it disposable to the country's mental health sector.

In the following pages, I begin by delineating the points of contention that arise from a gender critical lens. I discuss the dominant discourses that have populated the country's mental health landscape in the years following Erwadi, how these discourses have taken shape as policy and legal actions, and what these actions entail for women as users of mental health systems. Next, I look at how Indian women's mental health care pathways link to some of the key concerns in the international political discourse on women's health rights and how these concerns can inform the formulation of gender-sensitive mental health policies. I conclude by reiterating the urgent need to foreground women's mental health care strategies as a crucial factor in formulating future mental health policy in the country. In order to do so, a shift in perspective is required to see how women's help-seeking choices may signify a deliberate response to the positive role religiously based traditional mental health systems play in women's lives and well-being, rather than being considered an effect of their lack of choices, or ignorance, vis-à-vis psychiatric care.

Debating Gender, Psychiatry, and Traditional Healing

Psychiatric epidemiological data from urban India reveal low atten-
dance by women in public health psychiatric facilities.[6] By comparison, Indian women access traditional healing for their mental health
needs to a far greater extent. Women's predominance in traditional
healing sites is well documented not only in India but in other parts
of the world as well; research studies have found an overwhelming
presence of women in traditional healing settings across the globe
(Finkler 1985; Boddy 1994; Keller 2002; Seligman 2008). The fact
that women all over the world predominate in mystical–spiritual
healing sites points to an essentially gendered facet of these treatment
modalities.

The vast majority of traditional systems employ therapeutic techniques that derive from aetiologies of supernatural affliction and
associated mystical–spiritual beliefs and practices; rituals such as possession–trance, voluntarily chaining the body, and/or utilizing other
means of inflicting pain to the body as a form of religious penance
and as a means of 'exorcising' sickness out the body form an integral
part of the healing process at these sites. The Indian state considers these traditional practices violent and barbaric, and condemns
them for encouraging stigma and superstitious beliefs about mental illnesses. A number of healing rituals practised at these sites are
considered human rights violations of people with mental illnesses.[7]
A common ritual involving chaining people with 'divine chains' to
exorcise malevolent spirits or as penance, for instance, has become an
especially contentious human rights issue in India in the years following the Erwadi tragedy, since chaining was what led to the tragic
deaths at the dargah. The continuance of these practices is a vexing
concern for the Indian state that is pushing to discourage participation in traditional healing systems on the grounds that it is seriously
harmful to those engaging in them.

Much social science research on traditional healing systems across
the world, however, suggests that religious healing sites provide women
with the much-needed therapeutic spaces to ameliorate their psychological and social sufferings. How these indigenous healing practices
serve the therapeutic function has been extensively researched, and
multiple explanations have been offered for why they may become

the preferred mode of healing from psychological ailments (Kirmayer 2004). A great deal of anthropological scholarship tends to focus on the vastly different 'explanatory models' and therapeutic processes of the two systems that result in distinctive experiences of healing for women (Kleinman 1975).[8] Many studies have stressed the facilitative dimensions of culturally congruent beliefs and the use of local and contextual knowledge in the healing process that makes traditional systems especially attractive (Kakar 1982; Glik 1988; Csordas and Kleinman 1996; Sax 2009; Bellamy 2011). Cross-cultural mental health researchers suggest that women may be more likely to seek out traditional healers because they do not assign stigmatizing diagnoses or disease labels as psychiatrists may do, and involve the family and community in the healing process to a far greater extent (Pakaslahti 1998; Weiss 2001; Jain 2006). Traditional healing practices may even have greater 'aesthetic' appeal and more efficacious conceptions of cure and healing that make them attractive to women (Halliburton 2003, 2005).

Explanations that move beyond these general understandings about the distinctiveness of the therapeutic models focus specifically on 'gender' as a salient dimension of help seeking. These studies argue for a presumably empowering experience for women in mystical–spiritual healing practices (Boddy 1994; Keller 2002; Bourguignon 2004). Much of this literature focuses on women's greater affiliation for possession–trance states—psychological states that serve as the central idiom of distress and healing in mystical–spiritual healing. It claims that women's greater susceptibility to be possessed by malevolent spirits and propensity for inhabiting possession–trance states speaks of the mental and social distress they experience in patriarchal settings (Kakar 1982; Lewis 1989; Ram 1992; Bourguignon 2004).[9] Possession, these studies suggest, may become a language of resilience, resistance, or rebellion for women. Traditional healing sites, then, come to serve as safe spaces for the culturally permissible expression of distress and self-assertion for women.

Explanations for women's particular affiliation for traditional healing practices are complemented by feminist critiques that charge psychiatry with pathologizing and medicalizing women's social oppression, veering them away from psychiatric treatment (Dennerstein et al. 1993). Much of this literature has its roots in a critical psychiatry perspective. While some feminist researchers argue that women unable or unwilling to fit into socially prescribed gender roles may be labelled psychiatrically ill, others challenge the foundations of the science and institution of psychiatry itself, claiming that it is an essentially 'masculinist' enterprise structured to maintain and reinforce women's subordination (Davar 1999; Addlakha 2001, 2008; Caplan and Cosgrove 2004). The practice of psychiatry, these views suggest, may lack not only the cultural competence but also the gender sensitivity needed to address women's mental health concerns holistically (Pinto 2011). Much research, then, sides with the view that traditional healing has a great deal to offer women in terms of healing and well-being.

My own ethnographic research with women who seek healing for their psychological ailments in a Hindu healing temple and in a government psychiatric clinic in north India corroborates these findings. Women's experiences in the psychiatric system, I observed, tended to be tenuous and frustrating for the most part.[10] This resulted from the fact that the women's suffering arose not only from biological and psychological dysfunction but from deeply conflictive gendered engagements within their life worlds, which made the exclusively psychopharmaceutical management of their ailments in the clinic untenable. On the other hand, healing in the temple, I discovered, became efficacious for women because they conceived it as a self-propelled, agentive practice; as a 'process' of healing transformation that each woman individually tailored according to her therapeutic needs. The processual and fluid nature of healing in traditional healing settings, my research demonstrates, serves as an especially effective venue for addressing the vastly complex engagements of women in the transitioning gendered fields of family and society in contemporary India (Sood 2013).

Global health studies, in contrast to the aforementioned scholarship, view women's preponderance in traditional healing centres, by and large, as an indicator of underdevelopment. These views emphasize ignorance, stigma of psychiatric illnesses, as well as scarce mental health resources in low-income countries such as India as the primary factors in explaining women's preponderance in traditional healing centres (Murthy 2001). Women's attraction for traditional healing is perceived as a marker of the low priority accorded to their health needs in general, and of their incapacity to access modern health care (Patel *et al.* 1999). These views even go as far as to claim that the availability of accessible psychiatric care can eventually turn women away from traditional healing as psychiatric treatment becomes more readily available (Trivedi 2001). The most fervent proponents of this view advocate for a singular mental health policy approach that prioritizes the creation of more psychiatric services and efforts towards raising awareness about psychiatric illnesses and treatment among the public.

This latter perspective, that the popularity of traditional healing centres among women is a sign of underdevelopment, constitutes the primary framework for formulating mental health policies and practices in present-day India. The stance, as it translates in contemporary discourse, echoes a 'tradition–modernity dichotomy' that dominates the political/ideological landscape of many contemporary post-colonial societies, including India, characterizing tradition as adversarial to ideals of progress and advancement, while modernity is offered as the desirable goal of development (Ewing 1997). The polarity implies a moral judgement that considers all that is 'modern' superior to that which is 'traditional'. Traditional healing sites, thus, come to symbolize for the nation, the archaic, undisciplined spaces of the ignorant masses, in contrast to the progressive, regulated character of modern psychiatry. Traditional healing from such a perspective becomes a forced choice, a poor substitute for women when better modern mental health care is not available. This perception of traditional healing, construed within a 'tradition versus modernity' narrative, and consequently viewed as a less desired, 'forced' option for people in the absence of adequate psychiatric services, constitutes the normative discourse that has taken effect in India's mental health arena since the Erwadi tragedy.

Traditional healing centres, however, do not only attract the ignorant, uneducated, and poor; the demographic of attendees varies greatly across the diverse range of traditional healing practices that exist in the country. Studies indicate, for instance, that women attendees in many healing centres are relatively well educated and have equivalent access to psychiatric treatment, but may still prefer to seek traditional care (Pakaslahti 1998; Dwyer 2003; Sood 2013). While the structural constraints on women's access to health care in general cannot be underestimated, it is also true that these constraints alone fail to account for women's attraction for traditional healing. Women do deliberately 'choose' traditional healing practices over psychiatric care. A better psychiatric system is unlikely to lessen the popularity of this particular pathway to mental health care (Davar and Lohokare 2009).

The oppositional views about traditional healing that are reflected in scholarship and policy framing makes the field of gender and mental health in India a highly contested one. In my view, it becomes especially crucial in such a scenario to attend to what women's sheer numbers in traditional healing centres tells us about the value of these spaces for women, for these female healing spaces may not solely be a reflection of women's victimization, but instead, across varied contexts, even an expression of their agency.

Erwadi in the Media

The public rhetoric following the Erwadi tragedy pitted the 'archaic practices of traditional healing' against the advances of modern psychiatric treatment, clearly referencing a 'tradition versus modernity' polarity. An editorial in a national daily, for instance, carried the following comment about the Erwadi healing centre, 'It is hard to believe that a *modern* state can permit such *primitive* and inhuman conditions to exist' (*The Indian Express* 2001; emphasis added). News articles characterized traditional healing centres as backward, anti-progressive spaces frequented by an ignorant public, while psychiatry was projected as the panacea for the problems these spaces spread. Another news story about traditional healing centres reported: 'The treatment given in these centres is diabolic and inhuman. Although insanity is a mental disorder, people who bring patients here believe that illness has been caused due to the influence of ghosts...*desperate people fall for their evil designs*' (*The Times of India* 2001a; emphasis added). Yet another newspaper pronounced traditional healers 'quacks'; the story reported, 'Since quacks cannot be wished away in the Indian context...a mental health institute had actually tried to train them on the basics of *scientific* care, diagnosis, and treatment...' (*The Times of India* 2001b; emphasis added). It is interesting to see in the language of these news reports how traditional healing was projected as a clearly undesirable facet of the mental health system in the country, one that people were forced to make use of in the absence of psychiatric care.

Images of traditional healing centres as exotic, unintelligible, and cruel spaces were also commonplace in international media stories. In a notable report on the tragedy by a BBC correspondent, the Erwadi dargah premises were described in vivid detail, thus:

> The *dargah* itself, set in a sandy precinct, is a disturbing place. We watched men and women wailing and shrieking there, tearing at their clothes, beating their bodies against the sand or twirling, arms flying round and round, spinning out of control until they finally collapsed...One woman was stamping up and down the same narrow stretch, shrieking and rambling incoherently. Another was prostrate on the sand, moaning and rolling full length, over and over, crashing backwards and forwards in the crowd...The women's wailing was punctuated now and again by a young man letting out a piercing angry bellow. (BBC News 2001)

Another article in an Indian daily had the following lines describing a traditional healing centre, '...a frantic woman bangs her head against the *dargah*'s wall...several women huddle around a fire, some staring blankly, others positioned precariously close to the flames...' (*The Times of India* 2001b). The article described traditional healing practices, thus, 'Mentally ill people...are often beaten up mercilessly if the spirit refuses to come out...Some are even beaten to death, but these murders are usually not reported because the priest says the spirit was too strong and the family shrinks from social stigma' (*The Times of India* 2001b). These descriptions of traditional healing centres in the media portrayed these spaces as violent, barbaric, and harmful to healing seekers, their continuation an embarrassment to the modern Indian nation-state. Such media rhetoric clearly set the precedent for the state offensive against traditional healing centres that followed the Erwadi incident.

Legal Actions following Erwadi

Following the tragedy, the government initiated a series of legal actions against traditional healing centres with the express intent to reform the country's mental health sector.[11] Paradoxically, these reform initiatives were not directed at an ill-functioning state psychiatric set-up that had, over many years, been the target of grave allegations of poor quality of care and treatment and human rights violations of those incarcerated in state-run mental hospitals (National Human Rights Commission [NHRC] 1999). By targeting hostile 'reform' measures solely at traditional healing centres, the Indian state took on an explicitly adversarial position against these modes of healing, while claiming psychiatry as the sole rightful mental health care system for the country (Davar 2012).

The first set of legal actions against traditional healing centres began when the SC initiated *suo moto* action against the state government of Tamil Nadu and other states via the Writ Petition Civil No. 334 of 2001, ordering them to regulate the functioning of traditional healing centres within their ambit. This involved ascertaining if traditional healing sites were chaining people or committing other human rights violations, and shutting down the offending sites. One especially significant aspect of the SC order was the directive to all state governments to implement the Mental Health Act (MHA), 1987 in the sites where attendees sought shelter, and close down those that did not comply with the Act.[12] This required the healing centres to obtain licences from state mental health authorities and follow rules and procedures pertaining to admission, detention, and discharge of 'psychiatric patients' in their 'charge' in a manner similar to the functioning of psychiatric institutions. The Court's rationale for such a directive was that traditional healing sites that housed mentally ill people were akin to providers of 'mental health services' that consisted of, '...in addition to psychiatric hospitals and psychiatric nursing homes, observation wards, day-care centres, inpatient treatment in general hospitals, ambulatory treatment facilities and other facilities, convalescent homes and halfway homes for the mentally ill' (Government of India 1987). The decision to regulate traditional healing centres under the provisions of the Act was taken in accordance with this broad definition of what constitutes 'mental health services'.

This step to bring traditional healing centres under the purview of the MHA, a custodial act that pertains exclusively to the functioning of psychiatric institutions, is highly significant in chalking out the future of traditional healing in the country. Based on this order, state authorities gain the power to shut down and criminalize traditional healing centres under conditions of 'non-compliance' with the Act. The ruling is also highly contentious since, as Davar and Lohokare (2009) point out, traditional healing centres in the country function more as 'social institutions' where people seek psychosocial healing through participating in familial, communal, religious, and spiritual activities and not as custodial institutions to which the Act pertains (also, see Bellamy 2011). The Court order seeks to alter the character of these healing systems based on a philosophy of voluntarism and self-healing to one of custodial treatment. Such legal action comes across as reactionary and biased, instead of being grounded in the knowledge and reality of how traditional healing is practised by people.

Another critical set of actions taken in tandem with these SC directives involved the Writ Petition Civil No. 562 of 2001, filed by a civil society group, Saarthak, in October 2001. The petitioners sought to address the 'completely inhuman treatment meted out to persons suffering from mental illnesses' and demanded state governments to undertake a number of actions to ensure the protection of human rights of the mentally ill in the country.[13] The affidavits by various state governments to the SC in response to this petition provide critical insights into the emerging policy stance of the government against traditional healing centres. Even as points made in the Saarthak petition referring to the poor functioning of psychiatric settings were ignored by the respective states in their affidavits, most of these responses dwelt on the 'evils' of traditional healing and what actions the state had taken to end it. For instance, on the issue of the 'indiscriminate use of physical restraints' in mental health settings raised in the petition, the Ministry of Health and Family Welfare stated, '(T)he mental "asylum" at Erwady was an unauthorized one and conditions prevailing in *such places* may not be generalized to State mental hospitals' (emphasis added).[14] This statement of the ministry was contradictory to evidence obtained by the NHRC on the gross restrictions of movement of the incarcerated mentally ill in a majority of state-run mental hospitals in the country, including locking in 'isolation cells' and chaining the 'unmanageable' mentally ill for extended periods of time (NHRC 1999).[15] Further, while severely reprimanding traditional healing practices in such a manner, the affidavit defended psychiatric practices by arguing, 'Administration of ECT or any other treatment is a matter of *clinical discretion* of the treating physician… and any abridgement thereof, as sought by the petitioners, will not be in the interests of the patients and will have disastrous consequences for the doctor–patient relationship, which is based on *faith* and trust' (emphasis added). These statements beg the question of whether the state has different sets of criteria to judge what constitutes human rights abuses in a psychiatric setting as opposed to a traditional healing centre, and how a person's faith in psychiatric treatment qualifies as more legitimate than her 'blind' faith in a traditional healing system. The ministry's responses reflect the unquestionable legitimacy of psychiatric treatment in the state's norms, even as there seems to be little evidence to elicit such confidence given the dismal condition of psychiatric care available in the country.

The belief that seeking care in traditional healing centres constitutes a forced choice for the public was also reflected in a number of state affidavits, including the one by the state of Manipur that recommended the construction of a mental hospital in its response to the petition. The Manipur government stated, '(D)ue to lack of modern treatment facilities, people are following the traditional methods of treatment and families are losing confidence.'[16] The state of Andhra Pradesh similarly noted, '(P)rovision of such (psychiatric) services would go a long way in preventing society from utilizing services at unlicensed places such as *dargahs*, temples, churches and other religious institutions which do not have proper facilities and expertise.'[17] The decision of the states to expand the tertiary psychiatric care system and build more custodial mental health institutions in the country was supported by the Court that directed all states to establish a 'full-fledged State Government run mental hospital in the State/Union Territory and a definite time schedule for establishment of the same' (orders of the SC in Civil Writ Petition No. 334/2001 and 562/2001). This directive of the Court contradicts the international public health perspective vis-à-vis mental health care that stresses the expansion of community-based services and recommends *against* institutional care, not to mention the gross malpractices that custodial mental health care in the country has reared in the past, and continues to do (NHRC 1999).[18]

The final blow to the traditional mental health sector was delivered in early 2002, when the SC passed the following directive in the conclusive stage of the writ petition hearings:

> Both the Central and State Governments shall undertake a comprehensive awareness campaign with a special rural focus to educate people as to provisions of law relating to mental health, rights of mentally challenged persons, the fact that chaining of mentally challenged persons is illegal and the mental patients should be sent to doctors and not to religious places such as temples or *dargah*s. (Order dated 5 February 2002)

These writ petitions and state responses have since become important influences on the direction of future mental health policy.[19]

Mental Health Policy: A Gender Critique

The legal actions that were initiated against traditional healing centres in the last decade pose a challenge to the continuation of these sites, directly impacting the mental health concerns of Indian women who are the primary users of these spaces.[20] While the stance of the Indian state against traditional health systems in general, and in support of Western biomedicine in particular, is not particularly new, the mental health arena in recent years offers a unique venue for examining the rationale behind such policies (see also Nandy and Visvanathan 1990; Prakash 1999).[21] Two crucial sociopolitical concerns shape mental health policy directions in present-day India; the first pertains to the challenges of applying an international human rights framework to the country's heterogeneous mental health landscape, while the second relates to the Indian nation-state's adherence to development as a cultural and political project (Nandy 1988; Sivaramakrishnan and Agrawal 2003). Both these concerns affect, directly, how women's mental health needs are understood and, in turn, address the formulation of mental health policies and practices. I expand on each of these points in turn.

The allegation that traditional healing rituals are violent and in violation of the human rights of people with mental illnesses is a prominent reason for instigating the state's ire against these spaces.

Indeed, when viewed from a global health perspective that prioritizes bioethics, stigma reduction, and human rights in mental health care, mystical–spiritual healing systems seem to occupy a murky territory (World Health Organization [WHO] 2001). Understandings around ideas such as what constitutes bodily harm, consent for treatment, and the meaning of patient 'insight' vis-à-vis psychiatric illnesses become contentious and complicated in a scenario where much of the 'treatment' in religiously based healing traditions involves inflicting physical pain to oneself, and healing that proceeds through self-direction. Traditional healing practices can neither be accommodated within a medico-legal paradigm that pathologizes the practice of voluntary self-harm and deems people with mental illnesses incapable of self-determination, nor tolerated in a universal human rights framework that prohibits any form of violence on vulnerable populations such as those with psychosocial disabilities.

However, on analysing the state's stance against traditional healing in some depth, it becomes clear that the allegation that traditional healing is essentially violent and detrimental to people seeking such care is unjustifiable. First and foremost, malpractice and misconduct in any medical or social institution needs to be strongly protested, such as the case of chaining in the shelter at Erwadi, which was clearly unethical given the profit-driven activities of the place. The shelter where the tragedy occurred, while profiteering from the dargah's potential clientele, was not part of the dargah's therapeutic complex. The public outcry against traditional healing following the Erwadi tragedy did not take into consideration the critical distinction between malpractices that occur in the garb of traditional healing versus the therapeutic practices that constitute these systems. An act such as chaining that may constitute a gross human rights violation in one context may offer cultural nuances such that it ceases to be a human rights abuse when issues of voluntarism and intention are taken into consideration. A woman who chains herself to symbolically 'contain' her sickness is not the same as the destitute mentally ill who were barbarically killed in the Erwadi tragedy.

A series of research studies on traditional healing, in recent years, have called attention to how practices such as possession–trance, binding oneself in chains, head-banging, somersaulting, and a range of activities and rituals that involve the sufferer's body as a central facet of the therapeutic process may constitute ways of expressing physical and psychological angst for the sufferer, as well as for cultivating a deeply 'embodied' experience of the healing process itself (Csordas 2002; Seligman 2008, 2010). These bodily activities, combined with a belief in spiritual powers and divine healing, make for a potent therapeutic experience for users of these practices. As Davar and Lohokare (2009: 66) found in their research in traditional healing sites across Maharashtra, women reported feeling 'warm, light, fresh, peaceful and relaxed' after participating in a range of bodily practices at the sites. During my research with female healing seekers in a Hindu healing temple in Rajasthan, I found that a range of ritually informed, body-centred practices are utilized by these women as deliberate 'techniques' of healing that bring about concrete, discernible therapeutic effects over a period of active engagement (Sood 2013).

Cultural context, thus, plays a key role in deciding the culpability of traditional healing. The meaning of violence and abuse with respect to traditional healing methods may need to be reconsidered in light of the overall philosophy that guides these systems of healing. The language of universal human rights may not always translate neatly in culturally diverse situations (Visweswaran 2004). Critics may still warn that such a 'cultural relativist' argument on human rights can foreclose the possibility of recognizing inequitable power relations constituted within the 'cultural' as well (Howard 1993). However, the human rights rhetoric to shun traditional healing systems also seems situated within a particular sociocultural and sociopolitical context that privileges the 'modern' over the 'traditional', and can therefore be challenged. Moreover, concerns over malpractice and human rights violations have also plagued the functioning of public health psychiatry in the country for decades (NHRC 1999). Corrective action, however, has focused on condemning the malpractices rather than shunning the practice of biomedical psychiatry.

It can well be argued that the state's efforts at foreclosing women's options for seeking care in a variety of mental health systems may entail a form of human rights abuse as well. The human rights of people with psychosocial disabilities include not only protection from harmful and degrading treatment, but also the right to personal autonomy and freedom to exercise civil, political, social, and cultural rights, in accordance with the United Nations Convention on the Rights of People with Disabilities (UNCRPD), which the Indian government signed and ratified in 2007 (Davar 2012). Moreover, as Davar and Lohokare (2009) point out, if people with an affliction include an element of prayer or penance in a site of their choice as a significant contributor to their well-being, should law not protect that as a health right? Instead, current legal and policy formulations threaten such an option. Recognizing the coercion implicit in current mental health policies of the state is crucial to formulating gender-sensitive mental health policies that respect women's health-seeking choices.

There is a valid concern that women's mental health strategies, when touted as inseparable from the Indian nation-state's allegiance to development and modernity, may become the special target of state oppression and abuse (see also Das *et al.* 2000). Scholars have discussed, in the context of women's reproductive health rights in an earlier era of international public health measures to curb India's 'population explosion', how women's bodies came to embody modernity based on their reproductive choices (Van Hollen 2003). Public health became a way of ensuring disciplinary, and at times violent, control over women's bodies and health (Ram 2000). A similar process may unravel in the mental health arena if what women do and where they seek help in times of mental distress becomes a mirror to India's self-image as a modernizing society and its commitment to development. When women's mental health strategies come to be equated with the development and modernization of the country, mental health becomes the site for 'manoeuvring development' for the state intent on fashioning women's choices in the 'right' direction (Van Hollen 2003). In a sense, women, by choosing psychiatry over traditional healing, come to 'embody' modernity (also, see Lester 2005).

In such a discursive field, it is imperative to be cognizant of how larger discourses pertaining to public health and human rights impact the lives of women in a volatile mental health climate in the country. The practice of public health in the present-day world is one of the defining features of progress and development for a country; it is a cardinal indicator of the well-being of nations on the development index (Desjarlais *et al.* 1995).[22] The public health concerns of marginalized populations such as women become especially significant within such a global discourse on development. It is no surprise then that women's health movements across the world frame women's health concerns in public health terms and advocate with governments and international public health agencies for equitable and good-quality health care. This framing involves using the rhetoric of development to make claims legitimate and to shame governments in case they fail to provide for women's health needs. However, while the notion of development provides a powerful tool to further women's health-related concerns, it might be problematic when applied without critical analysis of the global political economy of health and without basing it in the complexity of local contexts. In the case of mental health policy in India and around the world, the idea of a modern public health system that only endorses biomedical psychiatry has become a tool for delegitimizing other local and cultural alternatives. While conceding that many modern health interventions have the potential to positively transform women's lives, equating 'all' non-modern practices with underdevelopment is still faulty reasoning that needs to be strongly resisted (Visweswaran 2004).

Recourse to biomedicine alone, feminists critique, tends to medicalize women's health concerns that might originate not in their bodies alone but in the structural inequalities they experience in their lives. Within the gamut of health concerns that women experience, the case of mental health is given to medicalization in unique ways (Vindhya 2001). Horacio Fabrega (1993) discusses how psychiatric discourse has historically developed in a manner that the mentally ill individual's needs are often overlooked, citizenship questioned and suspended, and credibility injured. He writes, '(B)y reducing human problems of the social, economic and political structure of the society to symptoms of illness to be treated with drugs and other physical measures, the potential of reaching a more humane amelioration of the "social pathology" that give rise to the deviant behaviour is aborted' (Fabrega 1993: 185). Insofar as psychiatry becomes the primary mode of understanding and healing mental disease within the institution of public health, the voices of women are likely to go unheard as a 'natural' consequence.

Women have resisted the medicalization of their social suffering in a variety of health sectors and mental health is an important arena in which to muster this resistance in present-day India (see, in this context, Davar's 2008 discussion of the use of a medicalized language versus one focused on disability among female users of psychiatry in recent years). It becomes vital, therefore, to acknowledge and understand how traditional healing offers women an efficacious alternative to address the social and psychological suffering they experience in patriarchal societies in a 'non-medicalized' way, and how its absence can potentially be detrimental to their lives and health.

Women's Rights and Human Rights: An International Policy Perspective

For those working in the field of women's health, the international human rights framework has proven to be a powerful policy and advocacy tool in recent decades, especially following the Fourth World Conference on Women ('Platform for Action'), in Beijing, in 1995 (United Nations [UN] 1995). As Peters and Wolper (1995) note, the framing of women's rights within a human rights discourse lends irrefutable legitimacy to women's concerns across a wide range of issues (also, see Visweswaran 2004). With respect to health rights, the human rights framework has helped construct women's health in public health terms, rather than as a solely individualistic, medical concern as previously imagined. Ensuring the good health of women has become a matter of justice and human dignity that all nation-states are liable to uphold (Mann and Gruskin 1995).

As far as the right to mental health goes, it has been articulated as a human right in a number of international policy documents, for instance, Article 12 of the International Covenant on Economic, Social and Cultural Rights and Article 25 of the Universal Declaration of Human Rights. These policy articulations, coupled with public health concerns over the rising global burden of diseases such as depression and anxiety that disproportionately affect women around the world, have led to renewed attention on the importance of women's mental health in the larger women's health and human rights arena. The women's movement has also been increasingly concerned with the social, political, and structural dimensions of mental health. The medicalization of women's bodies and health, and the structural inequalities that it signifies, has become an especially significant area of feminist research and advocacy in recent years (Inhorn 2006). For instance, a lot of attention is being paid to how structural gender inequalities interact in systematic ways to produce gender differentials in mental health. Gulcur (2000) mentions the 1999 General Recommendation on Health made by the Committee of the Elimination of Discrimination against Women (CEDAW) that relates directly to this aspect. I quote at length:

> ...An analysis of the right to health for women must address not only access to and quality of health care, but also the underlying gender-specific socioeconomic conditions that impact health. It (the Recommendation) discusses the effect of gender inequalities and violence on women's physical and mental health, as well as gender differentials in psychological conditions. It states that governments must report on factors that impinge on women's health needs, such as: socioeconomic factors that vary for women in general and some groups of women in particular. For example, unequal power relationships between women and men in the home and workplace may negatively affect women's nutrition and health. They may also be exposed to different forms of violence, which can affect their health. Girl children and adolescent girls are often vulnerable to sexual abuse by older men and family members, placing them at risk of physical and psychological harm... (Gulcur 2000: 48)

The General Recommendation highlights gender differences in psychological conditions, '(P)sychosocial factors that vary between women and men include depression in general and post-partum depression in particular as well as other psychological conditions, such as those that lead to eating disorders such as anorexia and bulimia' (Gulcur 2000: 49). Following these perspectives in the international circuit, a clear relationship is articulated between issues such as gender discrimination and violence against women and the ensuing mental health impacts on women. This linkage between gender inequalities, rights violations, and mental health is clearly drawn in Paragraph 100 of the Beijing Platform, which states: 'Mental disorders related to marginalization, powerlessness and poverty, along with overwork and stress and the growing incidence of domestic violence as well as substance abuse, are among other health issues of growing concern to women' (Gulcur 2000: 51).

In the Indian mental health arena, the articulation of women's health in a human rights language, while clearly emphasizing the state's responsibility towards securing women's mental health and highlighting the gender discrimination inherent in health delivery and resource allocation, presents a number of vexing problems. As a number of scholars argue, a universal human rights perspective when applied to the women's rights discourse offers many benefits but, in a variety of contexts, is also given to a special kind of co-optation and cultural imperialism (Berkovitch 1999; Visweswaran 2004). As Winter *et al.* (2002) note vis-à-vis the UN-driven international discussions on women's human rights and the notion of 'harmful traditional practices', the discourse draws a clearly hierarchical distinction between Western/non-Western and modern/traditional. When perceived within a universal human rights discourse, tradition is perceived as inherently and without distinction a violation of women's rights. Quite so in the Indian mental health sector, insofar as public health psychiatry and traditional healing are viewed in the binary of the Western/modern and non-Western/traditional, the latter is, by definition, vilified. The result is the unchallenged endorsement of biomedical psychiatry as the only mental health recourse for Indian women, and the shunning of traditional healing systems. Furthermore, as Visweswaran (2004) convincingly argues in the South Asian context, women's oppression at the hands of tradition often masks global structural features (also, see Davar 2012). Framing the legitimacy of biomedical psychiatry (and the illegitimacy of more popular systems of traditional healing) in the context of universal human rights rhetoric could, thus, obfuscate neo-colonial and neo-liberal development agendas that, in fact, exacerbate structural violence against women.

It is important, thus, that the stance on Indian women's mental health rights be formulated by taking into consideration the connection between women's mental health concerns and the medicalization of women's social suffering. The need of the hour, as Davar (1999) points out, is not only to situate mental health within the larger health movement by bringing attention back to the centrality of linking women's ill-health to their difficult lives, but also critiquing specialist, 'clinical' interventions that ignore the social suffering experienced by women. That also means recognizing the value of holistic alternatives to biomedical psychiatry, such as traditional healing systems, as especially and absolutely essential for addressing women's mental health needs.

***

The Erwadi tragedy and the mental health policy implications that ensued from it are likely to change the mental health landscape for women in the country. Women's preference for traditional systems of healing as opposed to state-supported psychiatry is viewed as anti-development and anti-modernization by an Indian state conscious of its image as a developing nation on the global stage. Modernizing agents of the state characterize the persistence of these centres as a development indicator, and cite the lack of access to modern health care and education in order to make informed choices as the main reason for the popularity of traditional healing among women (Government of India 2002). This stance also echoes similar discourses involving the tradition–modernity dichotomy that dominate the political/ideological landscape of many other post-colonial settings in present times (Ewing 1997).

Formulating gender-sensitive mental health policy requires that women's preferential use of traditional healing systems must not be viewed simply as an indicator of their inability to access modern systems of healing. While it is true that women are often systematically denied access to good-quality health care in patriarchal societies such as India, it is also critical to listen to why women make the health-seeking choices that they do, and what they say about why they seek healing at traditional healing sites in overwhelming numbers. The state's paternalistic attitude of foreclosing these options for women is a violation of women's rights to choose for themselves. A sole focus on psychiatric care for women is given to the medicalization of women's health that feminists have argued in other contexts. The state's policies are likely to amplify the issue of medicalization in the women's mental health arena as well. The intimate relationship of structural inequalities and violence in women's lives and their mental health is widely recognized, but responses to this recognition that advocate for biomedical interventions alone shift the focus from sociopolitical concerns to medical ones. This shift is likely to be detrimental to women's well-being in the longer run.

That traditional healing continues to be popular among women despite the state's condemnation of such practices suggests that they do provide 'abundant community-based resources' and may not be 'regarded as ineffective or indeed harmful without sufficient exploration and systematic examination' (Kapur 2004: 92). Framing mental health as a human rights issue also tends to complicate the arena of mental health in the country where traditional healing sites are seen as abusive of the human rights of people with mental illnesses. While malpractice in the biomedical and traditional healing systems must be strictly prohibited, there is a need for understanding the local and cultural complexities of traditional healing vis-à-vis women's health rights and human rights to design gender-sensitive mental health policy that does not foreclose women's help-seeking choices.

Notes

1. I am grateful for the encouragement and guidance that Dr Bhargavi Davar offered so generously, the research support provided by the Center for Advocacy in Mental Health, Pune, and the invaluable inputs of my colleagues in the Department of Anthropology and the Women, Gender, and Sexuality Studies programme at Washington University in St Louis.
2. Details of the incident are reproduced here by combining news reports from the national dailies, *The Hindu*, *The Times of India*, and *The Indian Express*, the fortnightly current affairs magazine, *Frontline*, and the BBC South Asia reports from the years 2001–2.
3. Anthropologist Joao Biehl (2008) introduces the concept of 'zones of social abandonment' to refer to an increasing number of spaces in the era of neo-liberal globalization that house people deemed unproductive and/or unsound in appallingly inhumane conditions. These spaces, Biehl notes, receive little attention from the state and society, functioning like 'dump' sites for the abandoned and destitute.
4. Studies on the preferential use of mental health systems in medically plural societies such as India point to a complex patterning of treatment choices, involving the use of multiple practices informed by a diverse range of sociocultural and pragmatic considerations. Even as an array of traditional systems, operating outside the official biomedical

psychiatric system, are preferred by the general Indian population, folk practices based on notions of mystical–spiritual healing are believed to hold special expertise and competence in treating mental afflictions.

5. A number of public interest litigations (PILs), from time to time, have brought to light the pathetic state of government-run mental hospitals in the country and human rights violations of the incarcerated mentally ill in these institutions. In 1999, the National Human Rights Commission (NHRC) of India set out to chart the condition of state-run mental health facilities in the country and reported abysmal, inhuman conditions for mental patients in the majority of these sites.

6. Studies from the 1990s have cited a ratio of one woman to every three men attending psychiatric outpatient clinics (Varma *et al.* 1992; Davar 1995). These statistics seem to hold up even against the fact that community studies indicate an equal, if not higher, distribution of psychiatric disorders among women (Chakraborty 1990; Jablensky *et al.* 1992).

7. For instance, a common trance-inducing technique employed in many of these healing sites involves vigorous movements of the head from side-to-side and in circular motion for an extended period of time, a practice that has been categorized as a form of torture by the Amnesty International (Glucklich 2001: 115).

8. Now an integral part of medical anthropological language, Arthur Kleinman (1975, 1980) developed the concept of 'explanatory models' to refer to the way patients and practitioners understand illness and healing, the causes that they ascribe to the ailment, and the treatments that they believe will ameliorate the condition.

9. There is often a clear distinction made across different cultures between possession states that are understood as a positive experience involving spirits that uphold the moral order and typically speak (though not always) through men, and those associated with experiences of affliction involving amoral spirits that typically possess women and other subordinate and marginal social groups (Lewis 1989). A number of researchers combine this literature with feminist perspectives to claim that women's preponderance as the afflicted in mystical–spiritual healing systems is an expression of the powerlessness that they experience in patriarchal settings.

10. This was especially true of illnesses understood to be predominantly 'female', such as women who presented with dissociative disorders, somatoform disorders, anxiety, and depression (Shidhaye *et al.* 2013).

11. Details of the legal actions initiated after the Erwadi tragedy have been accessed through the 'Erwady Case Study Files' at the library and documentation centre, Center for Advocacy in Mental Health, Pune.

12. The Mental Health Act, 1987 is a more recent replacement of the highly controversial Indian Lunacy Act of 1912. The Act pertains to the functioning of psychiatric institutions in the country, including admission, stay, and discharge procedures for patients and rules for regulating the functioning of such institutions. The Act is specifically focused on custodial modes of care for the mentally ill and does not engage the arena of community mental health (Dhanda 2000; Davar 2012).

13. Writ Petition (Civil) No. 562 of 2001, Saarthak and *Achal Bhagat* v *Union of India, Ministry of Social Justice and Empowerment, Ministry of Health, Disabilities Commissioner, and other State Governments.*

14. Affidavit filed by Under Secretary, Ministry of Health and Human Welfare, on behalf of respondents The Union of India and Director General of Health Services, Government of India, March 2002.

15. The NHRC (1999) report, *Quality Assurance in Mental Health*, provides a 'shocking revelation', for instance, of isolation cells in more than half of the government-run mental hospitals in the country where many patients are locked for long periods of time, with no water, bed, or toilet. At times, many patients may even be locked in a cell that can accommodate only one person (NHRC 1999: 39–40).

16. Affidavit filed by Chief Secretary, Government of Manipur, 26 February 2002.

17. Affidavit filed by Joint Commissioner and In-charge Special Officer, Legal Cell, Government of Andhra Pradesh, 18 March 2002.

18. The World Health Organization's (WHO) *World Health Report 2001* outlines recommendations for mental health service provision and planning, stressing the provision of treatment in primary health system and giving care in the community. It clearly disfavours institutional mental health care.

19. Another noteworthy development is the Anti-Superstition Bill (2005), still pending in the Maharashtra State Assembly, that sees mystical–spiritual healing centres as perpetuating superstition and causing harm to those who seek such help. The Bill declares these healing practices a punishable offence. The Bill is still awaiting passage as law, but may be adopted in other states as well. See http://www.legalserviceindia.com/articles/statl.htm.

20. Significant changes are already underway in the traditional healing sector. My ethnographic research in a Hindu healing temple in north India in the year 2009–10 documents how a number of key healing rituals carried out in the temple over many decades have completely disappeared in the last 10 years. Long-time healing seekers lament

the disappearance of these practices, which, they believe, were especially effective as therapeutic techniques for the alleviation of their suffering but are no longer allowed in the premises of the temple (Sood 2013).

21. The Indian nation-state has, since inception, favoured Western biomedicine as the legitimate health system for the country, despite a rich tradition of medical plurality in Indian society and a variety of healing systems such as the ayurveda, unani, innumerable folk forms, and even homeopathy competing for popularity (Khan 2005).

22. The Human Development Index of the United Nations Development Programme (started in 1993), for example, rates the countries of the world as developed, developing, or underdeveloped on the basis of a 'long and healthy life' of their populations, measured in epidemiological mortality and morbidity data, along with other criteria such as literacy and gross domestic product.

References

Addlakha, R. 2001. 'The Lay and Medical Diagnoses of Psychiatric Disorder and the Normative Construction of Femininity', in B.V. Davar (ed.), *Mental Health from a Gender Perspective*, pp. 313–33. New Delhi: Sage.

————. 2008. *Deconstructing Mental Illness: An Ethnography of Psychiatry, Women, and the Family*. New Delhi: Zubaan.

BBC News. 2001. 'Silent Suffering of India's Mentally Ill', BBC News South Asia, 6 August.

Bellamy, C. 2011. *The Powerful Ephemeral Everyday Healing in an Ambiguously Islamic Place*. Berkeley: University of California Press.

Berkovitch, N. 1999. *From Motherhood to Citizenship: Women's Rights and International Organizations*. Baltimore: Johns Hopkins University Press.

Biehl, J. 2008. 'Life of the Mind: The Interface of Psychopharmaceuticals, Domestic Economies, and Social Abandonment', *American Ethnologist*, 31(4): 475–96.

Boddy, J. 1994. 'Spirit Possession Revisited: Beyond Instrumentality', *Annual Review of Anthropology*, 23: 407–43.

Bourguignon, E. 2004. 'Suffering and Healing, Subordination and Power: Women and Possession Trance', *Ethos*, 32(4): 557–74.

Caplan, P.J. and L. Cosgrave (eds). 2004. *Bias in Psychiatric Diagnosis*. Maryland: Rowman and Littlefield Publishing Group.

Chakraborty, A. 1990. *Social Stress and Mental Health: A Social–Psychiatric Field Study of Calcutta*. New Delhi: Sage.

Csordas, T.J. 2002. *Body/meaning/healing*. New York: Palgrave Macmillan.

Csordas, T.J. and A. Kleinman. 1996. 'The Therapeutic Process', in C.F. Sargent and T.M. Johnson (eds), *Handbook of Medical Anthropology: Contemporary Theory and Method*, pp. 3–20. London: Greenwood Press.

Das, V. 1996. *Critical Events: An Anthropological Perspective on Contemporary India*. New York: Oxford University Press.

Das, V., A. Kleinman, M. Ramphele, and P. Reynolds. 2000. *Violence and Subjectivity*. Berkeley: University of California Press.

Davar, B.V. 1995. 'Mental Illness in Indian Women', *Economic and Political Weekly*, 30(45): 2879–86.

———. 1999. *Mental Health of Indian Women: A Feminist Agenda*. New Delhi: Sage.

———. 2008. 'From Mental Illness to Disability: Choices of Women Users/Survivors of Psychiatry in Self and Identity Constructions', *Indian Journal of Gender Studies*, 15(2): 261–90.

———. 2012. 'Legal Frameworks for and against People with Psychosocial Disabilities', *Economic and Political Weekly*, 47(52): 123–31.

Davar, B.V. and M. Lohokare. 2009. 'Recovering from Psychosocial Traumas: The Place of *Dargah*s in Maharshtra', *Economic and Political Weekly*, 44(16): 60–7.

Dennerstein, L., J. Astbury, and C. Morse. 1993. *Psychosocial and Mental Health Aspects of Women's Health*. Geneva: WHO.

Desjarlais, R., L. Eisenberg, B. Good, and A. Kleinman. 1995. *World Mental Health: Problems and Priorities in Low-income Countries*. New York: Oxford University Press.

Dhanda, A. 2000. *Legal Order and Mental Disorder*. New Delhi: Sage.

Dwyer, G. 2003. *The Divine and the Demonic: Supernatural Affliction and its Treatment in North India*. New York: Routledge.

Ewing, K.P. 1997. *Arguing Sainthood: Modernity, Psychoanalysis, and Islam*. Durham: Duke University Press.

Fabrega, H. 1993. 'Biomedical Psychiatry as an Object for a Critical Medical Anthropology', in S. Lindenbaum and M. Lock (eds), *Knowledge, Power and Practice: The Anthropology of Medicine and Everyday Life*, pp.166–88. Berkeley: University of California Press.

Finkler, K. 1985. *Spiritualist Healers in Mexico*. New York: Prager.

Glik, D.C. 1988. 'Symbolic, Ritual and Social Dynamics of Spiritual Healing', *Social Science and Medicine*, 27(11): 1197–206.

Glucklich, A. 2001. *Sacred Pain: Hurting the Body for the Sake of the Soul*. New York: Oxford University Press.

Government of India. 1987. *The Mental Health Act, 1987*. New Delhi: Ministry of Law and Justice.

————. 2002. *The National Health Policy*. New Delhi: Ministry of Health and Family Welfare.

————. 2003. 'Appendix H: Orders of the Supreme Court in Civil Writ Petition No. 334/2001 & 562/2001—Erwadi–Saarthak Public Interest Litigation (PIL)', in S.P. Agarwal (ed.), *Mental Health: An Indian Perspective 1946–2003*, pp. 503–20. New Delhi: Directorate General of Health Services.

Gulcur, L. 2000. 'Evaluating the Role of Gender Inequalities and Rights Violations in Women's Mental Health', *Health and Human Rights*, 5(1): 46–66.

Halliburton, M. 2003. 'The Importance of a Pleasant Process of Treatment: Lessons on Healing from South India', *Culture, Medicine and Psychiatry*, 27(2): 161–86.

————. 2005. '"Just Some Spirits": The Erosion of Spirit Possession and the Rise of "Tension" in South India', *Medical Anthropology*, 24(2): 111–44.

Howard, R.E. 1993. 'Cultural Absolutism and the Nostalgia for Community', *Human Rights Quarterly*, 15(2): 315–38.

Inhorn, M. 2006. 'Defining Women's Health: A Dozen Messages from More than 150 Ethnographies', *Medical Anthropology Quarterly*, 20(3): 345–78.

Jablensky, A., N. Sartorius, G. Ernberg, M. Anker, A. Korten, J. E. Cooper, R. Day, and A. Bertelsen. 1992. 'Schizophrenia: Manifestations, Incidence and Course in Different Cultures. A World Health Organization Ten-country Study', *Psychological Medicine Monograph Supplement 20*. Cambridge: Cambridge University Press.

Jain, S. 2006. 'Traditional Healing and Community Mental Health', Paper presented at the seminar on 'Faith Healing: Going beyond Medicine', a Seminar and Photo Exhibition at Balagandharv Kaladalan, Bapu Trust, Pune, 13 January.

Kakar, S. 1982. *Shamans, Mystics and Doctors: A Psychological Inquiry into India and its Healing Traditions*. New York: Alfred A. Knopf.

Keller, M. 2002. *Hammer and the Flute: Women, Power, and Spirit Possession*. Baltimore: Johns Hopkins University Press.

Kapur, R.L. 2004. 'The Story of Community Mental Health in India', in S.P. Agarwal (ed.), *Mental Health: An Indian Perspective 1946–2003*. New Delhi: Directorate General of Health Services.

Khan, S. 2006. 'Systems of Medicine and Nationalist Discourse in India: Towards "New Horizons" in Medical Anthropology and History', *Social Science and Medicine*, 62(11): 2786–97.

Kirmayer, L.J. 2004. 'The Cultural Diversity of Healing: Meaning, Metaphor and Mechanism', *British Medical Bulletin*, 69(1): 33–48.

Kleinman, A. 1975. 'Explanatory Models in Health Care Relationships', in *Health of the Family*. pp. 159–72. Washington, DC: National Council for International Health.

————. 1980. *Patients and Healers in the Context of Culture: An Exploration of the Borderland between Anthropology, Medicine and Psychiatry*. Berkeley: University of California Press

Lester, R.J. 2005. *Jesus in Our Wombs: Embodying Modernity in a Mexican Convent*. Berkeley: University of California Press.

Lewis, I.M. 1989. *Ecstatic Religion: A Study of Shamanism and Spirit Possession*, 2nd edition. London: Routledge.

Mann, J. and S. Gruskin. 1995. 'Women's Health and Human Rights: Genesis of the Health and Human Rights Movement', *Health and Human Rights*, 1(4): 309–12.

Murthy, 2001. 'Lesson from the Erwadi tragedy for mental health care in India', *Indian Journal of Psychiatry* 43 (4): 362–378

Nandy, A. 1988. *Science, Hegemony and Violence: A Requiem for Modernity*. New Delhi: Oxford University Press.

Nandy, A. and S. Visvanathan. 1990. 'Modern Medicine and its Nonmodern Critics: A Study in Discourse', in A. Marglin and S.A. Marglin (eds), *Dominating Knowledge: Development, Culture and Resistance*, pp. 145–84. Oxford: Clarendon Press.

National Human Rights Commission (NHRC). 1999. *Quality Assurance in Mental Health*. New Delhi: NHRC.

Pakaslahti, A. 1998, 'Family-centered Treatment of Mental Health Problems at the Balaji Temple in Rajasthan', in A. Parpola and S. Tenhunen (eds), *Changing Patterns of Family and Kinship in South Asia*, pp.129–66. Helsinki: University of Helsinki.

————. 2009. 'Health-seeking Behavior for Psychiatric Disorders in North India', in M. Incayawar, R. Wintrob, and L. Bouchard (eds), *Psychiatrists and Traditional Healers: Unwitting Partners in Global Mental Health*, pp.149–66. Chichester, UK: John Wiley & Sons.

Patel, V., Ricardo Araya, Mauricio de Lima, *et. al.* 1999. 'Women, Poverty and Common Mental Disorders in Four Restructuring Societies', *Social Science and Medicine*, 49(11): 1461–71.

Patel, V., Ricardo Araya, Sudipto Chatterjee *et. al.* 2007. 'Treatment and prevention of mental disorders in low-income and middle-income countries', *The Lancet*, 370(9591): 991–1005.

Peters J.S. and A. Wolper. 1995. *Women's Rights, Human Rights: International Feminist Perspectives*. New York: Routledge.

Pinto, S. 2011. 'Rational Love, Relational Medicine: Psychiatry and the Accumulation of Precarious Kinship', *Culture, Medicine and Psychiatry*, 35(3): 376–95.

Prakash, G. 1999. *Another Reason: Science and the Imagination of Modern India*. Princeton: Princeton University Press.

Raguram, R., A. Venkateswaran, Jayashree Ramakrishna, and Mitchell G. Weiss. 2002. 'Traditional Community Resources for Mental Health: a Report of Temple Healing from India'. *British Medical Journal* 325 (7354): 38–40.

Ram, K. 1992. *Mukkuvar Women: Gender, Hegemony, and Capitalist Transformation in a South Indian Fishing Village*, pp. 82–117. New Delhi: Kali for Women.

———. 2000. 'Rationalizing Fecund Bodies: Family Planning Policy and the Indian Nation-State', in M. Jolly and K. Ram (eds), *Borders of Being*. Michigan: University of Michigan Press.

Sax, W.S. 2009. *God of Justice: Ritual Healing and Social Justice in the Central Himalayas*. New York: Oxford University Press.

Sebastia, B. (ed.). 2009. *Restoring Mental Health in India: Pluralistic Therapies and Concepts*. New Delhi: Oxford University Press.

Seligman, R. 2008. 'Distress, Dissociation, and Embodied Experience: Reconsidering the Pathways to Mediumship and Mental Health', *Ethos*, 33(1): 71–99.

———. 2010. 'The Unmaking and Making of Self: Embodied Suffering and Mind–Body Healing in Brazilian Candomblé', *Ethos*, 38(3): 297–320.

Shidhaye, R., E. Mendenhall, K. Sumathipala, A. Sumathipala, and V. Patel. 2013. 'Association of Somatoform Disorders with Anxiety and Depression in Women in Low and Middle Income Countries: A Systematic Review', *International Review of Psychiatry*, 25(1): 65–76.

Sivaramakrishnan, K. and A. Agrawal. 2003. *Regional Modernities: The Cultural Politics of Development in India*. New Delhi: Oxford University Press.

Skultans, V. 1991. 'Women and Affliction in Maharashtra: A Hydraulic Model of Health and Illness', *Culture, Medicine and Psychiatry*, 15: 321–59.

Sood, A. 2013. 'Navigating Pain: Women's Healing Practices in a Hindu Temple', *All Theses and Dissertations (ETDs)*. Paper 1157. Available at: http://openscholarship.wustl.edu/etd/1157.

The Indian Express. 2001. 'Action Please', Editorial, 11 August. Accessed from Erwadi Case Study Files, Library and Documentation center, Center for Advocacy in Mental Health, Pune.

The Times of India. 2001a. 'Torture in God's Name: When Blind Faith Reigns, even the Sane Turn Insane', 8 August. Accessed from Erwadi Case Study Files, Library and Documentation center, Center for Advocacy in Mental Health, Pune.

————. 2001b. '*Dargah*s Play Ghost-busters to Demons of the Mind', Editorial, 11 August. Accessed from Erwadi Case Study Files, Library and Documentation center, Center for Advocacy in Mental Health, Pune.

Trivedi, J.K. 2001. 'Implication of Erwadi Tragedy on Mental Health Care System in India', *Indian Journal of Psychiatry*, 43(4): 293–4.

United Nations (UN). 1995. 'United Nations Fourth World Conference on Women, Beijing, September 1995, Platform for Action', available at http://www.un.org/womenwatch/daw/beijing/platform/health.htm, accessed 15 December 2008.

Van Hollen, C. 2003. *Birth on the Threshold: Childbirth and Modernity in South India*. Berkeley: University of California Press.

Varma, V.K., S.K. Avesthi, S.K. Mattoo, and A.K. Jain. 1992. 'Diagnostic and Sociodemographic Data of Psychiatric Patients at the National level', *Indian Journal of Psychiatry*, 8(3–4): 22–34.

Vindhya, U. 2001. 'From the Personal to the Collective: Psychological/ Feminist Issues of Women's Mental Health', in B.V. Davar (ed.), *Mental Health from a Gender Perspective*, pp. 82–98. New Delhi: Sage.

Visweswaran, K. 2004. 'Gendered States: Rethinking Culture as a Site of South Asian Human Rights Work', *Human Rights Quarterly*, 26(2): 483–511.

Weiss, M.G. 2001. 'Cultural Epidemiology: An Introduction and Overview', *Anthropology and Medicine*, 8(1): 5–59.

Weiss, M.G., S.D. Sharma, R.K. Gaur, J.S. Sharma, A. Desai, and D.R. Doongaji. 1986. 'Traditional Concepts of Mental Disorder among Indian Psychiatric Patients: Preliminary Report of Work in Progress', *Social Science and Medicine*, 23(4): 379– 86.

Winter, B., D. Thompson, and S. Jeffreys. 2002. 'The UN Approach to Harmful Traditional Practices', *International Feminist Journal of Politics*, 4(1): 72–94.

World Health Organization (WHO). 2001. *The World Health Report 2001—Mental Health: New Understanding, New Hope*. Geneva: WHO.

9

Identity Constructions for 'Mentally Disturbed' Women

Identities versus Institutions

Bhargavi V. Davar[1]

User/Survivor Identity

This chapter describes my reflections on questions of self-identity of 'mentally disturbed' women and their complex relationships with institutions. In this chapter, I am writing self-reflectively, as a childhood survivor of psychiatry and its institutions; as a philosopher who has engaged with epistemologies concerning 'madness' (Davar and Bhat 1995) and their gendered dimensions (Davar 1999, 2001); and also as a political agent active within both the women's movement and the mental health movement in India. My own journey of trauma, depression, and struggles with staying well is recorded elsewhere (Davar 1998, 2006). Briefly, my trauma dates back to repeated and intense early childhood exposure to psychiatric violence: mental institutions, shock treatments, solitary confinement, police arrests, chaining, and other brutalities that existed (and continue to exist) in the mental health sector; experiences of enduring parental abandonment and childhood depression following the irretrievable loss of my mother to the highly coercive mental and allied penal institutions; profound depression after sustained exposure to domestic violence and the loss of a child; intense engagement with myself for over a decade, as a 'mentally disturbed woman' of meaningless medical denominations trying to understand what it is that I am suffering from, and trying to 'get cured' of it; and then later, evolving a self having the strong intent to shed childhood traumatic memories (particularly relating to the 'smell' of asylums), keep myself well, and live a fulfilling life as an adult woman, a healer, and a mental health advocate. After all these experiences, something has remained as 'my sel(ves)' worthy of preserving, and even though I was always profoundly preoccupied with the topics of death and dying, I never did attempt suicide.

In this chapter, other than my own experiences, I draw from Sanchit, an oral history archive of people living with a mental illness,[2] and particularly from the stories of four women, Abha, Anu, Chrysann, and Urja.[3] 'Sanchit' is a collection of women's stories of mental distress and disturbance, and their experiences with various institutions: family, psychiatric, and other mental health services, work, education, etc. There were about 25 stories in all in the collection at the time of writing this chapter. Sanchit has a well-developed programme protocol of inclusion in decision-making by the person giving the interview at every stage: consent, confidentiality, time, and space where the interview will be done, interview process, recording, transcription, editing, the final production as personal diaries, and follow up. Sanchit has resulted in the build-up of a user/survivor community and collectivization in Pune, extending beyond the city limits into other cities, with support from other organizations and individuals. The Sanchit collection also includes a small selection of books, films, audio-visuals, letters, arts and artifacts, and other memorabilia, testifying to user/survivor experiences in India.

A 'survivor of psychiatry' is someone who has been through and has survived mental illness, and may also mean surviving psychiatry and its institutions. This usage by clients of a health care system is peculiar to the mental health sector. Women do not usually build a lifelong marginalized identity around health care violations. Nobody self-identifies as a 'survivor of gynaecology', for example, even though women may have had traumatic experiences with these services. There are reasons why users/survivors of psychiatry feel profound trauma about the way we have entered and exited the mental health system, and in particular, psychiatry. When requested to contribute her story to Sanchit, Ciera Louise, a survivor, writes: 'We might not want to remember the details of our younger years in the '70s, locked down like animals to be feared and punitively treated rather than embraced with care.'4 Chrysann, another survivor from her recent experiences, says, 'You can't just get out of that door. It's all locked. You don't have any freedom there. You cannot run away or anything. I didn't even think of running away. After a few days you are just drugged and dazed. I don't know what it was. I cannot express it in words.'

Children who lost their parents, particularly the mother, to psychiatric institutions are often traumatized and hurting lifelong (Gombos and Dhanda 2009; Gopal Chandu in Sanchit 2009; Sandhu 2009). In the Indian context, where family bonds are strong, we can also talk about intergenerational trauma with respect to psychiatry and psychiatric institutionalization. I identify as a survivor largely because during my early childhood days, my mother's deep trauma within mental asylums was experienced as my own and my life has been an enduring struggle to survive this primary trauma; and I identify as a user because the disability linked with these experiences returns on and off, decentring me, making me seek different therapeutic routes excepting psychiatry. I believe I carry scars from childhood abuse caused by the biomedical system, though this spectrum of experiences has not been included in the extant diagnostic usage of childhood or psychosocial trauma. Many of us with this sense of hurt and injury spend a lifetime working to challenge the mental health system politically, even as we worked on ourselves to deal with our drained selfhood, mourning a lost childhood.

Very recently, during a visit to the Manila mental asylum, I had to sit down with nausea and giddiness, because of an overwhelming flash of 'sensory' memory about the 'smell' of the asylum. Once the trauma of mental health care and its institutions is established in our bodies and minds, enduring almost as biological in experience, concerned others have to literally drag us into treatment using force, where the primary trauma of mental institutions, terror of shock treatment, solitary, and other forced psychiatric treatment, is never addressed (Minkowitz and Dhanda 2006). We try to resolve the primary trauma with its psychosocial and biological consequences through political action. We create our own spaces for sharing, and storytelling, about our 'psychiatric institution trauma'.

Trauma from psychiatry can be experienced in other ways too. Chrysann and Anu, survivors of psychiatry, are both self-advocates and will remain so for a long time to come because of their deep sense of personal violation by an insensitive, if not punishing, mental health system and by intimate family relationships. Recently, a member of one of the mental health peer support group, of which I am a part, was struggling to deal with her nose hallucination (that her nose was constantly moving and changing): a 37-year-old who had only minimum exposure to the asylum, she linked her hallucination to traumatic experiences of being in a very smelly and dirty solitary cell, with naked and unkempt women locked in a closed ward. With such profound experiences of disempowerment through sensory and other memories, our survival and recovery is in relation to psychiatry and its institutions, as they seemingly consume our lives, relationships, and worldviews. This is, in itself, a site to tie our self-identities with, and when possible, to celebrate over our small victories. Such long-term emotional scars do have a creative dimension, even a world vision for self and well-being, and advocacy lessons to give to the mental health and allied medico-legal systems, if only it were recognized as such. Being a user/survivor of psychiatry is a legitimate identity construct for some of us, like being lesbian or Dalit, which we celebrate by being a part of the 'mad pride' movement worldwide.

The post-war period in the West, during the 1960s and early 1970s, was historically significant for the user/survivor movement because of the widely prevalent spirit of dissent, and the subcultures that it led to (Hirsch et al. 1974). A policy of deinstitutionalization in the 1960s and the 1970s around the Western world led to the closure of many mental hospitals and consequently, hundreds of men and women were left abandoned on the streets, homeless and job-less, severely discriminated by the local communities (Grob 1983, 1987). These men and women organized on the streets, coped with their trauma memories, wrote poetry, held protests, and collectively mobilized against psychiatry and its institutions, leading to the rise of 'mad pride' movement in the West, celebrated every year in July.

Users/survivors of psychiatry have used various terms, such as 'madness', 'mental distress', 'disability', and 'disturbance', to refer to what we experience and live with (while psychiatry offered only one term, 'disorder'). Each of these terms created new possibilities of constructing oneself and one's identity as well as new critical questions. Within the user/survivor movement, each term has had its own use as well as nuance to allow for choices. It must also be said that not everyone who has entered the mental health system has profound identity questions of having done so and are willing to let go of such interruptions as a part of life (Estroff *et al.* 1991). For other women, the identity is deep-rooted and can exhaust itself only through direct political action as self-advocates. A variety of identity constructions and political actions are possible in between these two polarities. Urja, living with extreme states since young adulthood, says, 'I don't see myself as either a user or survivor. I just see myself as a different person. I'm not really looking for an identity because there is so much that has made me much of who I am.'

It may also be difficult to find highly individualized users/survivors in India, who, as a part of retrieving a sense of well-being and community, do depend, albeit with great ambivalence, on their primary family relationships and networks. Also, as Das and Addlakha (2008) have pointed out, women living with a disability do seek traditional gendered identities as daughter, mother, or wife, as a way of self-fulfilment, because this is often denied to them.

In this chapter, I write about three gestalts on the question of self, identity, madness, and institutions, by making sense of some of the Sanchit stories. These were presented in other papers or versions thereof (Davar 2002, 2008) as chronological developments, as if one view was in contest with the others. But, to present them as simultaneously present in the gender and disability discourse, and as possibilities for women living with or contesting mental illness, is probably more epistemologically satisfactory. This presentation, emphasizing simultaneity and diversity, increases identity choices for women users and survivors of psychiatry, who experientially occupy every epistemological position described herein depending on our own life process, our insights about it, our choices, as well as our identity politics. Each choice also comes with its own dilemmas and life questions.

1. One gestalt challenges the very existence of something called 'mental illness'. In this view, mental illness is seen as a communication we have used to challenge patriarchy. Our search here is for our rationality, saneness, strength, autonomy, and resilience; our dissent misinterpreted by the medical profession as 'madness'.

2. Another gestalt comes from the reality of women users who engaged with their own emotional states, naming their experience as 'disturbance', and wanting to find a 'cure'. The right to good-quality mental health care is the need of the hour for these women. In making this choice, we choose to build our lives on recognition of our vulnerability.

3. A third view, which is an epistemological as well as experiential choice for me at the moment of writing this chapter, bridges the body, imagination, reason, and experience to reach a knowledge of an embodied, spirituality-seeking, resilient, and connected self in madness. Here, the label of 'mental illness' does not matter as much as 'the mindfully lived reality of madness' (which may seem a contradiction to some).

Survivors Protesting Patriarchy

One position that women survivors of psychiatry have taken is that an experience of total well-being, including psychosocial well-being, can happen only in a socially just society, which orders all people (including women) on an equal basis and provides everyone with equal opportunity and freedom of expression, without discrimination (Astbury 1999). We have understood that personal struggles, that is, the loss of self-identity, marginality, and living amidst violence, discrimination, and privations, are the causal factors for mental disturbance and disability. In the health sector, a social justice environment is important too, but is not causal to the problem or its cure. For example, if a given protocol is followed, a malaria drug will work irrespective of the quality of the delivery process. However, in mental health care, the 'specific agent' cannot be separated from the environmental factors: if the mental health delivery system is of poor quality, it can cause or exacerbate mental disturbance, as testified earlier. In this view, sociopolitical empowerment and the creation of a justice environment through political action is per se psychologically empowering. In this way, social justice is considered to be essential to the experience of mental health.

Feminist writers, while not raising the identity question, have noted that the women's movement is a mental health movement of this sort. The women's movement gave women safe emotional spaces, support and belongingness, much required for rescripting and reclaiming the self. The women's movement gave 'mad' women a chance to relocate their lives within patriarchy, understand their social powerlessness, and engage with rescripting their mad experiences as political identities. The therapeutic value of political activism was evident, as we established our sanity using the spaces by developing a different kind of women's knowledge, reason, autonomy, and praxis (Sathyamala 2005). We were able to appreciate our socially non-conforming selves, channelize anger, and rebuild our sense of 'normalcy' on a feminist epistemology. Users/survivors often find healing spaces in other political movements, particularly being close to the environment, disability, and queer movements.

Legal feminist writings are evidence that non-conforming women have been abused by psychiatry: psychiatry colludes with various institutions, including mental institutions, the police, the prisons, the judiciary, and the family. Once labelled with a 'mental illness', very soon we realize that legal institutions are highly depriving. It seems that 'mental illness', unlike other kinds of health problems, is more like a crime than a disorder. We become legal subjects first, before becoming health care subjects. When in crisis, we, unlike other health patients, run the risk of being accused, arrested, sedated, kidnapped, or otherwise 'caught' (Cremin 2007) and hauled in, rather than being escorted with love and care to the hospital. It is also easy to 'insanitize' someone and keep them involuntarily committed for long periods, through adopting a legal route. It seems that mental illness could be granted, but patienthood could not; and many institutional and private players are taking undue advantage of this, due to profit motives.

Chrysann continues to be distraught by the way she was dragged before the divorce court through a highly manipulative process of 'insanitizing' her, by methods which included defrauding, sedation, kidnap, forced hospitalization, and electroshock, much against her will, because, as she says, she was always plain-spoken in her marriage. She suspects a nexus operating between high-profile lawyers and psychiatrists in this process, which she wants to expose through a 'sting'. To some, it may remain to be 'proven' whether this is her 'paranoia' or is based on 'facts'; but an important Sanchit protocol is that we stay with lived experience and its narrative coherence, and do not look for so-called 'objective' facts.[5]

Advocacy experience and legal data suggest positive evidence of her doubts. Women get a raw deal in any civil court when diagnosed with a 'mental illness'. Since 2001, media has been exposing atrocities in both private and public mental hospitals (for example, see *Mumbai Mirror* 2012). A shocking 40 per cent of the divorce cases that come to family courts are filed on insanity petitions.[6] *Tehelka* exposed a psychiatrist from the Agra Mental Hospital for issuing false certificates of insanity to husbands wanting to relieve themselves of their wives, at the cost of Rs 5,000 per certificate (*Aaina* 2004: 1). A news report described the connivance of a brother with the magistrate in order to institutionalize his sister for trying to marry a man not approved by her family (Indian Social Institute 2005). A recent exposé in *Mumbai Mirror* (2011) describes the overuse of shock treatment, fraud, and wrongful commitments made by a very popular and century-old psychiatric facility in the heart of Mumbai. Chrysann's husband fraudulently and forcibly institutionalized her in this facility by conniving with psychiatrists; and this was later used as evidence of her insanity in the family court. Students, friends, well-wishers, relatives, therapists, and activists have also started a campaign to save women from insanity petitions, as it were, following the unscrupulous and illegal detention of a woman within the context of a long-drawn-out divorce and custody battle using the loopholes in law.

The undue legal advantage taken of 'mentally ill' women within the family court has been recorded by Nagaraj (Chapter 3 in this volume). Cremin's (2007) report describes the ground realities of unregulated custodialization, even within community mental health outreach services, where people are 'caught' and taken to the hospital. Law regularly pronounces upon the 'dangerousness', 'incapacity', and 'incompetence' of persons, especially women, labelled with a mental illness; and this can be applied to universal legal contexts, leading to total loss of citizenship (Dhanda 1987, 2000). No other doctor, except in psychiatry, has the great power to 'certify' the 'fitness' of a woman to be married, to have children, to care for children, and so on. Neither the sciences nor the courts seem to be able to differentiate the two types of instances, namely, where someone is 'actually' mentally ill and where someone is 'charged with' mental illness. Such a difference would be demanded within a framework of scientific rigour: if we could not differentiate someone 'having' diabetes and someone 'accused of having' diabetes, would we not question the medical diagnosis of diabetes and consequent actions taken in the name of 'treatment'? We also need to appreciate the gravity of medico-legal labelling within this legal context: any woman charged with or diagnosed with a mental illness, going before the court, runs the risk of serious civil disempowerments and loss of most rights. Significantly, a woman who is stripped of civil rights on a count of mental illness is at higher risk for forced institutionalization. If she desires to save her fundamental rights and liberties, the denial of mental illness, questioning its very foundation, and restoring her self as sane seems the only route to take.

Chrysann, a woman now in her late thirties, has no doubt that she is 'normal'; and that she had been insanitized through a fraudulent and humiliating medico-legal process. She admits to standing up to her own rights in her decade-old marriage and was dragged into the psychiatric system by force. Her husband had her institutionalized for 'hallucinations', which she vigorously denies. She is deeply affronted as to how anyone can liberally attribute hallucinations to another person, much contrary to their own lived experience. There is a tinge of humiliation at being compared to 'mad people'. Her husband forcibly treated her against her will, or even knowledge, with many electroconvulsive therapies (ECTs) and medicines over a period of three years. Such forceful collusion between patriarchy, psychiatry, and the family court literally drove her crazy. Even though a vigorous advocate for the rights of women 'like her' who are accused of mental illness, she has not anchored her personal knowledge or advocacy around an identity as a woman living with a mental illness. She denies truth value to any 'finding' of mental illness; and therefore, is incredulous that anyone can be 'cured' from it. She is clear that she was an angry wife, that there were logical reasons for her anger (her husband's extramarital affair), and that she got insanitized for this. She does not feel the need for any kind of help or therapy, even though she is shattered by all the recent psychiatric traumas in her life and is dealing with it using natural methods of healing as well as political action. Her tenacious struggle on divorce, custody, maintenance, and share over joint property continues, and she is striving to establish her reasonable interests through this process by challenging patriarchy and psychiatry at every step.

Herein lies the dilemma: in order to be politically active, Chrysann is forced to act within the realm of reason. She is pressured to always manifest as a strong and logical-thinking woman, a normal woman survivor of an Indian marriage, without vulnerabilities. As part of her self-advocacy through the court process, Chrysann made several 'expert' contacts and meticulous efforts to collect evidence of her 'normalcy' from various sources. If she exposed her fragility, that would be seen as a symptom of her insanity, not only by biomedicine and the courts but also by society at large. The insanitizing process, that is, the various visits to clinics, the medication, the hospitalization, and the shock treatments, also left an obsessive self-doubt— 'Am I crazy?'—leading to renewed actions of seeking remedies and proving her rationality. She depended, once again, on biomedicine to re-sanitize her. This proved to be difficult because doctors turned her away saying that she did not have any 'problem'. A question which kept arising for her was: 'If psychiatry can label someone as "insane", why can it not label a person as sane? Why are doctors not giving normalcy certificates?' She had no answer to the question: which authority will now redeem her as sane?

Dissenting women get insanitized; but when diagnosed with a mental illness, their political dissent gets invalidated as part of the mental illness. So they have to work double hard and often keep their distress a secret, to manifest themselves as studious, logical, and reasonable people. Chrysann joined a course on human rights to build that expertise. To be able to study hard, prepare a great report, make presentations in class, earn respect from teachers, and to do better than the rest in the final exam was a determined goal for her. For women survivors, insanity is the risk and limit of their protest. We cannot expose any degree of disability and still hope to be considered as a well-reasoning political dissenter. We take undue societal pressure and responsibility in maintaining the balance between the two: the distress remains an untold story; and the dissent becomes the public manifestation. Chrysann's lawyers, gender and rights-sensitive media reporters, and supporters from women's groups raised an eyebrow or two in interacting with her. Her high-profile feminist lawyer called her 'crazy' because she was expecting too much by way of settlement: her lawyer did not add the psychological and material costs of the insanitization, and her justified anger. Media reporters wanted to talk to her husband and his lawyer to 'verify' her story! Fellow protestors within movements and friends also keep this pressure up on us, to continually establish our reasonableness and 'normalcy', leading to overprotection and/or exclusion. Since we are constantly exposed to oppressive state regimes (police, custodial authorities, courts) and prejudice elsewhere, this pressure to be operating primarily within the realm of reason is not meagre.

However, remaining sane in insane places is not easy to do. People in what Goffman has called 'total' institutions, private or public, are allowed no contact with the outside world. If forcibly institutionalized, as one often is, access to friends or other support systems becomes negligible. Writing or receiving letters, phone calls, and other communication, become highly restricted. Within institutions, management of patients overtakes caregiving responsibilities (*Aaina* 2001: 10). ECT deletes memory and causes cognitive brain damage in some patients, thereby compromising the capacity to partake of political actions. For most, the use of force in giving this treatment is hard to accept. Gita Ramaswamy testified about being isolated by her family and forcibly given ECT as punishment for her radicalism and involvement in the Naxalite movement in the early 1970s (Ramaswamy 2001: 17–18). She wrote about losing her memory. Anecdotally, the fear and terror wrought by shock treatment is widely narrated. Abha, also involved in the feminist movement, was hyper-suicidal, had repeated ECTs, and came out of it feeling emotionally good. However, she could not remember anything that had happened to her between the ECT episodes, including the ECT treatment itself. She also lost the ability to concentrate on her work. Tajnees, a women's rights activist who contributed to Sanchit, said: 'They called me about twice for the shock treatment. After that my condition was very bad and actually got worse than it was before. Before the treatment, I would understand things better, but after the shock, I wouldn't understand anything.' Receiving care through the mental health system, therefore, unlike other health care systems, compromises the capacity to be a political agent and in fact, one's sanity. The fictional quality of 'insanity' (Szasz 1974) as a patriarchal discourse and a power display upheld by various institutional players can well be concluded from these discussions.

Users Acknowledging Vulnerability

For some of us, holding up a wall of reason for public purposes, when internal spaces are largely fractured, fluid, and hurting, is difficult. We have needed safe spaces to share and connect and express our madness and its disabling effects on our selves and lives. In the women's movement, we have questioned the value of 'privacy' specifically in the field of mental disabilities, because it has allowed the state and scientific institutions to silence the abuse done to us. However, women who contribute to our Sanchit collection are very careful in their expectations of confidentiality, safety, and privacy, leading us to develop several methodologically protective measures.[7] Until now, and for these reasons, Sanchit remained a closed-access collection in the Bapu Trust archive. Women tell their stories in order to have a listening and caring Other, to rescript their stories, to be mad safely, and to restore their own sense of perspective and balance, rather than to give mileage to a political movement or to prove their dissenting rationality. Women who access public spheres to build a feminist politics around their identity as women accused of or living with a mental illness are rare; they weigh their odds keenly before doing so. While being involved in the user/survivor movement, I have found it a dilemma, about pushing other user/survivor peers one way or the other. It is also a personal dilemma for me, in public spaces, when and where to expose and resource my political identity as survivor: it is just so much easier to resource the safer 'expert' identity. By doing so, you also face less risk of having your professional views undermined.

Movement work, whether challenging patriarchy or the mental health system, is emotionally demanding. To be aroused in anger, to give it a full-blooded embodied manifestation, and to create holding spaces and rhetorics for this, is politicizing our emotions within public spheres. Anger has been of great personal, pragmatic, rhetorical, and theatrical[8] use to all political movements. This strategy of acting out anger is very useful for psychiatric users, who often have a problem about self-assertion. We, while wanting to keep one foot inside this door of political action, weigh this against our disability, our need for loving ourselves, our inner peace, and our search for affirming relationships, emotional stability, self-integration, and well-being. The lived experience of anger, a self-depleting force, is something we often struggle with: it is not enough to rebuild our shattered selves on any single overwhelming emotion. Love, shelter/belonging, touch, surrender, connection, devotion, pleasure, desire, joy, and so forth, are other emotions we want deployed in our lives.

Many of us do carry an identity as a woman with a disability. The disability is an experienced reality, leaving us emotionally needy, dissociated, lonely, hopeless, sad, powerless, angry, yearning, and not able to do anything. The body is reduced to weakness, pain, fatigue, sensory overload, feelings of being disembodied, and other bizarre experiences and general sickness. While psychiatry reduces mental pain to something in the head region, particularly the brain, we feel it all over our bodies. The digestive, endocrine, and reproductive health systems are usually disturbed. It is an equally disabling situation for women with 'disturbance', experiences such as hearing voices, delusions, mania, obsessive thoughts, addictions, or wanting to end life. 'Someone is in the living room, and I do not know whom,' writes Urja, talking about her illness. Anu, a women's rights activist and teacher, says: 'Actually I am not empowered at all, I get teary eyed and all that. But I fought it out. I did fight it out.' While 'fighting' for 'empowerment', we experience the mismatch of this value against our personal experiences, and we are fighting, as Anu is, the depression or the extreme states, not patriarchy. A sense of internal empowerment does not come with just having an empowerment language about social equality.

Some women find psychiatric diagnosis and medications useful. Anu says, '(I) have always had a sense of not being satisfied with myself, not liking myself. I never understood why this is happening at all. That is one of the major reasons for depression, this constant fear of failure and low self esteem which slowly develops into the psyche.' Particularly for the many women who have been helped by medications, the diagnosis is a site to anchor and develop their identities. Andreason (1984) went against the tide of user–survivor advocacy to argue for the role of medications in staying well. When the selective serotonin reuptake inhibitors (SSRIs) hit the markets in the United States (US), many thousands of women who were prescribed the drug loved the magical self-transformation they brought about, from depression to highly effective, socially skilled, and beautiful women (Wurtzel 1999). It was only later that the magic of the drugs wore off, leading to many class action suits against the manufacturers, making the situation comparable to the tobacco tragedies (Breggin 1993; Wurtzel 1999; Szasz 2001; Menzies 2004). A similar situation prevails with respect to the newer class of antipsychotics. It is by now widely known that these drugs bring on type II diabetes and cardiovascular disease prematurely (*Aaina* 2005). While it is problematic to advocate against the use of medicines, we did have several problems about psychiatry's casual approach to medicines, its side effects, iatrogenic damage caused by them, and so on. Women who were finding the drugs useful rarely had the opportunity to know from their doctors about optimizing its efficacy (Glenmullen 2001). Women were puzzled why the doctors 'never' informed them about the side effects. Experience with medicines also resulted in our adopting various self-taught strategies of optimizing its use, for example, with diet and lifestyle changes or exercise. What we advocated for was 'choice' and having adequate information about the diagnosis and treatment plan to effect it.

Anu, while not diminishing the role of social and economic deprivations within her marriage and family, has a strong view that '...the depression was definitely chemical imbalance, though it was definitely deepened, lengthened, as well as made serious by incidents in my life'. Yet Anu says, '(I) am not saying that all who are depressed should cry on each other's shoulders. But they need to learn about their illness, to put their heads up and face the world and tell people that, "Yes, I am depressed, and what are you going to say about it". That is what I am trying.'

For Urja, '…it was a lot of voices in my head basically. I never realized at that time but I realize now that they were voices…It was a lot of confusion. There was a lot of anger and I didn't know where the voices were coming from…The illness just came and went. It was never stable until now.' Urja was very amused when her highly paid doctor suggested a sex change for her. It seemed to show up her parents' incompetence in dealing with the voices and they had to pay for such nonsense! Abha said:

> …knew I was ill. The colour of my world changed. I lost weight. I stopped eating and cried continuously. There were times when I just cried and cried. There is something about depression, which gives you a very sick, and closed feeling. It is very internal. I knew that I was extremely unhappy in my mind…That was the first episode of depression.

Through supportive friendships, we have engaged with the specificity of each of these personalized 'idioms of distress', a phrase made legacy by Mark Nichter (1981), and built our own everyday language and philosophy about the experiences (Chadwick 1997; Davar 2002). A voice-hearing friend educated us that not all voices were disturbing and some had been supportive through growing up years. Another voice hearer made amazing paintings when she heard voices, because she lost her own voice during this time and the paintings allowed her to express herself. She would hear loud music through ear phones to drown out the voices, leave home with her sketch pad and pens, and create amazing metaphysical paintings. In our peer support group, a woman who was under excessive control of, and faced criticism by, her mother vented her own anger with furious voices every time she felt unsafe (Firestone 1997). Another used her poetic and drawing skills to 'negotiate' or 'talk back' to the voices, bringing down the 18-odd voices she heard to a more manageable three or four. Some of these people were given up by the medical system as incurable or drug resistant. All were resigned to the categories of 'severely mentally ill' and 'lacking insight' (see International Voice Hearers Network; Stastny and Lehmann 2007, for coping with voice hearing). The doctors never engaged them in conversation with the genealogy and phenomenology of these voices in that person's life. It is also an untold story as to how many women with epilepsy, general health problems, or childhood sexual-abused women get misdiagnosed with severe mental illness (Firestone 1997; Klonoff and Landrine 1997).

Mental disturbance does not have a universal formula applicable to all women charged of or living with a mental illness, and 'empowerment' needs to match internal needs. The personal advantage in naming and managing mental illness is that it brings women with similar experiences and identities together, while making us acknowledge and appreciate individual experiences of disability. Building support networks, peer support, and friendships for women living with a mental illness has helped in sharing and connecting, and also served our self-nourishment. Groups of women users and survivors, along with various friends, supporters, and advocates within the women's movement, have met in their homes, cafes and schools, in offices, as well as in conferences[9] (Sadgopal 2005). Sanchit is now such an informal support network in Pune. We built knowledges based on our experiences both of self and of psychiatry. The knowledges established that 'mental illness' included a personal experience of distress and disturbance, which psychiatry never understood. There is a 'disease' of voice hearing within psychiatric nosology; but the Indian mental health system suffers from the disease of 'not hearing voices' when it comes to users/survivors' experiences, even though for over a decade, as users of available care and support systems and as survivors with imaginative ideas on humane care and support, we have shared our experiences and advocated for inclusive and humane mental health services.

To mark oneself as an ill person, while beginning the insightful process of self-discovery, is a choice that people with psychosocial disabilities do make. This situation is not uplifting always, and may include coping with and surviving the mental health system and the associated normative structures (family, community, work) for many years. Anu describes in detail her hard negotiations with the series of psychiatrists and therapists who treated her. She met unscrupulous doctors, and narrates with horror a person who continues to use sodium pentathol and other such psychoactive drugs to extract his clinical information. Another one would put all his clients to sleep in a common room, giving them an 'injection' for 'relaxing', while he, a chain smoker, went out to smoke! Anu, Urja, and Abha's struggles with medication, doctors, and other mental health professionals continued. We are the 'voluntary patients', as defined by the law, but the voluntarism has to be constantly negotiated in institutional, community, and professional spaces.

The doctors we approached would look at and talk to our accompanying spouse, child, or relative while making a treatment plan for us. Abha says:

> I thought a psychiatrist is someone whom you can talk to. I didn't know head or tail of what psychology or psychiatry was. He would look upon it from a personal level. He was very patriarchal. He would say, 'You must not think like this. You must cook for your husband, you must look after your home and doing so will give you a sense of pride'. He was telling me to do everything that I didn't want to do.

They had little time for discussing our life situation. They left us with little choice of treatments. They had no knowledge of how the medicines they prescribed affected our mental health, our daily life, work, health and reproductive health, relationships, and caregiving functions.

Abha says, '(N)one of the anti-depressants seemed to make any difference except for the different side effects. They all did the same thing to me. My depression did not go. But my emotions were flattened. My thought processes were numbed.' Often they did not even ask nor provide adequate information. Anu says:

> '(T)his is what these people (psychiatrists) do when they realize that this patient is not going to go through the therapy as they want it or are questioning the medicines. I asked him about the medicines. They were related to schizophrenia. I asked him why he was giving me these. He said that these are to calm me down. I said ok, but you must tell me about these, because I want to know.

Anu was not given appointments when she asked all these questions.

Urja says, '(T)he psychiatrist that I first saw here, never really told me what my problem was. She just prescribed drugs and she said, "(C)ome and we'll talk about what is disturbing you". Every time I asked her what was going on in my head, she could never answer me. I was astonished thinking that do you even know what you're doing?'

Being a male-dominated fraternity, they had no understanding of women's psychology nor for that matter, biology. The sexual abuse of female clients by their doctors was also reported by peers. One of the earliest Sanchit stories was of a set of women clients being seduced by their psychoanalyst in Mumbai, in the late 1990s. In psychoanalytic circles, this became a scandal, and a part of the skeleton in the psychiatrists' cupboard. The story was withdrawn due to fear of safety. Eventually, it was fictionalized as a story in the rather obscure book, *The Waiting Room*, by someone who was affronted by the whole affair and perhaps wanted to expose it (Mehta 2007). Anu says:

> '(I) went to many (psychiatrists) and some were absolutely callous. I went to _____. He gave me medication but he found that it was not working. He tried to counsel me…and I hated it because somebody was telling me something and it wasn't gelling and I couldn't apply it to myself. What was the use of that terribly erudite language? I used to get angry and one day I tried to commit suicide.

Wanting to commit suicide after meeting your psychiatrist or therapist is not an unknown experience and sometimes, it is linked to the trauma of the clinical experience itself. Anu also experienced many psychiatrists who looked down upon women's depression, 'who first pull you out of it and then tell you that now its two years and now you must be all right, so get on with life'.

Chrysann was not even informed that she was given multiple ECTs. The doctor to whom she was forcibly taken by her husband said that her blood was taken for doing 'blood tests'.

> I just felt as if I'm dying. I knew that now I'm going to get injected and get unconscious. I could feel that thing entering my brain as though I was drunk or something. That feeling was terrible. I've never had this. It was a dreaded thing. I used to tell my husband that I was really scared about what was happening, even though I had no idea (what they were doing)…

We had to face the fact that psychiatry was in its very foundation, a discourse of exclusion, systematically stereotyping, judging, and marginalizing women, other than going well beyond the ambit of ethical medical care.

When brought within psychiatry even as a willing beneficiary, we confronted multiple family pressures and attitudes. Middle-class communities slot the person into the label of a 'mentally ill patient' and validate little else. Particularly the younger women within a traditional family set-up come under a lot of surveillance on a daily, if not hourly, basis. Everyday decision-making as women, especially as young and 'mentally ill' women, is near impossible. Friendships, contacts, and operating in public spaces are highly controlled by well-meaning family members. Urja's parents firmly discouraged her from pursuing her great painting talent and diminished her for not consistently holding a job. Anu's family kept harking back upon her emotional highs and lows or her medications if she was expressive. For both, to 'tell or not to tell' their employers, and taking the consequences of either, was also a dilemma. Abha's spouse allowed himself to be subjected to her anger, violence, and abuse through the depressive episodes, stroked her hair endlessly, and reminded her about the medications. He didn't know what else to do.

In the community, as women self-identified as living with a mental illness, we walked on thin ice. We were never believed. Kendra, compiling the stories of homeless women with psycho disabilities, had a really hard time going on a 'truth'- finding mission about each of the women as they told their stories to her (Kendra 2002). Did she really live there? Work there? Did she really…really…and so on. She may have had less difficulty compiling abled womens' stories, for she would not have made any assumptions about the truth value of those stories, as she did about the stories of mentally disturbed women. A different style of non-judgemental personal story writing is adopted by Chadwick (1997) when he recounts stories of diagnosed people. These stories are rich with magic, miracles, strange beginnings, perceptions, sensations, beliefs, experiences, and so on. Chadwick is clear that he is not the one who will make the choice between truth and falsity, and that should be left to the people themselves. What is the truth value of stories that women of 'unsound mind' tell? Should they be believed?

Our stories were deconstructed at every step: friends and family members accepted us better if we continually affirmed our disability status and were willing to admit that our deviation from social conformity, or our dissent, was a sign of the illness. But this was a double-edged sword. While our edginess and mania were tolerated, even with humour, they also set limits for us for the same reason. Abha and Anu, who by now has grandchildren, both talked about being treated like children by close family members. Establishing our 'capacity' in private as well public spheres was often difficult. The evergreen questions, '(D)id you take your medicines today?' and '(A)re your symptoms coming back?', are annoying, which if expressed, only strengthened their conviction that you have defaulted on your medicines. Neighbours and relatives were sometimes unrelenting in their criticism and humiliation. At least two people who contributed to the Sanchit collective had been so hounded by neighbours that this was an enduring part of their madness stories. Women friends living with a mental illness for a number of years were more at risk for being isolated, sedated, and picked up as 'lacking insight' and put away within institutions forcibly. Someone or the other was constantly 'disappearing' in this way from our friendship or peer support groups. We have now started calling them 'enforced disappearances', as the ambush strategies used to isolate and 'catch' people are not dissimilar from those disappearances which originally led to this political category. We grieved their loss, but despite hard efforts, could do little to connect back due to the oppressive medico-legal institutional system which prohibits all social contact. The most invisible were the lesbian women who were in treatment and women with physical disabilities. It was difficult to convince friends in the women's movement that a woman did not need to be put in a penal institution and that it was no way of providing 'mental health' care. These institutions just need to be finally vanquished and replaced with more humane designs (Davar and Lohokare 2008).

Survivors Speak Out

There is no universal answer to the question, 'Is mental illness a myth (Szasz 1974) or a fabrication by patriarchy?' Different women have answered these in their own unique ways. However, we have come to understand that we cannot be fragmented into mind, body, and spirit by medico-legal labelling. We are all this individually and together. Psychiatry or the mental health and behavioural sciences can do only so much for us. When we do approach these disciplines, we expect that they will deliver the sciences with care. It is not only that we felt let down by the mental health system and its institutions; the very foundation of the mental health system was shaky, which is a global experience. Proposing solutions or firefighting mechanisms, such as finding less cruel physical or chemical restraints, better ECT machines, or more humane custodial hospitals, often referred to euphemistically as 'safeguards', were inappropriate. Some practices are inhuman, degrading, and even torturous, and just have to go. The situation regarding solitary confinement and direct shock treatment within the asylums, both private and public, is the darkest side of the mental health system, contested before the Supreme Court by Saarthak, a Delhi-based non-governmental organization (NGO), in 2001. The enormous legal power vested in psychiatry and its neo-colonial institutions has to be seriously challenged with new treatment formats that assure and protect health care rights and healing practices that are holistic.

At its present stage, psychiatry is an infant pseudo-medical science, with a very poor burden of proof and evidence (cf. Davar and Bhat 1995; Biswas, Chapter 2 in this volume). It is a statistical science, as all the diagnostics found in the discipline have been developed statistically, significantly in the war and post-war period. The physiological, biological pathways needed to establish any evidence of disease is far from being met in psychiatry. The integration with general medicine is only just beginning to happen in the West, and psychiatry operates on the fringes of general medicine.[10] Psychiatry in India has not addressed the larger integrations of medicine (nutrition, endocrinology, reproductive health, cardiology, sports medicine) with mental health. For example, does any doctor advise his client on diet changes for better emotional health? There is overwhelming medical evidence for the application of Omega 3 and other diet therapies in cures from depression and other mental disorders. Experts from around the world have established the value of nutrition, sports, arts, and other ways of healing and recovery (Arem 1999; Stastny and Lehmann 2007). Still others have studied the uses of indigenous healing methods, including spiritual and shamanic healing in the recovery process (West 2000; Winkelman 2000). The Sanchit collection is also testimony to this. We have helped each other drop psychiatric drugs *or* use alternatives to optimize the effects of the drugs we are using (Lehmann 1998).

The 'gene' factor even for the so-called dreaded mental disease, schizophrenia, has proved to be elusive. Schizophrenia, often misdiagnosed as purely psychiatric, defines a set of sensory, perceptual, embodied, psychological, and social experiences, the causes of which are multifarious, including, importantly, urbanization (McKenzie 2008; Morgan *et al.* 2010), childhood physical and sexual abuse, isolation, other early trauma, drug use, and malnutrition. These experiences create life contexts, meanings, and lifestyles in women living with them. An experiential basis for dealing with mental health problems needs to be developed (Davar 2000).

We are named 'violent' and 'dangerous', yet, the thriving peer support system in the world is witness to the fact that many of us also know how to build relationships back with love, humility, forgiveness, and grace. Connecting back to people who we have hurt is an important ritual and skilful practice, something that movement leaders pass on to us, and something that will be of great use to the destructive world at large found among the abled. The violent world of the abled leaves us feeling unsafe. Some of the inspired users/survivors I have met, who lead movements in their own locality/country, have the insight of the wisest in the world. Yet, we are named as 'lacking insight' by the system. Many of us in the user/survivor movement have developed embodied methods of self-expression as well as healing, using various physical activities, sports, meditations, visualization of better health, martial arts, music, dance, ritual, movement, and theatre and performance (Statsny and Lehmann 2007; West 2000).

The mental sciences and the professionals basing their faith on them do not know how to deal with women's lived experiences, their embodied subjectivity, diversity, the creative and survival potential of non-reason, the strengths of living in suspense and uncertainty, the insights brought by vulnerability, and the experience of surrendering to the unpredictable—all that is a part of our everyday self-experiences as people living with a mental illness. It has taken me many years, and a personal engagement with mental disability and disability-inspired spirituality, to accept an embodied non-reason (intuition, imagination, desire, creativity, and so on) as part of consciousness and human connectedness with the human and non-human world. If living life from a non-rational creative space is 'insanity', I accept that as a gift and a blessing.

'The main thing is that I'm still depressed but not frightened of it. Because I am not frightened of it, I can cope with it. I think being sentimental or emotional is considered to be a weakness. I feel that it is not weakness, it is strength. The most depressed people have written and done the most wonderful work.' (Anu)

'There are lots of things, which are there. Being mentally ill means being outside the permissive levels of normalcy and I feel that it gives me leverage as well. I know I can look at things differently. That power is there within me.' (Abha)

'I have seen dreams no mortal would ever dare…
I have learnt to be brave and not be in scare.' (Urja)

Notes

1. I thank all those who contributed their stories to Sanchit, the oral histories archive. I thank my programme team, Deepra Dandekar, Madhura Lohokare, Puja Modi, Vrushali Athalye, Chandra Karhadkar, Maitreyee Desai, Seema Gaikwad, and Reshma Val, for their creative contributions to the project. I thank the Center for Advocacy in Mental Health, its library, and Yogita Kulkarni for administrative support. Sir Dorabji Tata Trust provided financial support for Sanchit.

2. 'Sanchit' is a collection of women's stories of mental distress and disturbance. The stories have been collected through in-depth interviews, and tape recorded, transcribed, and published as personal diaries. The collection rests in the library of the Bapu Trust for Research on Mind and Discourse, Pune, India (www.bapucamhindia.org) and is available for reading and research at the library archive.

3. Names have been changed to protect identity.

4. Personal communication.

5. In the development of the Sanchit study design, we were repeatedly advised by women activists that we cannot believe the woman's stories alone; that the 'archive' is complete only when we take interviews of the caregivers and psychiatrists as well! We have rejected this advice as patronizing and diminishing of persons with psychosocial disabilities.

6. '40% of Divorce Cases Involve People with Mental Health Issues', *Times of India*, 11 September 2011. Available at: http://articles. timesofindia.indiatimes.com/2011-09-11/chennai/30141640_1_ mental-health-divorce-cases-indian-psychiatric-society, accessed 23 March 2015.

7. Relating to where the interview is given, who is taking the interview, where the tapes are stored, who is transcribing them, whether identity is preserved or erased, who accesses them, and so on.

8. This is not written in a disparaging way, but rather in appreciation of how skilful this is to the movement.

9. JAGORI organized a small study circle in Shimla, in October 1995, called UNMAD, which went on to collect 'stories' of women labelled 'mad'. Anveshi organized a national seminar on 'Women and Mental Health' in 1996. A pre-Beijing meeting was organized by Priti Oza in Shimla, in the summer of 1995. Reports, bibliographies, and advocacy notes were circulated in these meetings. IFSHA organized a meeting on 'Violence and Mental Health' in Delhi in the year 1999. Various others have since organized around the theme of women and mental health.

10. An indicator of this is the fact that public health journals in India till date have not covered the mental hospitals in their scope.

References

Aaina. 2001. 'Be a Good Patient now', 1(3): 10.

―――. 2004. 'Editorial', 4(2): 1.

―――. 2005. 'Atypical Anti-psychotics, a Research Review', 5(2): 9–10.

Andreason, N.C. 1984. *The Broken Brain: The Biological Revolution in Psychiatry*. New York: Elsevier.

Arem, R. 1999. *The Thyroid Solution: A Mind–Body Program for Beating Depression and Regaining Your Emotional and Physical Health*. New York: Ballantine.

Astbury, J. 1999. 'Gender and Mental Health', Working Paper Series No. 99.18, Harvard Center for Population and Development Studies, Cambridge, MA.

Breggin, P. 1993. *Toxic Psychiatry: Drugs and Electroconvulsive Therapy: The Truth and the Better Alternatives*. London: Harper Collins.

Chadwick, P. 1997. *Schizophrenia: A Positive Perspective. In Search of Dignity for Schizophrenic People*. London: Routledge.

Cremin, K. 2007. *General Hospital Psychiatric Units and Rehabilitation Centres in India: Do Law and Public Policy Present Barriers to Community-based Mental Health Services?* Pune, India: Bapu Trust.

Das, V. and R. Addlakha. 2008. 'Disability and Domestic Citizenship: Voice, Gender, and the Making of the Subject', *Public Culture*, 13(3): 511–31.

Davar, B.V. 1998. 'Of Schizophrenic Mothers and Depressed Daughters', *Indian Psychologist*, 3(1): 5–8.

———. 1999. *Mental Health of Indian Women: A Feminist Agenda*. New Delhi: Sage.

———. 2000. 'Writing Phenomenology of Mental Illness: Extending the Universe of Ordinary Discourse', in A. Raghuramaraju (ed.), *Existence, Experience and Ethics*, pp. 51–82. New Delhi: D.K. Printworld.

——— (ed.). 2001. *Mental Health from a Gender Perspective*. New Delhi: Sage.

———. 2002. 'Dilemmas of Women's Activism in Mental Health', in R. Khanna, M. Shiva, and S. Gopalan (eds), *Towards a Comprehensive Women's Health Programmes and Policy*, pp. 460–82. Pune: Sahaj for WAH.

———. 2006. 'Natural Healing from Depression', in Peter Statsny and Peter Lehmann (eds), *Alternatives to Psychiatry*. Germany: Peter Lehmann Publishing.

———. 2008. 'From Mental Illness to Psychosocial Disability: Choices of Identity for Women Users and Survivors of Psychiatry', *Indian Journal of Women's Studies*, Special volume in R. Addlakha (ed.), *Disability, Gender and Society*, 15(2), May–August.

Davar, B.V. and P. R. Bhat. 1995. *Psychoanalysis as a Human Science: Beyond Foundationalism*. New Delhi: Sage.

Davar, B.V. and M. Lohokare. 2008. 'Recovering from Psychosocial Traumas: The Place of Dargahs in Maharashtra', *Economic and Political Weekly*, 44(16): 60–8.

Dhanda, A. 1987. 'The Plight of the Doubly Damned: Mentally Ill Women in India', in P. Leelakrishnan (ed.), *New Horizons of Law*, pp. 187–98. New Delhi: Indian Law Institute.

———. 2000. *Legal Order/Mental Disorder*. New Delhi: Sage.

Estroff, S., W.S. Lachicotte, L.C. Illingworth, and A. Johnston. 1991. 'Everybody's Got a Little Mental Illness: Accounts of Illness and Self among People with Severe, Persistent Mental Illnesses', *Medical Anthropology Quarterly*, New Series, 5(4): 331–69.

Firestone, R.W. 1997. *Combating Destructive Thought Processes*. London: Sage.

Glenmullen, P. 2001. *Prozac Backlash: Overcoming the Dangers of Prozac, Zoloft, Paxil, and other Anti-depressants with Safe, Effective Alternatives*. New York: Touchstone.

Gombos, G. and A. Dhanda. 2009. *Catalyzing Self Advocacy: An Experiment in India*. Pune, India: Bapu Trust for Research on Mind and Discourse.

Grob, G. 1983. *Mental Illness and American Society, 1875–1940*. Princeton: Princeton University Press.

————. 1987. 'The Forging of Mental Health Policy in America: World War II to New Frontier', *The Journal of the History of Medicine and Allied Sciences Inc.*, 42(2): 410–46.

Hirsch, S., J.K. Adams, L.R. Frank, W. Hudson, R. Keene, G. Krawitz-Keene, D. Richman, and R. Roth (eds). 1974. *Madness Network News Reader.* California: Glide.

Indian Social Institute. 2005. 'Madly in Love, Couple Ends up in Mental Asylum', *Human Rights Bulletin*, 29 June.

International Voice Hearers Network. Available at: http://www.intervoiceonline.org/.

Kendra. 2002. *Out of Mind, Out of Sight: Voices of the Homeless Mentally Ill.* Chennai: East West Books (Madras) Private Limited.

Klonoff, E.A. and H. Landrine (eds). 1997. 'Preventing Misdiagnosis of Women: A Guide to Physical Disorders that have Psychiatric Symptoms', in *Women's Mental Health & Development, Vol. I.* Thousand Oaks: Sage.

Lehmann, P. 1998. *Coming off Psychiatric Drugs.* Germany: Peter Lehmann Publishing.

McKenzie, K. 2008. 'Urbanisation, Social Capital and Mental Health', *Global Social Policy*, 8: 359–77.

Mehta, A. 2007. *The Waiting Room.* New Delhi: Penguin.

Menzies, K.B. 2004. 'The Rising Tide of Pharmaceutical Lawsuits: What the Practitioner Needs to Know about the Future of Psychiatric Drug Litigation', presented at Safe Harbor's Third Annual Medical Conference. Safe Harbor: Los Angeles.

Minkowitz, T. and A. Dhanda (eds). 2006. *First Person Stories on Forced Treatment and Legal Capacity.* Pune: World Network of Users and Survivors of Psychiatry and Bapu Trust.

Morgan, Craig, Kwame Mckenzie, and Paul Fearon. 2010. *Society and Psychosis.* London: Cambridge University Press.

Mumbai Mirror. 2011. 'Health Chiefs Raise Alarm on Masina's House of Horrors', 3 January. Available at: http://www.mumbaimirror.com/article/15/20110103201101030853502491dd077d5/Health-chiefs-raise-alarm-on-masina%E2%80%99s-house-of-horrors.html.

————. 2012. 'Asylum Treats Insane Inmates like Dogs, 2 Held', 4 January. Available at: http://www.mumbaimirror.com/news/india/Asylum-treats-insane-inmates-like-dogs-2-held/articleshow/16194272.cms, accessed March 2015.

Nichter, M. 1981. 'Idioms of Distress: Alternatives in the Expression of Psychosocial Illness: A Case Study from South India', *Culture, Medicine and Psychiatry*, 5(4): 379–408.

Ramaswamy, G. 2001. 'A Remembered Rage', *Aaina*, 1(1): 17–18.

Sadgopal, M. 2005. 'Sihaya Samooh: A Mental Health Self-help Support Group in Pune', *Psychological Foundations: The Journal*, VII(2): 41–2.

Sandhu, A. 2009. *Sepia Leaves*. New Delhi: Penguin.

Sathyamala, C. 2005. 'The Loving and the Telling: Perspective on a "Mad" Actress', *Psychological Foundations: The Journal*, VII(1): 47–52.

Statsny, Peter and Peter Lehmann. 2007 (ed.). *Alternatives beyond Psychiatry*. Berlin: Peter Lehmann Publishing.

Szasz, T. 1974. *The Myth of Mental Illness: Foundations of a Theory of Personal Conduct*. New York: Harper and Row.

———. 2001. *Pharmacracy: Medicine and Politics in America*. Connecticut, US: Praeger.

West, W. 2000. *Psychotherapy and Spirituality: Crossing the Line between Therapy and Religion*. London: Sage.

Winkelman, M. 2000. *Shamanism: The Neural Ecology of Consciousness and Healing*. Westport: Bergin & Garvey.

Wurtzel, E. 1999. *Prozac Nation: Young and Depressed in America: A memoir*. London: Quartet Books.

Index

Editors and Contributors

Renu Addlakha is Professor at the Centre for Women's Development Studies, New Delhi. She completed her doctorate from the Department of Sociology, Delhi School of Economics, University of Delhi. Her areas of interest include the sociology of medicine, mental illness and the psychiatric profession, public health, anthropology of infectious diseases, bioethics, gender and the family, and disability and society. She has worked as a research consultant for a number of international organizations such as the World Health Organization (WHO), DANIDA, the World Bank, and the McArthur Foundation in India. She has published widely in peer-reviewed journals. She is the author of *Deconstructing Mental Illness: An Ethnography of Psychiatry, Women, and the Family* (Kali for Women, 2008) and *Contemporary Perspectives on Disability in India: Exploring the Linkages between Law, Gender and Experience* (LAP LAMBERT Academic Publishing, 2011), and the co-editor of *Disability and Society* (DK Agencies, 2009). *Disability Studies in India: Global Discourses, Local Realities* (Routledge, 2013) is her most recent edited publication. She can be contacted at: addlakhar@gmail.com.

Ranjita Biswas is a psychiatrist who divides her time between research, teaching, and therapeutic support. She is associated with the School of Women's Studies, Jadavpur University, Kolkata. She has published in the areas of mental health, sexual violence, and sexuality; and has recently co-edited a volume on marriage and sexualities in India. She can be contacted at: ranjitabsws@gmail.com.

Bhargavi V. Davar is Director, Centre for Advocacy in Mental Health, Pune. Her publications include *Psychoanalysis as Human Science: Beyond Foundationalism* (with P.R. Bhat, Sage, 1995); *Mental Health of Indian Women* (Sage, 1999); and *Mental Health from a Gender Perspective* (ed., Sage, 2001). From 2001 to 2008, she edited *Aaina*, a mental health advocacy newsletter; and edited volumes for the Bapu Trust under the title of *Mental Health Advocacy Resources*. She has published book chapters and journal articles in her areas of research interests: gender, traditional healing, social legal studies, human rights and mental health. She is the clinical director of Bapu Trust's 'Seher, Urban Community Mental Health Programme', whose vision is to 'create emotionally sustainable communities'. She is a qualified arts-based therapist and a certified international trainer on the Convention on the Rights of Persons with Disabilities. She can be contacted at: bvdresearch@gmail.com.

Yogita Hastak has a Masters in clinical psychology and has been involved in research in the fields of adolescent identity development and lesbian, gay, bisexual, and transgender (LGBT) mental health. She has also worked as a school counsellor, primarily working with children having learning difficulties and addressing students' personal/social and career development needs. Currently, she is living in Pune and raising her one-year-old and working with 'The Paws Pack' as head for 'Paws for a Cause—An Animal Assisted Activities and Therapy Initiative', while pursuing an advanced course in animal-assisted therapy. She can be contacted at: yogita10@hotmail.com.

Jayasree Kalathil is an independent writer with a background in critical humanities and cultural studies. Her areas of interest and expertise include mental health, race equality, and cultural representations of madness. Her publications include: *Recovery and Resilience: African, African Caribbean and South Asian Women's Narratives about Recovering from Mental Distress* (London: Survivor Research and Mental Health Foundation); *Dancing to Our Own Tunes: Reassessing Black and Minority Ethnic Mental Health Service User Involvement* (London: NSUN); and the children's book, *The Sackcloth Man* (Kottayam: DC Books). Dr Kalathil was the editor of *Open Mind* magazine (London: Mind, 2010–12), a co-chair of the Social Perspectives Network (2009–12), and is currently a coordinator of the independent 'Inquiry into the Schizophrenia Label'. She lives in London and runs Survivor Research, a virtual collective of researchers interested in issues of marginality, representation, and human rights in mental health. She can be contacted at: jayasree@survivor-research.com.

Shazneen Limjerwala is an academic researcher, and psychotherapist. Her expertise spans the following areas: mental health, qualitative research methodology, women's issues, narratives, communication, management, and psychotherapy technique. She received her PhD from Lancaster University (United Kingdom) as an overseas research student and J.N. Tata scholarship for her research on sexual violence. She has taught at Lancaster University, Sophia College, and Indian Institute of Management (IIM) Ahmedabad. She contributes to understanding through writing, teaching, creating study and workshop modules, and conducting workshops. She can be contacted at: dr.shazneen@gmail.com.

Vasudha Nagaraj worked in Anveshi, Research Centre for Women's Studies, Hyderabad. She is a practising lawyer in the family courts in Hyderabad defending women in various registers of marital rights. Her primary interest lies in theorizing issues of contemporary practices of the law which include women's experiences with the courts, structure of the law and legal institutions, and the scope and effects of special legislations. She can be contacted at: vasudhanagaraj13@gmail.com.

Ketki Ranade works as Assistant Professor, Centre for Health and Mental Health, School of Social Work, Tata Institute of Social Sciences (TISS). Her research interests include marginalization and mental health, specifically LGBT mental health, and gender and mental health. She is currently involved in research projects related to developing gay affirmative counselling practices in India and familial response to same-sex sexuality in a family member. Ketki is also pursuing her doctoral studies at TISS on 'growing up gay' in a heterosexually constructed world. She is a member of a queer feminist LBT collective, 'Lesbians and Bisexuals in Action' (LABIA;

www.labiacollective.org) in Mumbai. Before dabbling in academics and research, Professor Ranade worked at the Bapu Trust, Pune, in developing and implementing mental health service programmes in urban slum communities as well as institutions. She can be contacted at: ranade.ketki@gmail.com/ketki.ranade@tiss.edu.

T.K. Sundari Ravindran is Honorary Professor at the Achutha Menon Centre for Health Science Studies, has a PhD in applied economics from the Centre for Development Studies, Trivandrum, India. Sundari is a founding member and secretary of a grassroots women's organization, Rural Women's Social Education Centre (RUWSEC), India, founded in 1981; and a member of the steering team which launched, in 2006, the Coalition for Maternal–Neonatal Health and Safe Abortion (India). She has worked as a consultant with the WHO, Geneva, since 1984, and was a gender specialist in its Department of Gender and Women's Health during 2001–3. She was a co-editor of the Journal, *Reproductive Health Matters* from 1993–8. She is co-editor (with H. de Pinho) of *The Right Reforms? Health Sector Reform and Sexual and Reproductive Health,* 2011, by the Initiative for Sexual & Reproductive Rights in Health Reforms [School of Public Health, University of the Witwatersrand]; and of WHO's training manual, *Transforming Health Systems: Gender and Rights in Reproductive Health*; and has authored a number of WHO publications, including *Women in South-East Asia: A Health Profile,* and WHO's gender and poverty training resource for medical educators on domestic violence, ageing, and gender-sensitive and pro-poor health policies. She can be contacted at: ravindrans@usa.net.

Anubha Sood has a PhD in anthropology and a graduate certificate in Women, Gender and Sexuality Studies from the Washington University in St Louis, United States (US). Her research sits at the intersection of medical, psychological, and psychiatric anthropology, the anthropology of religion, and gender studies. Her most recent research project involved 15 months of ethnographic research with female attendees in a Hindu healing temple in north India, popular for treating psychological ailments that manifest as spirit possession. She has also conducted anthropological research in government psychiatric settings in north India and worked extensively with women incarcerated in state-run mental institutions in the country. She has been involved with policy and advocacy work in the gender and mental health arena in India for over a decade. She can be contacted at: anubha.sood@gmail.com.